Next Steps in Parenting the Child Who Hurts

Tykes and Teens

Caroline Archer

Adoption UK

Jessica Kingsley Publishers
London and Philadelphia

First published in the United Kingdom in 1999 by
Jessica Kingsley Publishers Ltd,
116 Pentonville Road, London
N1 9JB, England

and

325 Chestnut Street,
Philadelphia PA 19106, USA.

www.jkp.com

Second impression 2000

Copyright © Adoption UK and Caroline Archer 1999
Illustrations Copyright © Joy Hasler

Library of Congress Cataloging in Publication Data
Archer, Caroline, 1948–
    Next steps in parenting the child who hurts : tykes and teens /
Caroline Archer, Adoption UK.
        p.   cm.
    Includes bibliographical references.
    ISBN 1 85302 802 9
    1. Adoptive parents Handbooks, manuals, etc. 2. Child care Handbooks, manuals, etc. 3. Parent and teenager Handbooks, manuals, etc. 4. Parenting Handbooks, manuals, etc. I. Adoption UK (Firm) II. Title.
HV875.A683   1999   99-41637
649'.145--dc21   CIP

British Library Cataloguing in Publication Data
A CIP catalogue record for this book is available from the British Library

ISBN 1 85302 802 9 pb

Printed and Bound in Great Britain by
Athenaeum Press, Gateshead, Tyne and Wear

Contents

Acknowledgements

There are many people I would like to remember and thank for their ideas, support, active criticism and advice during the incubation and realisation of *Next Steps* over the past year. Some I will mention by name whilst others, especially all those members of the After Adoption Network within Adoption UK (PPIAS) who have shared a piece of their lives with me, will, out of expediency, remain anonymous. A special, silent thought should go to them as they struggle each day to live with the hurts of adoptive family life.

In particular my thanks go to Beth Gibb and Judith Mulcahy for their sound advice, to Lynda Gilbert and Margaret Robertson for reading and commenting on all the various drafts of *Next Steps*, to Ian Cockburn and Melanie Bush for their help in developing the illustrations, to Joy Hasler, who turned my fantasy ideas into brilliant graphic reality and to Philly Morrall, National Co-ordinator of Adoption UK, who as usual found time to be encouraging and supportive – even when she had no time!

Professor David Howe of the University of East Anglia in Norwich and Dr Vera Fahlberg of Forest Heights in Colorado, USA, have both been tremendous sources of encouragement, for which I am very grateful. I would also like to thank Dr Gregory Keck and Mrs Regina Kupecky of the Attachment and Bonding Center of Ohio, and authors of *Adopting the Hurt Child*, for their generosity and their inspiration and for allowing me to develop their idea of the 'hurt child' into 'the child who hurts'. On a more personal level I would also like to thank them for helping my own family with such humour, enthusiasm and love.

Which brings me once again to the most important people in my life and those to whom I have most to be grateful. My heartfelt thanks go to my husband, Allan, for his ability to remain unflappable when all around him are flapping wildly (and for sorting out my floppy disks!), to my grown-up and growing up children, Jenny, Danny, Tom and Jo, to my grandchildren Chloe, Sophie and Connor and to my dog Olive – even though she doesn't like my new 'office' and no longer keeps my feet warm so regularly!

What is Adoption UK?

Adoption UK, formerly known as Parent to Parent Information on Adoption Services, was formed in 1971 by a group of parents who were involved in adopting children with special needs. Twenty-something years on, membership stands at over 2500 individuals and families, which includes existing adoptive parents, prospective adopters and child care practitioners.

Adoption UK is a registered charity which aims to provide information, support and advice for prospective and existing adoptive parents and long-term foster parents. Through its computerised Experience Resource Bank (ERBIE), and its parents' networks, families can also share experiences with each other at every stage of adoption. One of these networks, the After Adoption Network (AAN), came about as a direct response to members' very real needs for on-going post-placement support and advice on dealing with a wide range of behavioural, emotional and relationship difficulties within their adoptive families.

Adoption UK has its office base at Lower Boddington, Daventry, Northamptonshire NN11 6YB (telephone 01327 260295), and has over 130 local volunteer co-ordinators throughout the UK, all of whom are experienced adopters. Adoptive parents who wish to have further opportunities to get in touch with other parents whose children show difficulties around attachment, trauma, separation and loss may also become involved with the After Adoption Network groups regionally.

From its inception, adoptive parents have been the prime movers in establishing Adoption UK as a support and information service, with effective links with adoption agencies, and has been able to raise issues of concern for all adoptive families. I am proud to be part of such a unique organisation and to have the opportunity to contribute to its ground-breaking traditions.

Foreword

The success of adoption as a piece of social legislation has been recognised for many decades. However, recent changes in social mores and in adoption practice have complicated what once seemed a relatively simple picture. Today, the typical child placed for adoption is a toddler or of school age. In many cases he or she will have suffered some form of abuse or neglect at the hands of at least one carer and now exhibits behavioural or emotional problems and has been disoriented by many moves between a large number of carers. These children still need parents; they need family life. Yet many of them, possibly the majority, pose considerable challenges to the skills, love and understanding of their adoptive mothers and fathers. We have learned that parents need a good deal of preparation and support, help and advice if they are to meet these challenges with skill and confidence, patience and humour, compassion and resilience.

As a researcher, I have had the privilege of meeting many parents, and children who have been adopted or looked after by foster carers. Slowly, I have learned to understand the long-term damage and disturbance that early trauma can have on children's psychological and behavioural development. I have recognised the huge demands that such children can make on their parents' competencies and commitment. I have appreciated that the needs of both the children and their parents are special and peculiarly demanding, needs often not understood by professional helpers based in the mental health, education and social services.

Adoption UK (formerly PPIAS) has been consistently at the forefront in recognising and understanding that children who have experienced early and severe distress in their lives require unusually high and subtle levels of parenting skill when placed in substitute families. Adoption UK's closeness to adopters and adopted children has meant that they have picked up, earlier than most, on what it is like to care for children who hurt. Being a very practical organisation, Adoption UK has also developed a range of very useful resources to help parents, including support networks, a telephone helpline and a range of literature. *Parenting the Child Who Hurts – the First Steps*, published by Adoption UK in 1997 (and now published in a new edition as *First Steps in Parenting the Child Who Hurts: Tiddlers and Toddlers* by Jessica Kingsley Publishers for Adoption UK), is an extremely useful guidebook for parents looking after children who have suffered trauma, abuse and neglect. I have recommended it to many parents who, without exception, have reported that they found the guide absorbing, reassuring and helpful.

The sequel, *Next Steps in Parenting the Child Who Hurts: Tykes and Teens* is a natural follow-on. It contains all the insights and experience that the first book offers but moves the action on. Adoption UK and Caroline Archer have managed to pull together a wide range of firsthand personal experience and research to produce an excellent guide for parents looking after older children with histories of disruption and disturbance. The book succeeds on two levels. First, it paints very familiar and recognisable pictures of children who pose great challenges to parents. Adopters and foster carers find this recognition of their child very reassuring and supportive. Second, it offers a vast range of practical advice given by people who have lived and worked with children who have been hurt. *Next Steps in Parenting the Child Who Hurts: Tykes and Teens* promises to be every bit as valuable to parents as *First Steps* and I wish it every success.

Professor David Howe
University of East Anglia, Norwich
January 1999

Introduction

Welcome to *Next Steps in Parenting the Child Who Hurts: Tykes and Teens*, the second guidebook of philosophies, insights and strategies for adoptive and long-term foster parents living with 'children who challenge'. As with *First Steps*, the use of 'the child who hurts' in the title acknowledges the hurts, of separation, loss, abuse, neglect and inconsistent parenting, which many adopted children experience in their young lives. These traumatic experiences of early hurts can make it more likely, although by no means inevitable, that they in their turn will attempt to hurt those closest to them, as a way of expressing their inner pain.

Patterns of adoption placement over the past decade have changed enormously; we are now seeing an increasing proportion of children who have survived overwhelming emotional pain, often suffering distress on a chronic basis, being placed in permanent families. In other words, they have experienced repeated traumatic hurts which will affect their perceptions of the world for the foreseeable future – **unless we can effectively interrupt their patterns of social interaction, their thinking and their reacting in their inside and outside worlds.** Many of you will have found from experience that this is not as easy as it sounds and that, although love and patience are essential ingredients, they are often not enough to alter a child's blueprint for 'surviving' family life.

What I hope to offer in this book is a continuing outline of the effects of **traumatic hurts** on a child's ability to function, to feel safe, to feel comforted and comfortable, to learn about themselves and about other people, to think, to trust and to deal with the unknown. The foundation to finding effective strategies for living with children who hurt is to understand why they do what they do, and why they carry on doing what they do, even though *we* feel they are now in a safe family. **So if you have not already done so, please obtain a copy of** *First Steps* and take time to familiarise yourself with the fundamental developmental processes through which all children must pass, alongside a discussion of the difficulties which may arise if all does not go well for a child in her earliest years.

As you will be reminded throughout both books, a child organises her nervous system, and her responses, thoughts and beliefs about the world, around her experiences as a baby or very young child. So that, **even if your child is a teenager now, she may well continue to struggle with earlier developmental issues.** This can affect her growth and development on many levels (physical, psychological, social, intellectual and spiritual), and may be particularly marked at important developmental stages, such as at adolescence. **I hope that you will find many fun suggestions in *First Steps* which you could successfully adapt to suit the current needs of your child who hurts.**

I believe this book is an essential sequel to *First Steps* for parents of older children because being a parent to an under-five, even a young child with serious emotional and relationship difficulties, does not pose the same degree of difficulty as being a parent of a fifteen-year-old struggling with the same issues. For one thing, there is a social expectation that parents should be in charge and should take decisions for a young child; parents also have the advantage of a larger physique. This is frequently not the case for the parents of teenagers today. Moreover, in the current socio-political climate, as increasing emphasis is being given to child protection issues and children's rights, sight is sometimes lost of young people's responsibilities, and of the discrepancies between chronological age (how old they are) and functional age (how old they act) in youngsters who have been hurt.

I trust you will enjoy reading both these books and that you find them helpful in enabling you and your child to come to terms with your lives together. If you do not find what you really need, then I wholeheartedly apologise and remind myself, and you, that I am only human! I am intensely aware of how much I have left out, how much still remains to be said, about the extremely complex puzzle which is life with a child who *hurts*. In particular I know that I have barely touched on strategies for children who have 'shut down' – who may show 'passive resistance' in their families, or whose compliance is so total that it feels unnatural. We hope to cover these areas in a series of 'occasional papers', to be published by Adoption UK beginning in 2000, which will include other relevant issues such as depression, addictive behaviours and eating disorders, teenage parents and adoptive grandparenthood.

I realise that I have also not specifically addressed the impact of being black in a white family. Adoption UK embraces an equal opportunities policy and has been active in its support for same race placements. However, the reality for children of black and mixed parentage is that this is an ideal which has yet to be achieved. In the meantime we have a responsibility to support and encourage all racially mixed families. As a member of such a family myself, I am aware of the additional challenges which face children who have been trans-racially adopted and of the tireless efforts of members of the black community to raise awareness about racial and identity issues for adopted children and young people.

The pressures of appearing 'different' can certainly contribute to a child's weak sense of self – and hence to his sense of self-worth and his identity. However, I firmly believe that this is only a part, though admittedly a very significant part, of the struggle every adopted child has to define himself and to accept himself for all that he is. Certainly black children need positive, black role models, opportunities to build connections with their ethnic roots and culture and to take an informed pride in their differences. They also, like every child who hurts, need parents to love and care for them and a family in which they will feel secure and to which they feel they belong.

I also believe that parents who can actively acknowledge, accept and reflect back the outstanding uniqueness of a child, whatever the similarities or differences in their race and cultural heritage, will undoubtedly meet all their child's needs well enough. Certainly they may require additional help and support to make specific ethnic links and to 'get it right' but they will succeed! It is up to us all to give them every encouragement in this challenging, life-long and life-giving task: to be good enough parents to children who hurt.

Coming Home

Words in bold and italics can be found in the glossary

Parenthood does *not* begin at the moment you bring your child home but at the point of conception of the *idea* of extending your family. This is true whether you are planning to conceive a home-grown baby or to find room in your home, and in your hearts, for an older child who has experienced multiple previous caretakers, abuse or neglect, and intense emotional pain. Of course, just as it is possible to become pregnant without planning or thinking things through, so it may be feasible to bring an older child into your home without a lot of preparation and forethought. However, many clinicians recognise the common sense in ensuring the good all-round health of both partners prior to conception of a baby and of making the nine months' waiting time a time for preparation, sustained self-care, and a thorough exploration of the possibilities of parenthood.

The assessment and preparation period, prior to an adoption placement within the UK, will ideally parallel this invaluable **developmental** process. For would-be adopters from overseas, requirements may vary considerably, according to the countries with which you are working. However, whichever way you do it, there will probably be many aspects which are not covered by an initial assessment, or which are not to be addressed in sufficient detail. **Use the waiting period, that time which feels so full of unnecessary delays and frustrations, to move gradually, from the original concept of the idea of adoption in the abstract, towards the reality of a particular child (or group of children) coming into your life.**

However good your social worker is, unless she is herself an adoptive parent, she may be unable to get across to you how it *really* feels to be an adoptive parent. One of the best ways to find out what adopting a school-age child feels like is to get in touch with other adoptive parents who are further along the same road. Through Adoption UK you will be able to locate other adopters close to you, whom you can meet face to face. If you would like to be put in touch with other parents who have taken on a specific age of child, or one with particular past experiences, our computer resource bank, ERBIE, can make this a *reality*.

Better still, you can join your local Adoption UK group (local co-ordinators' names and telephone numbers are published in our quarterly journal, *Adoption Today*) and become part of our self-help support network, the After Adoption Network. This will give you many valuable opportunities to hear a variety of different experiences and, often, to meet the children first hand, at some of the events which Adoption UK members arrange. It may only be through seeing and hearing some of the challenges that adoptive families may face on a daily basis that you can begin to take on board the joys and sorrows a child who *hurts* may bring. Later on, when your child does finally come home, you will already have a well established network of friends with whom you can share your own feelings and worries, surprises and puzzles.

It can also be invaluable to begin to get an idea of the sorts of questions you may need to ask about a child and the social work agency's range of resources before 'delivery'. Once again, Adoption UK has produced an essential checklist for would-be adopters, which is available free to members. Do remember that any child coming into your family beyond babyhood probably has a long and complicated family history. It is to be hoped that the placing social worker will have access to a good deal of documented information which she will do her best to share with you. However, what has actually happened and what is documented may be two very different things. This situation can become complicated further where a specialist preparation and placement agency is working on behalf of a placing local authority to find a family for the child. In this case, some information may be withheld, or overlooked unintentionally, which could be vital to your family's future well-being.

Even with the best will in the world, your placing social worker will be unable to tell you everything that is known about your child. Quite probably she will attempt to select what she considers the most important information and will try to present it to you in what she feels is the most acceptable way. She may have issues of confidentiality to consider, may try to be very sensitive to your feelings, not wishing to distress you with unpleasant details, or she may not recognise the significance of particular pieces of information at the time.

Sometimes, reading descriptions of 'children who wait' may have much in common with estate agents' advertisements for accommodation – although I understand that recent legislation requires estate agents to verify all the information they now provide. Just as you would use your common sense to decode the 'des. res.' advertisements, so you would do well to practise translating the brief descriptions of waiting children into real terms. Features in the 'Children Who Wait' section of our journal *Adoption Today* are preceded by a page which alerts would-be adopters to some of these issues – **read it!** Beyond that, do bear in mind that almost all children currently being placed for adoption have experienced a number of past *hurts*. **Be prepared to ask lots of questions and to consider the implications of what you learn for your whole family, over the next twenty years or more.**

As I hope you will have learned from *First Steps*, **the earliest years of a child's life are the most crucial for healthy development. They are the foundation years, upon which all subsequent experience will be built.** When you are house-hunting you will, initially, pay most attention to the appearance of the house, to whether the rooms feel warm and sunny, and whether you like the present decor (even though this is easily changed). However, if you are serious about buying the house, you will then go on to ask a surveyor to undertake a formal inspection of the foundations and structure of the property, to find out whether it is a solid financial investment. You are also likely to engage a solicitor to examine the legal aspects, including the past history of the property and any persisting obligations and agreements. **Just because this is a child you are considering, you should not allow your heart completely to rule your head or fail to undertake basic safeguards.** The decision you make now has implications for your whole future, and that of the child.

Finding out about the foundation years, especially information about the pregnancy and birth, is likely to be difficult, increasingly so the older the child is at placement. Unfortunately, much of this information may not have been well documented by social services departments, although medical records may indicate potential areas of concern, if you can access them. From our own experience, we know that placing social workers tend to pay most attention to what has happened to a child in the past year or two, gaining most of their information from the child herself, and from current carers and other significant adults. These details are indeed vital, although talking to the previous caregivers personally, armed with a checklist of essential questions, will provide you with a much clearer picture of the way the child is currently functioning in a family. **However, this snapshot needs to be fleshed out by pen pictures from the past.** It may be ten years since this child was in her mother's womb, but her experiences then may well form the basis of her present belief system – especially about mothers, and about family life (see Part 4: Through the Looking Glass).

I do not believe that any number of insights (or cautionary tales) from seasoned adopters, or full disclosure of information about a particular child, will change your mind about the concept of building your family by adoption. Nor should it! However, I do believe that **you will do what you wish to do best if you know where you are going** *and* **have made as informed a decision as possible about the right child for you.** This is certainly not just a rational, *left brained* activity (see page 48) devoid of emotion. On the contrary, the intuitive chemistry of *goodness of fit* is an essential component, without which your relationship may never truly take off. **What is vital is that you find a balance between informed decision-making and trusting your 'gut feelings'.** That way you all stand the best chance of **'getting it right'** – rather like house buying really!

Bringing a school-age child into your family is undoubtedly going to have profound effects on your life. Whilst having a new baby at home can consume all your waking (and sleeping!) hours, at least for home-grown infants, there are rituals and ways of doing things, in those first few weeks and months, which are expected and sanctioned by 'society' at large. You tend to do what your own family did, or what your friends and neighbours are doing, or to use that information consciously to change the way you do it.

For most of us who build our families by adoption, there are fewer precedents, and even fewer opportunities to make contact with other adoptive parents in the same situation. Extended families and social networks are also likely to be 'new' to adoption. You will need to be ready to prepare them for this out of the ordinary addition to your family at the same time as you are getting used to the idea yourself. With fewer norms, less defined working models and less established guidelines upon which to base your lives as adoptive parents, it makes sense to keep in close touch with other adopters and their families along the way.

Misconceptions about adoptions beyond babyhood are very common. You may already have become aware of some unspoken messages, implied criticisms or words of warning when you broached the subject of taking an older child into your home. Conversely, you may have faced excessively admiring comments, along the lines of: 'You are wonderful. I couldn't do that!' There are often inter-generational differences of perspective, cultural variations, class and political differences, of which you may not have really been conscious, until the moment you start talking about adoption. In addition, where you already have children born into your family, wider family members may suddenly seem over-protective towards their 'own' grandchildren, feeling that they may be sidelined or 'pushed out of the nest' by 'an invading cuckoo'.

Society as a whole tends to be quite ambivalent about adopters and adoption. So whilst they may think we are saints or martyrs, or just plain weird for choosing to do what we do, there is also a tendency to look for ulterior motives and even to take some comfort from signs of difficulty and stress, along the lines of 'I told you so' or 'Well, what did you expect?' It is to be hoped that you will have had opportunities to work through some of these issues with your social worker in the preparation period – but it is often difficult to predict people's reactions before the child has been placed with you. You may find that you will need to re-consider how you handle such responses at some length, over the coming years, should you hit really sticky patches with your youngster.

Whatever anyone else thinks, you will almost certainly still choose to go ahead and expand your family. That's great! With luck you will also have time to explore some of your own expectations, motives and preconceptions. It is very difficult to be *realistic* and objective about adding a child to your family, since if you did not have a dream and believe that you have something valuable to offer, you wouldn't have considered doing it in the first place. There are, after all, plenty more financially rewarding and socially valued things to do with your life! Please do not be tempted to let go of your dream – but, equally, do your best to prevent it turning into a sleepless nightmare by preparing for the worst, whilst continuing to hope and strive for the best. **The current *reality*, for almost all children placed for adoption beyond infancy, is that they will have been seriously *hurt* in the past, that their future depends on your commitment, and that they are likely to test you to the limits and beyond, over and over again.**

Finding the *'right balance'* in your expectations for yourself and for your child can be very difficult. Many parents want their children to grow up to 'be something' – be it a brain surgeon, a social worker, a craftsperson, an opera singer, an architect or a creator of computer software. You may want your children to achieve this for themselves, so that they feel valued, fulfilled and successful, and perhaps also because it helps you to feel that way too. Whilst most youngsters do *not* grow up to be famous or wealthy, you might *realistically* expect them to be honest, hard-working, respectable and to reach their full potential.

Whatever your private dream you will certainly wish your child to be happy in her life, both as a child and as an adult. **What you will probably not have expected is a child who gives almost nothing back, who can be hateful, abusive, rejecting and destructive and carries on that way for years and years.** If you had known it was going to be like that, you might have chosen to do something else instead. Now you may have to accept that your child's life will always be very difficult and try to set your sights on more *realistic* targets – that she will leave the cat alone today, for example. Yet, knowing that adoption is part of the solution for a child who *hurts*, you will never give up hoping that she will 'come out the other end' able to hold her own in the world.

Your social worker may have spoken to you of the 'honeymoon period', after your child first comes home, when you are all on your best behaviour, and you are trying to find out about how the relationships will work at close quarters. Indeed, you may well have already noticed this pattern during the introductory period, although common sense will probably have told you that these 'getting to know you' meetings are hardly *real* life or *really* about 'getting to know you', except at a very superficial level (like judging the structure of a house by the wallpaper in the front room). However, you may have hoped that once the child was with you, in your home, in your care, then things would be different: that it would all start being more *real* for both of you. **Yet, in many ways, the 'honeymoon period' can be best understood as an extension of the unreality of the introductory period. It is up to you to start out, on your own terms, as you mean to go on.**

Many children who have been *hurt* have had many previous experiences of 'families', most if not all of whom will have let them down, by being absent, inconsistent, neglectful or abusive. Parents may also be perceived this way if, for other very valid reasons, they have been unable to keep on taking care of the child. Whatever the circumstances, the child coming into your home is likely to be feeling bereft, bewildered, scared, confused, sad, angry, resentful, unloved and unlikely to believe that he will be safe with you. If you remember that his whole survival, so far, has been based on living through danger and staying alive, then you can expect that things are not going to be easy, nor are they going to change overnight. **It will also help you to begin to make sense of his behaviour, although not to excuse it.**

Some people have referred to the honeymoon period as 'the stalking out period' – a time during which the child is trying to find out how the land lies and how best to take care of himself. During this time he may indeed seem quiescent, co-operative and inconspicuous: he may be 'keeping his head down *and* keeping his nose clean' because he needs all his senses fully *functional*, if he is to work out what is going on in your family, and not get hurt again. This is a child's 'safety shield', which may not reflect how he *really* feels, or give you any *real* idea of his usual way of being. (See Part 4: Through the Looking Glass.)

A child coming into a family needs to know where she stands and what the house rules are, right away. So, you will want to start giving clear messages, right away, that you are going to care for her safely *and* that you are going to do it your way. Given what we know about the beliefs of children who *hurt*, it is likely to be just as hard to show that you can be loving as to show you have safe, workable limits. It is essential that you can keep on doing both. Remember that the two things that any child coming into a family will be looking for and fearing, in equal parts, are indications that you are trying to get close, and that you are able to take charge.

Since a child's past experiences are for the most part going to colour her perceptions of the present, **there will be no room for inconsistency or 'letting things pass because she's** new'. Any hint of uncertainty on your part will feed into her belief that you, like everyone else in her life, will be unreliable. This will reinforce her view that only she can take care of her, and that getting close to people is dangerous. Be prepared for this push-pull of neediness and fear of closeness, the search for secure *boundaries* whilst fighting the system, to persist almost indefinitely. It goes with the job! However, if you can stick to your guns, eventually your child will begin letting down her defences and letting you in. **Meantime, firm *boundaries* form a safe containing field, within which a child can begin to experience change.**

Don't be tempted to let a youngster get away with things you don't really like at first, just to make him feel at home. Try to think how you feel when you go to stay with someone for the first time. If your hosts leave you to your own devices for too long, because they think that you need some space, then you may well begin to feel not wanted, or that you are in the way. You may then try to keep out of their way even more. If they also let you help yourself to everything in the house, whilst not encouraging you to help with simple tasks like the washing up, then you would assume that that's how they always want it to be. Depending on your personality you might feel quite rejected, or you might feel that you had fallen on your feet, had found 'suckers' to wait on you hand and foot! **A child whose thinking is muddled from experiences of *hurts* and inconsistencies in the past is even more likely to pick up 'wrong messages' like these, if there is any ambiguity in your home.**

It will be very much harder to establish your ground rules with a child after a period of 'anything goes' and allowing him to settle in than to start as you mean to go on. When a child coming into your family has already learned one system of house rules the hard way, by painful trial and error, he will not only have a very fixed idea of how things are, he is even more likely to believe that you are going to let him down too, or that he can do what he wants. Changing the rules as you go along will only compound the problem. **Unfortunately it is only too easy to confuse what a child wants with what he needs: you as the adult must be able to trust your instincts on this one.** If you start out firm but fair, and stick with it, your youngster may come to respect you, and, to begin with at least, he will be able to recognise that you believe your way is the 'right way'.

Of course, you will, at the same time, be looking for ways of making your child feel at home, perhaps by including some of her favourite foods and doing some of the things you know she likes. Speaking to previous caretakers should fill you in on these, and perhaps provide you with some familiar clothes, bedding and toys. For some children who have been seriously *hurt* in the past, eating beans on toast or watching *Home and Away* may be the only reliable events they have *ever* known in their otherwise chaotic life. They may cling to them like a drowning man to a lifeboat in a stormy sea! Whilst you can understand this and will want to respect this, you will also want to extend her nutritional, recreational and social 'diet' as time goes on.

Again, this is a balance that you will wish to apply to all areas of your child's life. **Too much change too soon can be overwhelming but too little change will leave her where she is,**

stuck in an out-moded, *dysfunctional* pattern. It is likely that you will also find there are times when a youngster is less open to change, or when she may even go backwards, demanding certain foods or toys you thought she had outgrown. This will usually be a sign that there are other stresses in her life, which she is finding difficult to cope with right now. A little leeway at this point can go a long way, as long as you are able to keep giving the message that you do expect your child to let go of these 'babyish' things again, in time.

Try not to show your disappointment when you do perceive relapses, since your child will sense you are upset and may well believe that you will now want to get rid of her, just like her parents did in the past. For, whatever the reason for her leaving her birth family, your child will, very deep down, believe it is because she wasn't good enough. She will be waiting for the criticism and rejection to happen again and may even try to make it happen sooner, rather than later, by acting the part. **When a child's early experiences have led her to believe that she truly is unloveable, worthless, damaged or bad, then she will tend to perceive confirmation of these beliefs in everything which happens to her.**

You will have to work very diligently to change these *selective perceptions*, whilst simultaneously keeping your feet firmly on the ground – **for much of what your child actually does may well feel unloveable, worthless, damaged or plain bad. This emphatically does not mean that you have to accept unacceptable behaviour or carry on as if it isn't happening.** On the contrary, showing your child that you are not prepared to let her go on *hurting* herself or others, by her words, actions or lack of thought, can give her a very powerful message that you believe she is a valuable young person and that she is capable of, and deserves, better. At first she will probably not be able to hear this invaluable message but at least you will be establishing some ground rules and giving her opportunities to try out what it feels like to do it differently. Any positive habits you can begin to set in place now can form the essential foundations, on which you can continue to build.

Remember, too, **that a child's blueprint for survival is likely to become more firmly entrenched, and more resistant to change, over time.** This will have the effect of skewing every aspect of her *development* increasingly with age. It may take more love, more patience and more ingenuity for you to come up with effective parenting strategies, to provide your older child with corrective life experiences and to encourage a willingness to let go of old, destructive ways, than for a pre-school child.

Adolescence can itself raise further troublesome issues, at a time when all feelings are likely to be heightened by the 'rampant hormones' of puberty and when social and peer pressures may be pulling your child in different directions. In addition, as with every new developmental stage, adolescence can pose particular challenges to young adoptees whose development has already been put at risk. Its associations with the vital issues of separating, growing up and becoming an individual make this a period of great potential turbulence and challenge.

However daunting this may make your parenting task, it certainly doesn't make it impossible. At this stage you may not be able to contain your youngster in the same ways you could with an eight-year-old, and he may be very much bigger than you, but you are still the adult(s) and can still find ways of showing him who is ultimately responsible, in the family, for the family. You can also hope that he will accept at least basic responsibilities for his own life and can try to treat unexplained absences, or days in bed, as time off for you too. Even an adolescent's leaving home (or threats to leave), although distressing, can bring you a well deserved rest from the 'in your face' responsibilities of family life with a youngster who *hurts*. **Don't worry – he will always be back!** (See Staying a Family and Being Apart in Part 7.)

More Beginnings – Continuing Child Development

We tend to think of child *development* as something which happens in the early years – perhaps before a youngster starts school. In terms of *neuro-biological* development it is certainly true that the vast majority of brain cell growth and maturation occurs during the first few years of life, which is why so much emphasis is placed on developmental processes in *First Steps* – but it doesn't just stop there! Each one of us goes on growing and changing throughout our lives, to a greater or lesser extent. It continues to be possible to influence the quality and direction of change – particularly if we understand these developmental processes and how they can be influenced for better or worse.

A child who *hurts* will, by definition, have experienced some serious challenges to her early development at one or more levels – physically, emotionally, psychologically, intellectually or spiritually. How far her development is affected will depend on many factors. Some children cope with adversity far better than others. Some, perhaps, may appear not to have been affected in any obvious way. Whilst this may be so, it could well be that such a child has learned to cope and to cover up her weaknesses, especially through her early childhood. However, continued attempts at *compensation* can place extra stress on the child and, just like Harlow's rehabilitated monkeys (see *First Steps*, page 78), further *distress* can lead to *de-compensation*, i.e, a child who has appeared to be coping well may 'lose it', perhaps following another move, on changing schools, or during adolescence.

Whether your youngster is six or sixteen, whether he has just come home or has been with you for ten years, he may still be trying to compensate for the breaks in his development during those early years. It may be helpful to remind yourself, at this point, that it is never too late to 'start again', although, like learning a foreign language, it becomes harder as you grow older. Whilst you may feel that you have missed out on vital periods of development, it will often be possible to find ways to encourage a youngster to reach his full potential.

Certainly, it may not be easy – that's why the 'right times' are called *critical periods* – but is still feasible, with a little luck, lots of patience and a liberal dash of ingenuity! The *brain and nervous system,* like your child, has tremendous *resilience* : a great capacity for flexibility and continuing growth. So, whilst it is true that the bulk of growth, learning and development *does* take place in the first three or four years following conception, **you can reduce the lasting damage and increase the extent of healing – if you can recognise areas of difficulty and work with them positively, as soon as possible**.

Below I have listed a number of areas in which a child's development may have been slowed down or altered. Of course, a child may show signs of difficulty in more than one area, since **development is multi-faceted and changes are often occurring simultaneously.** The degree to which a youngster is adversely affected can also vary widely and may depend on her current age and developmental stage, as well as upon her past experiences and inherited characteristics. Trust your own instincts on this, since you are the one who sees your child most, and in the widest variety of situations. If you are worried about any areas of your youngster's development, you are probably more than justified in being concerned. However, try to keep things in proportion – to find that delicate *balance* between acknowledging limitations and still believing change is possible. (See also page 19 in Part 1.)

It is also important that you consider consulting your GP, to discuss some of your anxieties with her. If necessary, you can request a referral to a specialist in child development, such as a paediatrician, clinical neuro-psychologist or paediatric occupational therapist. The number of experienced practitioners who are able to recognise and work effectively with sometimes subtle developmental difficulties unfortunately remains limited, but this should still be your first line of approach.

Being able to establish, with some degree of accuracy, 'where your child is' currently, in developmental terms, is essential. This knowledge can help you see 'where your child is going' and what he needs to 'get him back on track'. (See Part 5 of *First Steps*.) **The pointers below are derived from the personal experience of a number of adoptive parents and are intended as broad guidelines only.** It is vital that you bear in mind your child's chronological age and remember that some degree of variation will exist naturally.

Things to Look Out For (If Age Inappropriate):

- poor concentration*
- short attention span*
- high *impulsivity**
- tendency to 'day-dream', or to seem 'spaced out'*
- inability to remain still, always 'on the go'*
- disruptive behaviours
- difficulties with social interaction, e.g. making eye contact, physical contact, engaging in reciprocal conversation, taking turns in games and activities
- over-sensitivity to noise, movement, touch, smell or visual images (sensory integration difficulties)
- tendency to talk excessively or to chatter nonsensically
- lack of natural curiosity, or 'into everything' (beyond toddlerhood)
- co-ordination problems, such as clumsiness (*dyspraxia*), developing handedness/ dominant eye or ear (laterality)
- problems associated with memory – short/long term, or selective

*these characteristics, when occurring together, are often associated with Attention Deficit Disorders [ADDs] or Disorders of Attention, Movement and Perception [DAMP]

- lack of self-awareness, such as not recognising when cold or hungry, or difficulty distinguishing wants from needs

- poor organisational abilities, such as inability to take care of *self* appropriately e.g. washing, getting ready for bed, school – may be selective

- tendency to be *over-compliant*, silent or lacking spontaneity

- specific learning difficulties, such as in reading and writing (dyslexia) or in numeracy (dyscalculia)

- speech and language difficulties, including problems with articulating words (dysarthia), difficulties taking in audible information and difficulties processing and using that information (auditory processing deficits)

- persistent wetting (enuresis) and/or soiling (encopresis)

- younger than actual (chronological) age behaviours, e.g. play, choice of playmates

- sleep problems – including difficulties getting to sleep and night wakefulness

- obsessive or repetitive play or drawing, especially if this involves the portrayal of violence

- clingy behaviour, including over-dependence on adult caregivers (beyond toddlerhood)

- over-*in*dependence, competence (the 'parentified child'), or weakened ability to demonstrate/accept dependency

- marked preference for adult or older company

- difficulties in distinguishing between fantasy and reality

- extreme reactions (e.g. tantrums at ten) or absence of expected reaction

- inability to accept reasonable limits

- specific or generalised fears (intense, e.g. of the dark, or of being alone)

- lack of appropriate fear

- tendency to engage in dangerous or destructive play or activities

- other repetitive behaviours, including excessive verbal repetition

- self-stimulating behaviours, such as head-banging, poking, picking

- self-soothing activities, such as rocking, thumb-sucking, stroking a 'blankie'

- tendency to damage clothing through picking, poking, tearing, cutting etc., or to be 'hard' on shoes or clothes

- *self-harming* activities, including hair and skin cutting, eating foreign bodies, lack of awareness of danger, sexual inappropriate behaviours

- self-medicating activities, such as the use of tobacco, drugs, alcohol – too much, too soon.

I am grateful to After Adoption members for the following examples, from experiences within their own families, which illustrate some of the above points:

He would repeatedly wreck any activity in which any other member of the family was engrossed. He soon found that switching off the computer mid-game, when his brother had carefully paused it in order to go to the bathroom, created a great stir and was guaranteed to destroy the peace. **(disruptive behaviour)**

Often when we spoke to our daughter she seemed to be in another world. Much of the time she stared into space and twiddled tiny pieces of paper between her fingers. We grew used to touching her gently to attract her attention, before we spoke. **(difficulties with social interaction/tendency to 'day-dream'/obsessive or repetitive play)**

She talked incessantly – and even answered when we spoke to her younger brother. 'No, he doesn't want marmite. He wants jam. Red jam. Lovely. I like jam. I'm spreading it now. He likes it. It's red. Yummy! Shall I have jam?' … **(tendency to talk excessively/the 'parentified child')**

He never seemed to know when he was hungry or respond when he had had enough. At two and a half he would scream for food, then, when it was put in front of him, refuse it. If I took it away, he would scream again, and so it went on. Sometimes he would eat without cease all that was there. **(lack of *self-awareness*)**

Our eight-year-old was always tripping over her own feet. She couldn't catch or kick a ball and her handwriting was a mess. **(co-ordination problems)**

Even in Year 10 our son never seemed to have the correct books for his lessons, but he never forgot his lunch money! **(poor organisational abilities/problems associated with memory – selective!)**

Our school-aged son's speech was very indistinct and quite idiosyncratic. He never seemed to be able to follow even simple instructions. He would also muddle up words like 'back' and 'front', 'up and down', 'bring and take'. **(speech and language difficulties/problems associated with memory)**

My daughter came to live with us at seven years old. It took us almost a year to get rid of a plastic dummy. She insisted on sucking it, especially on visits to the supermarket. **(younger than actual age behaviours/self-soothing activities)**

I couldn't leave my daughter (aged eight years) in the car whilst I posted a letter or bought a car park ticket. She clung to me all her waking hours and was frightened to go to sleep. **(clingy behaviour beyond toddlerhood/sleep problems/specific fears)**

He would never let us help him or show him how to do anything. He couldn't stay close enough, or still enough, to pay attention. **(over-independence/difficulties with social interaction/short attention span/inability to sit still)**

My son finds it difficult to get on with his peers. He tends, instead, to monopolise adults, or older adolescents, whenever possible. **(marked preference for adult company)**

Whilst staying with friends I went into my eight-year-old's bedroom and was greeted by a 'pooey' smell. I suggested she might need clean knickers but she just said: 'It's chocolate!' **(difficulties in distinguishing between fantasy and *reality*/lack of *self-awareness*)**

At fourteen he was cross that I was busy when he wanted my attention. I asked him to wait but he chose to go outside and let all my car tyres down instead! **(extreme reactions – 'tantrums at ten')**

She was very finicky about specks of dust and hairs, especially at bath-time. Washing her hair was a nightmare, as inevitably hairs came out and floated past. One day she absolutely screamed blue murder as her own 'poo' floated by! **(specific fears/extreme reactions/lack of** *self-awareness***)**

On one occasion, when my teenager was missing for four nights, he was found tied up to some railings in a local park. He made allegations of rape and kidnap to the local police but eventually admitted it was all a pack of lies. **(high** *impulsivity***/lack of appropriate fear/difficulties in distinguishing between fantasy and** *reality***)**

When he was out playing with other children we always had to be on the look-out, because he always played 'to kill'. He did not seem to be able to understand that he could hurt someone. **(tendency to engage in dangerous play/inability to accept reasonable limits)**

I was always careful to make sure there were no loose threads on his clothing, as you could guarantee they would be pulled and the item completely unravelled. One day I found him sitting on his bed, a pair of scissors in his hand, and several very careful, neat cuts across the front of his jumper. **(tendency to damage or wear out certain parts of clothing)**

He was thirteen when we found him completely unconscious on the bathroom floor. It was late one Sunday morning and we had assumed he was having a lie-in. Unknown to us he had gone downstairs very early and drunk everything in the cabinet. Fortunately he was violently sick when we moved him and regained consciousness. **(self-medicating activities/high** *impulsivity***)**

When Things Don't Seem Quite Right

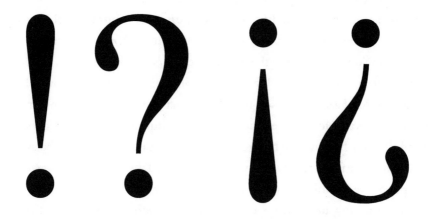

Understanding why your child acts as he does is one thing, living with difficult behaviours can be quite another. In fact, it is vitally important that you, as parents, do pick up on the seemingly 'crazy' challenges of your child – it is often the only way a child has of communicating major difficulties in his life. **If you don't let your kids 'get to you', then you truly cannot get in touch with them and begin 'getting to them' in newer, more healthy ways!** Moreover, if you are too understanding or too tolerant of their current difficulties, you may not be providing your children with sufficient opportunities for change.

Remember that the very behaviours which may have kept your child alive in the past could be preventing him from being truly alive in the present. So, the secret is to feel the apparent craziness, without actually going crazy yourselves. It may then become possible for you and your child to find a different way of being, which doesn't seem so crazy to either of you. This will be a very difficult concept for most people to grasp but it will probably make a lot of sense to you. It may help other people outside your family to think of this in terms of transference, one of the most widely recognised therapeutic concepts, by which therapists pick up on their clients' feelings through their personal interactions and through the feelings they engender in the therapist. Transference is recognised as an extremely useful therapeutic tool, if it is used well and with appropriate *empathy* and understanding.

Of course, not only is every child uniquely different in themselves, but they may often appear to be a very different child with different people. This may be particularly noticeable in children who *hurt*. In this case, **it is very likely that the person with whom a child will act most hurtful, most crazy and most difficult is with the current *mother* figure.** Irrespective of what actually happened to your youngster in the past, his *perception* is likely to be that his mother, the first and most important person in his life, has *abandoned* him, has let him down, has failed to protect him – in fact, has *hurt* him. He will then expect that you, his adoptive mother, will behave in precisely the same way. He may well interpret your nurturing and supportive behaviours as threatening and, at times, he may even bring up some of those same rejecting or abusive feelings in you (see Part 4). These are features of two other well recognised therapeutic phenomena, known as projection, or projective identification, and counter-transference.

So, if you are picking up feelings or experiencing behaviours with your child that no-one else is, not even your partner, then you are probably very much closer to the child's *real* feelings than anyone else. Hang on to that knowledge when you are feeling overwhelmed or horrified by the depth of your angry or destructive feelings, or experiencing disbelief, from yourself or from others. It is vital that you believe in yourself and that you still remain open to your child's deepest needs. **It is also essential that you do not in any way act on those projected negative feelings or beat yourself up unnecessarily for feeling them.** We all have positive and negative emotions within us; it is how we learn to deal with them that is important. Your child will be very sensitive to expected *hurts*, and even the merest hint of negativity from you is likely to consolidate his already *distorted perceptions* of you.

It is also essential that you learn to call a spade a spade. **For whilst you need to understand why your child acts the way she does, being open to, and open about, their difficulties can offer the clearest way towards healthy change.** In the past, the *hurts* your child experienced were most probably concealed, denied, minimised or made out to be the child's fault. This will have created major *distortions* in her ways of thinking and of relating to other people. If she is to be able to correct these *cognitive* errors, and the consequent challenging behaviours, you will have to be patently clear and unambiguous in your own thinking and responses. **The child was NEVER to blame for the *hurts* of the past but she must accept responsibility for her actions in the present.**

Again, this may be a *very* difficult concept for relatives, friends and child care practitioners to take on board. This is not only because we are talking about a child, but also because we are talking about an extremely vulnerable child, a child who has been *hurt*, and who deserves our understanding and love. **Absolutely true.** However, we may also be talking about a child who regularly steals, lies, manipulates, bullies, destroys belongings, abuses other vulnerable people, including other children, or does his best to ignore us completely. **If you as the parent are the only one picking up on these negatives, then you are the only one who can really describe these behaviours – and they are as bad as they feel to you!** It may take others a lot longer to see your child in this way, or to hear what you are telling them you see.

Difficult behaviours may also increase as you begin to get closer to your child. You can interpret this in several different ways – she may be beginning to trust you enough to let you know how she is feeling, or perhaps the closer you get the more that intimacy threatens her stability, or perhaps you are beginning to feel more like 'parents' to her – with all the inherent dangers she *associates* with that. Whatever the underlying reasons, **it is emphatically not because you are the 'wrong parent'** (except in the sense that any parent other than the birth parent is not the 'right parent'), nor because you have too high expectations, nor because you haven't yet come to terms with your own infertility – **although it may be worthwhile re-examining some of these issues with a supportive friend, or a social worker or counsellor you can trust.**

Each of you *has* to have expectations or you would never achieve anything – and you are the best hope your child has! **What you have to offer is good enough, although it probably doesn't feel like it to your child, or to you yourself, at times!** The fact that you see, and pick up, on difficult or *distorted* behaviours is because you *are* moving closer together and because you are 'tuning in' your body and mind to your child's. At this point, you may often find yourselves in a 'crazy dance of *attachment*', a 'push-me-pull-you' experience, where you try to move closer to your child, as you sense his neediness, and he immediately draws back. Then, just when you feel you can't take any more and are ready to stop trying, he rushes towards you with arms (metaphorically) outstretched. This pattern can go on and on, leaving you feeling even more like 'a crazy parent in crazy land'. (See also Part 4: Through the Looking Glass.) **Don't give up at this point!**

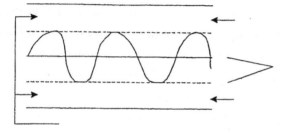

over-aroused 'hyped up'

normal variation in arousal
within comfortable limits

under-aroused
'switched off'

outside comfortable limits

Figure 3.1 Normal pattern of arousal

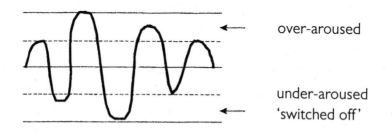

over-aroused

under-aroused
'switched off'

Figure 3.2 Pattern of extreme variation in the child who hurts

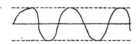 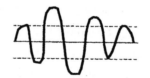 

comfortable levels +
in parent

uncomfortable levels =
in child (temporary)

comfortable levels
for both parent and
child

Figure 3.3 Using your own body rhythms to 'bring down' your child

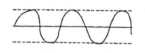 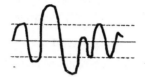 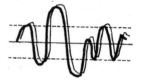

comfortable levels +
in parent

uncomfortable levels =
in child (more or less
permanent or chronic)

uncomfortable levels for
both parent and child
(can become more or less
permanent)

Figure 3.4 What can happen in families with a child who hurts

It is vital that you go on picking up on the craziness of your child's world (which comes from the *real* craziness of his crazy past) **and yet remain in touch with your own sanity and the *real* world you both now inhabit** (see also page 189). When things 'don't feel quite right', when you are continually being knocked out of kilter by your child, it can be very hard for you to keep things in proportion and to retain ways of finding peace in your life. It then becomes ever more important for you to work out ways of taking care of yourself, which feel right for you. Some good, simple ideas on physical self-care can be found in the tiny pocket book *Take Care of Yourself – Inspiration and Advice for Body and Soul* by Penelope Sach. See also the section on health and well-being in your local book shop or health food store.

Through the Looking Glass

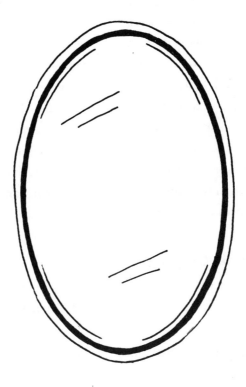

You may take it as read that your child has experienced serious, on-going *distress* in the life-time before he came home to you. In this section, with the curious title of Through the Looking Glass, I would like to take a closer look at some of the *distortions* in *perception* (what goes in), *cognition* (what is thought) and responses (what comes out), which can make it difficult for us to communicate clearly with a child who *hurts*.

When Alice visited Wonderland her varied experiences included becoming different sizes and conversing with strange individuals, who appeared to be speaking the same language – and yet often did not mean the same things. The Mad Hatter's Tea Party epitomises this dream-like, or *looking glass* effect, where things Alice heard, saw and felt could not be relied upon to be *real*, or what she expected. For example, some creatures appeared and disappeared at will, whilst other characters spoke largely in riddles, which appeared to make perfect sense to them but which seemed quite incomprehensible to the bewildered Alice.

I would like you to hold on to the idea of this surreal *looking glass* effect in relation to you and your family. In many ways, it is as if your youngster has stepped out of one world, which she has done her best to make sense of, and now inhabits another – where the rules, patterns and beliefs she has 'sorted' in her head no longer seem to work. The *looking glass* effect can work in both directions, so that what your child does or says can seem 'off the wall' or just plain difficult to you whilst for the child it can make perfect sense. To her, it is you who seem crazy or 'haven't a clue'. In *reality*, you are seeing the world from your 'normal' perspective and she is seeing it from her 'normal' perspective, each based on your previous individual experiences.

Your youngster's early experience of what is 'normal' will almost certainly not be consistent with yours, and the ways she has learned to survive (and even do well) in her world make her way 'normal' and absolutely *real* to her. As you can see, we are beginning to enter a *looking glass* world, where the same words may have opposite meanings – yet each makes perfect sense to the person using them. **With this knowledge in mind, perhaps you can begin to make more sense of your child's responses within your family.**

Speaking the Same Language

Even in 'ordinary, everyday' life, there may be a good deal of mis-matching and misinterpretation of what we say and what we do, which can lead to difficulties in otherwise healthy relationships. Let me give you an example:

> Recently my little grand-daughter came to spend the night with us at very short notice, whilst her baby sister was rushed into 'hopsital'. Not only was this an unplanned stay, but we already had one extra adolescent staying, so bedroom space and our energy supplies were already stretched. Eventually we got Chloe to sleep on the sofa-bed in my youngest son's room, covered in an odd assortment of bedding which was thrown over her once she had fallen asleep. Some hours later we were

awakened by a loud cry of distress and rushed in to discover that she had been violently sick over everything within throwing distance!

I saw the extent of the mess and smelled the nauseating smell without turning the bedroom light on, since I did not wish to wake my son. Since Chloe was sitting up, I tried to make her more comfortable by wiping her face and removing some of her soiled clothing. She reacted quite violently and, after pushing me away, went and crouched down in the far corner of the darkened bedroom. Although I spoke quietly to her and brought her back to her bed, she did not want me to touch her. (I felt at this point that she was afraid I was going to be angry with her for making such an awful mess.) She did, however, allow my husband to clean her up and sit with her until she fell asleep once more. Meanwhile, I retired to my own bed feeling sad and nauseous myself but (being human) also relieved that there was someone else to sort things out!

In the morning my grand-daughter was still very pale. She also remained reluctant to talk to me or get close to me – which is quite unusual, since we have a very warm relationship. She returned home later that morning and in the afternoon I telephoned my daughter's house to see how both grandchildren were now feeling. My daughter informed me that Chloe was reasonably well and had said 'I made a big sicky mess at Granny's house.' Further enquiry from me revealed that she had, indeed, perceived me as being very cross with her for being sick and making a mess – whilst what I had actually said and done was intended to be gentle and reassuring.

In fact Chloe had picked up on my body language, even in the dark! My tired and intensely nauseated reaction to this rude, midnight awakening, which I thought I was hiding quite well, had had a much more powerful and immediate effect. Fortunately, I was able to speak to my grand-daughter on the telephone, to say that I was sorry and let her know that everything was clean and O.K. again. She seemed to find this reassuring and was then very willing to chat to me in her usual, friendly manner.

If this degree of misunderstanding and distress can occur between an adult and small child who know each other pretty well and usually *speak the same language*, how much more difficult will it be for relative strangers, with little background in common, to 'get it right'? **If we take into account a child's previous *traumatic* experiences, then we are indeed likely to find ourselves living in a *looking glass* world** – where we say what we mean, yet the child does not perceive us as meaning what we meant to say (if you see what I mean). Throw in the inverse scenario, that we will not interpret our child's words and behaviours correctly either, then we may be in for a good number of mis-matched *perceptions* and responses – or what my middle son likes to call 'chaos theory'.

There are frequently several 'conversations' going on at the same time between parent and child and we cannot always predict which of these will be 'heard' by the child, or which we, ourselves, will 'hear'. Whilst, clearly, we would like our adopted children to be able to *speak the same language* as we do much of the time (since it is the 'first language' of our friends and neighbours and of the society we are all living in), we cannot necessarily expect them to know find it easy. Think how much harder it is to learn a foreign language when we are grown up than as young children. Over and above this, your child may not believe that she needs to change, since *the language she speaks* now is the language she learned from the cradle and is therefore the only *real language* to her. She will probably expect you to speak her language – and try to give you a 'crash course' right away! **It can help to recognise this potential for mutual lack of comprehension and misunderstanding from the moment your child comes home.**

As we have seen, one of the lasting effects of *trauma* is a tendency to react to innocuous experiences in the present as if they were the *hurtful* experiences of the past and it certainly doesn't take much to *trigger* a full-blown fear or panic response once the *neural networks* have been organised that way. **It may be that you look at your child only a little sharply,** because he is doing the same irritating thing for the hundredth time today and you have had enough. All you want is for him to stop. **Your child picks up on your expression but instead of seeing a gentle warning signal, perceives a major threat.** His *nervous system* immediately goes on full alert, *adrenalin* pumps round his body and he prepares for *flight, fight or freeze.*

If we could represent this graphically in terms of visual *perceptions* it might go something like this:

child's misperceptions (1)

You become a monster, capable of *hurting* or destroying the vulnerable child. Depending on his predominant response pattern you may be greeted by a 'whirling dervish' (fight), a child who runs away (flight) or a 'spaced out' child (freeze), who may lose all contact with the *real* world for a period of time. Remember that at this moment, for this child, this is his experience, his *reality*, his truth.

Be aware, too, that a child may equally easily misinterpret positive, loving messages from you as signs of weakness and hence unreliability. If your child's previous experience of family life has been one involving repeated incidents of verbal or physical aggression, he is likely to have deduced (albeit unconsciously) that being tough 'wins' whilst showing signs of gentleness is an invitation to be abused or manipulated. Graphically the scene could look something like this:

child's misperception (2)

Hence, if you are going to learn to communicate meaningfully with each other you will both need to learn to interpret each other's messages. **Being the adult, it is up to you to start 'getting it** right', to provide 'simultaneous translations' and to 'talk your child through' what went on, at a more appropriate time later! (See point 3.1 on page 62.) Only gradually will it be possible to alter the established patterns of response of a child who **hurts** – but, like everything else, it is possible, particularly if you can begin to understand the underlying mechanisms.

Learning the Language

A child learns language, spoken and unspoken (including body language), 'at his mother's knee' (or breast). More precisely, he is learning to make sense of all the sensations and interactions between himself and his environment from the moment he comes into the world. It is through his mother's eyes (initially his windows to the world), his mother's body (through the 'mother tongue' of touch), and his mother's responses to him, that he also learns to know himself. It is not surprising, therefore, that a child who **hurts** may have as many **distorted perceptions** of himself as he does of the outside world.

During a child's first months of life, his whole world is shared with his mother. It is she who responds to the infant's earliest sensations – soothing him when he cries, feeding him when he is hungry, holding him when he feels alone. So, clearly, the quality of a mother's responses will be directly **reflected** in the baby's feeling of well-being and his ability to learn basic trusts. (See page 112 in Part 7.) In fact, as we have seen, it is through the mother's sensitivity to, and **mirroring** of, the child that he truly learns to see himself and to take his place within the world. Put another way, **the quality of very early experience forms the basis for the formation of blueprints of life, from which predictions and expectations continue to be drawn.**

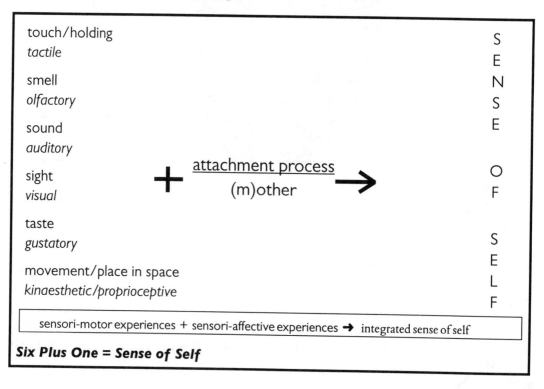

touch/holding		S
tactile		E
smell		N
olfactory		S
sound		E
auditory		
sight	+ attachment process →	O
visual	(m)other	F
taste		S
gustatory		E
movement/place in space		L
kinaesthetic/proprioceptive		F

sensori-motor experiences + sensori-affective experiences → integrated sense of self

Six Plus One = Sense of Self

NOTE: The information in the box below contains some complex, technical language. If you would rather not tackle it right now, please feel free to skip it. Perhaps later on you will feel more confident and familiar with some of the terms and will be ready to come back to it.

It is no coincidence that clinical research indicates the importance of the eyes to very young infants. The tiny, suckling infant focuses his eyes best at a distance of around eight to ten inches (20 to 25 centimetres) – just the distance from the breast to a mother's eyes! New-born babies will also track the image of a human face in preference to any other visual image – especially a face where the eyes are clearly visible. However, it is important to remember that *all* incoming information, through *every* sense, is 'seen' through the ***mothering figure's*** responses – so that the eyes and the concept of ***mirroring*** become a metaphor for (***reflect***) ***everything*** the baby perceives.

There is a growing weight of evidence which demonstrates that ***perceptual*** organisation of all information derived from early experience has both a biological and an emotional basis. Hence ***sensori-motor*** experience (see Six Plus One = Sense of Self above) is also ***sensori-affective*** (emotional) experience, and becomes 'hardwired' into the developing ***brain and nervous system***. For example, Allan Schore has shown that the right half of the ***limbic*** area of the brain matures earlier than the left: thus emphasising the emotional loading of very early (***state dependent***) learning, at a pre-verbal level. In ***real*** terms this means that the quality and accuracy of information ***reflected*** back from mother to infant is of prime importance in influencing the quality of ***attachments*** and in determining a child's ***self-awareness*** and ***self-esteem***.

Schore has also suggested that the ***internal working models*** (first proposed by John Bowlby almost fifty years ago (see the Reading List at the back of the book)) are formed at a subsequent developmental stage, as a *consequence* of the infant's ***attachment*** experiences and earlier ***neuro-biological organisation***. These ***internal working models*** then provide a more ***cognitive, psychological*** framework within which the child can fit himself, and into which he will continue to fit other significant people in his life. Since the young child's expectations and predictions about his social environment (primarily his family!) have such a firm ***developmental, physiological*** basis it is not surprising that they are so difficult to change.

I would like to suggest a more readily accessible way of thinking about these complex phenomena. As we have seen, the organisation of the ***brain and nervous system*** is profoundly influenced by what happens early on – in fact the ***neural pathways***, along which all information passes to and from the brain, are strengthened and consolidated through repeated use. So, just like a footpath, a ***neural pathway*** which is used well will remain open and ready for action, whilst one which is rarely used will be hard to access. Whilst it will always be possible to establish new 'footpaths', there will be a continuing tendency to stick to the old, well used ones – particularly when feeling lost or *distressed*.

In relation to the concept of *mirroring* (or 'parent–infant inter-subjectivity' as it is understood clinically!), it can help to consider concrete examples and to represent some of these graphically, in hedgehog form – with the aid of *mirrors*! As you will recall from *First Steps*, the hedgehog for me represents the child who *hurts*, being extremely prickly on the outside but retaining a soft and vulnerable underbelly. Combining this with the visual imagery associated with *reflections* in a *mirror*, it becomes possible to see what happens when the *attachment process* is disturbed or interrupted – how the *reflections* which an infant perceives through his mother's eyes can cause complex *distortions* in his developing *perceptions* of himself and of the world.

The reflected image matches the young hedgehog well enough.

The youngster receives an accurate and complete reflection of himself, feels accepted just as he is and valued for himself. Healthy **neural networks** will be established, he can therefore learn to see and know who he **really** is.

Here the hedgehog appears only to have one arm and one leg.

If he is persistently treated as if he has only one upper and lower limb he will not recognise the second pair and will fail to develop their use, or to **associate** their sensations with a part of himself. In **physiological** terms, the **neural pathways** relating to those limbs will fail to be consolidated and the hedgehog may eventually lose the ability to use those parts.

Here the hedgehog's outer prickles are enlarged, his vulnerable underbelly underplayed and his face becomes distorted and ugly.

Similarly, this **hedgehog** will develop an image of himself as ugly. He will also perceive himself as 'hard and prickly' and may be unable to relate to, or accept, his own childish vulnerability. He thus has no *realistic* idea of himself.

Often the picture will not be so clear cut: confusing and conflicting reflections can result.

The parent's responses to the baby hedgehog are inconsistent – sometimes he is seen as a baby needing to be taken care of. At others he is punished for his tears and his weakness. He may then develop several contrasting images of himself – images which he will be unable to reconcile. Since his *self-image* underpins his actions, he may show wildly inconsistent behaviour, or tend to favour one 'image of *self*' over another.

Getting Real

For a child for whom infancy goes well, who has been accurately *mirrored* and has established healthy *neural pathways*, the prospects are *realistically* good. If there have been inconsistencies they have been small and he has been able to bring them together (integrate them) into a meaningful image of himself. He has learned that being small and vulnerable is O.K. and that growing up and becoming independent is also O.K. In fact he is an O.K. hedgehog!

Where his mother's *mirroring* has been 'far from ideal' the youngster develops *distorted* images of himself. If his mother 'was not there for him', more often than not, then the young child will have very little idea of himself at all. He may not recognise even basic feelings of hunger and fatigue and may be unable to distinguish between different discomforts and *distresses*. The *reflection* he sees in the *mirror* of his mother's eyes will be quite faint and shapeless. Such a child would be 'hard to get a handle on' and could have difficulties responding to *good enough* parenting.

Alternatively, if the infant's small size and weakness were not valued in the past, if he did not feel nurtured and secure, he might devalue and deny that *part* of himself. He may see himself, highly *unrealistically*, as 'big and tough'. His *distorted perceptions* of himself then influence his thinking about the world so that he becomes convinced that only by acting as if he were 'big and tough' can he avoid being *hurt*. Hence he acts 'big and tough' (Superkid) – even when he has 'little and needy' (Scared kid) feelings (see illustration below).

Since the gap between these two *self-images* is so great, it may become impossible for this hedgehog to reconcile them. Often, one becomes far more powerful than the other and will tend to dominate his thinking and behaviour as, biologically-speaking, the *neural networks* organise around his (mis-)perceptions. However, traces of the 'little and needy' child (Scared kid) are likely to persist: these will, at times, frighten and confuse him. He will then have to try even harder to be 'big and tough' (Superkid) – to fit his own *self-image* and to keep on reassuring himself that he is O.K.

'Scared kid'   'Superkid'

Who am I Really?

The sad thing is that this hedgehog is far from O.K! He is out of balance, 'one-sided'; and his behaviour keeps everyone at a distance – even those who would like to get close to him. That is why **it is so vital that you try to keep a 'two-sided' picture of your hedgehog at the fore-front of your mind.** If your child is to *get real* he has to see more *realistic reflections* of himself in your eyes (the input) – over and over and over again. He also has to be helped to change his output (his actions) if his internal *cognitions* are to alter. Inevitably this will take time, faith and commitment, since the underlying *neuro-biological pathways* will also need altering.

Giving your child a *realistic self-image* means seeing and responding to *all* of your child. Focusing on containing or disciplining his 'bad' or 'tough' superkid behaviours will only reinforce his negative image, whilst paying attention only to his 'good' or 'vulnerable' scaredkid side, will likewise fail to provide him with an accurate image of himself. Instead, as we have seen, it is likely to confuse him, since it doesn't fit with his own *self-image*, or frighten him into greater feats of 'toughness', to reassure himself that he is not *really* weak and needy.

You might be surprised at how relieved your child may feel to be introduced to the idea that the *self*, for every one of us, is made up of many *parts*. In an emotionally healthy individual this *differentiation* of the *self* allows freedom and flexibility of thought and action, whilst retaining a *core identity* and an *integrated* sense of 'who I *really* am' (Goulding and Schwartz). In a child who *hurts,* the *parts* tend to be disconnected (*dissociated*) more extreme and more conflicting: it then becomes far harder to hold on to the belief that somewhere beneath 'all this stuff' is a great little kid trying to get out!

Furthermore, it often appears that each *part* denies the *reality* of the other – as if 'the left hand doesn't know what the right hand is doing'! If you remember that the *left brain* is the logical, reasoning part and the *right side of the brain* is the intuitive, emotional side, then this can begin to make a good deal of sense. Yet, irrespective of the extreme nature of some *parts*, there always remains an intact *core self*, untouched by the *trauma* the child has experienced, however overwhelming. It may be very difficult to get in touch with, since one of the reasons for the extreme behaviour of some *dissociated parts* is to protect this inner *self*, but it is always there. I like to imagine the *core self* as a glimmer of light, an essence which is never extinguished – although it may be very well hidden under a bushel. Have faith and you will see it too!

Whilst this may all sound quite strange (and complicated) to you at first, it could well give meaning and encouragement to your child. The important thing to remember is that **if you can embrace (acknowledge and *reflect* back) all *parts* of your youngster's character, then he can learn to accept all of himself too.** Even the most bizarre and disconnected aspects of your child's thinking and behaviour are there for a reason: they helped him to survive. Viewing these as *adaptive* makes them understandable; finding more appropriate ways for them to connect and to work for the child will harness their energy and survival power. (Just think how much energy your child currently expends acting 'big and tough' (Superkid) and struggling to contain the 'little and needy' (Scared kid) *parts* of himself!)

You must also continue to believe that your youngster already has within him 'what it takes' to become a *really* beautiful human being. This is certainly easier said than done – but it is essential if your child is to stand a chance of ***getting real*** and seeing himself as a whole person. Moreover, ***looking glass*** logic can be extremely hard to resist because you yourselves can get sucked into its pseudo-logicality. You may then find yourselves feeling as crazy as the child. Any difficulties here are likely to be compounded by outsiders' ***perceptions*** since, superficially, you are more likely to appear ***distressed*** than your child. In trying to think well of a child and help him to feel loved, a caring child care practitioner may play down his 'tough' or '***hurtful***' side – and see these characteristics only as ***projections*** in you.

Seeing the whole picture

Whilst it might seem logical to make excuses for a child who has been a victim, or to appeal to his 'better nature', **unless ALL around him see and respond to EVERY side of him, your youngster cannot feel fully connected and 'get *real*'.** The dominant characteristic for many children who ***hurt***, of the tough Superkid (see page 47) will not release its hold until its power is recognised and validated consistently. For a sizeable minority of children you may see more ***passive resistance*** or silent ***non-compliance***. A very small number will portray themselves predominantly as the thoroughly 'nice', wholly ***compliant*** children (Stuffed kids), almost as if they have no ***reality*** of

Scared kid   Stuffed kid   Superkid

The Three 'S's

their own, other than what they are trying to be for you. Although this is very difficult to put into words (which is a *left brain* function) *you* will know it – something will feel 'not quite right' (gut feelings are connected to *right brain* functioning) – if you are living with children like this. (It is intended that both passive resistance and compulsive compliance will be included in the proposed series of 'occasional papers' to be published by Adoption UK beginning in 2000.)

Irrespective of which way of acting is your child's *'part* of choice', once *you* can see it and accept it as a *real part* of your child – but not the *only part* – you can begin to reflect the broader *reality* back to him – and begin to alter the *balance of power* within. For, when you are able to be wholly honest with your child, he can begin to be more honest with himself, with you and with the outside world. **Moreover, since 'where your child is' at any given moment is his** *reality* **at that time, that is the place from which you have to start working**. (The Fundamental Principles in Part 5 and the strategies for Sensitive Situations (Part 7) are designed to *reflect* this.) Being able to keep in mind the broader image of your child allows you to respond to even the most horrendous situation with more equanimity, more *empathy* and more *real* faith that things can change.

Starting from the Right Place (or Getting Real Yourself)

As well as recognising that you and your child may be starting off from very different places, it is imperative that you keep reminding yourself that your own place is *good enough*. It is a place to which you will need to return time after time when you feel you are being knocked out of balance, through living alongside your child. Over and over you may find yourself becoming uncontrollably angry, unbearably *hurt*, inexplicably confused, inconsolably sad, overwhelmingly anxious or utterly lost. **At these times it is absolutely vital that you remind yourself of several things:**

- **This is the way your child is feeling too.**

- **You have the experience and the ability to move to a more comfortable place.**

- **You will feel better for doing so and be much better placed to deal with your child.**

- **By showing your child how to handle these feelings you are providing him with the tools to change, to join you in a more comfortable way of being.**

- **We are all human and 'blow' it sometimes. Being able to recognise and admit your mistakes is healthy. This can also be a very good learning experience for your child.**

Of course, it might be better never to allow yourself to slip that far along the 'crazy road' but intense feelings are part of being human – and if you weren't human you wouldn't have the humanity you need to come through! So it is pretty fundamental that you establish comfortable ways of bringing yourself back 'on line' and that you make them a regular part of your life. **You will need endless supplies of love, patience, understanding, time, firm *boundaries* and belief in yourself if you are to make a difference with your child** – and these are the very qualities which are most likely to become *distorted*, when you are face to face (in the *looking glass*) with a child who *hurts*.

First and foremost you will need this love, patience, understanding, time, firm *boundaries* and belief in yourself FOR YOURSELF. A parent is the single most important and most influential factor in any child's life and you are unlikely to be able to correct the palpable *distortions* in your child, and help him to make new connections, unless you are coming from 'the right place' and can find your way back there, as many times as it takes. Of course, you don't always have to do this on your own and there are many different ways to get back to 'the right place'. It's up to you to choose the ones with which you feel most comfortable. As long as you remain kind to yourself and find the space to check out 'where you are' regularly, you will still have enough to give to your child and to begin pulling him back from the *looking glass* craziness of his *distorted* world – a world where he, like Alice's acquaintances, may appear to change in size or to speak in riddles.

Speaking the Language of Diagnosis
(or What Is This Really All About?)

It is often very hard to find the 'right words' to describe how it *really* feels to live with a child who *hurts*. It is very hard, too, to find the words to describe the child herself, in a way that is *real*, honest and respectful. There are also a number of clinical diagnoses which attempt to describe discrete groups of behaviours, which may appear to fit your child more or less accurately. You may find that your child receives several such diagnoses as she passes through childhood into young adulthood. As a family you may then be passed from pillar to post and offered conflicting explanations and advice, depending on the skills and areas of interest of the diagnostician. Sometimes two or three diagnostic terms are applied simultaneously – until you begin to wonder how such a small child can have such a large number of labels!

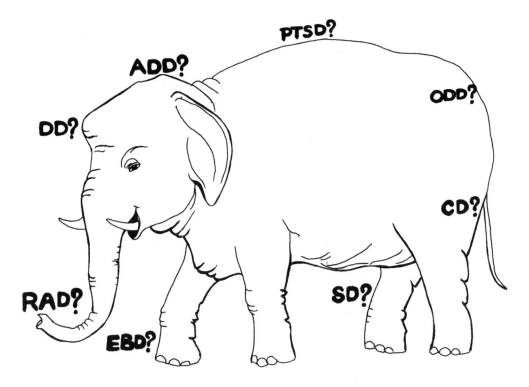

What is This Really All About?

Figure Note: A brief explanation of the diagnostic initials shown above may be found in the Glossary.

NB These are just some of the most common clinical diagnoses given to adoptees during childhood and adolescence. In adulthood, common diagnoses include: Borderline Personality Disorder, Anti-Social Personality Disorder, Schizophrenia, Bipolar Disorder (manic depression), Post Traumatic Stress Disorder, Major Depressive Disorder (and Dysthymia – mild to moderate depression), Anorexia and Bulimia Nervosa, Obsessive–Compulsive Disorder, Anxiety and Panic Disorders. For more information on diagnoses in adulthood, write to Adoption UK at Lower Boddington, Daventry, Northamptonshire, NN11 6YB, enclosing a large s.a.e.

This can be very confusing for all of you. Please try to bear in mind that the common link between every one of these diagnoses may be the effects of repeated early childhood *trauma* on *attachment* and *development*. You might like to visualise your child like the proverbial elephant – being identified by whatever part of him comes to hand when he is being examined. Just as an elephant is not just a tail, a trunk or a leg, so too the diagnostic picture for your child needs to take every aspect and area of his being into account. **As long as you can try to see the whole of your child and maintain a flexible approach based on an understanding of *trauma*, you will not become lost in the diagnostic maze and will be able to find 'the right help' for your family.** (For further information on specific diagnoses, please contact Adoption UK at Lower Boddington.)

Fundamental Principles

This is not intended to be a Do It Yourself, 'How-To', manual, more a collection of philosophies and suggestions, backed by parents' own experiences and by current theories of *attachment, development* and *trauma*. It should help you to find what you need for yourselves – in particular it should strengthen your belief in your own *perceptions*, feelings and intuitions. This will give you the essential foundations from which to make your own choices with self-confidence, courage and love, for yourself and for your child. **If it doesn't feel like love at first, try it anyway – you may be pleasantly surprised.** Just 'doing the right thing', irrespective of how you feel, can help to make you feel good about yourself – and then you may well find you are 'doing the right thing' because it is what you really want to do!

Please try not to skip over the preparatory sections to find the 'right answers' in the sections on specific strategies; perhaps you may not always be asking the 'right' questions. This may be especially true if you are not 'starting from the right place' (see Part 4) or if you are only looking at the 'presenting problem', without looking at what lies beneath. You, too, may be caught in the *looking glass distortions* of your child's world. Until you have been able to step back and give yourself some space, you may not be best placed to help your child.

Because I know how difficult it can be to think clearly when you are living under stress, I have tried to devise graphic illustrations and snappy headings which you may find easier to absorb and recall when you are in danger of 'losing it'. It is not just children who lose the ability to think when they are distressed – our brains can go into 'action mode' too, where we tend to be governed by powerful feelings, rather than by reason and thoughtfulness. It takes a good deal of preparation and practice to get to a point where you will automatically start from the 'right place' and say and do the 'right thing'.

It would be very presumptuous of me to tell you, as the experts on *your* child, exactly what to do. However, knowing how easy it is to lose your way and to feel overwhelmed by your child's *distress*, some sort of guidelines can be invaluable, especially when you have found out the hard way that 'doing the usual' often doesn't work with children who *hurt*. Perhaps the difference with these guidelines is that they are designed to empower *you* to choose *what* you do and *how* to do it.

There is no single way which will be effective with every child all the time. These fundamental principles offers a 'mix and match' selection from which you can create a strategy to suit a particular problem, as and when you need – building on your own inner strengths and existing resources. They will also allow you to ring the changes, which may encourage your child to begin to think, since you are not always being entirely predictable, and eventually to change. When a strategy which has served you well becomes familiar, and as in the proverb breeds contempt in your child, you can set it aside and put together some more ideas which just might be 'the right thing'.

Although these fundamental principles are varied and extremely flexible, they embody certain basic rights, that all children, however challenging they may be, deserve at all times:

- to be cared for

- to be protected

- to be treated with respect

- to be encouraged to develop to the best of their ability.

It is vital to keep reminding yourself of this and to keep on remembering that your child is not to blame for the *hurts* she has experienced. All her behaviours have evolved as the best way she knows of staying safe in an unsafe world – and clearly they have worked well or she wouldn't still be here! **However, that does not make her present behaviours acceptable or excusable.** You, her adoptive parents, the wider community and society as a whole, owe this child the opportunity to begin to feel safe and to change. Your child's resilience is to be commended but this ***resilience*** implies the channelling of vital energies into self-protection, keeping the dangerous outside world safely outside, at the expense of healthy and flexible relationships. You are now reaching a position from which you can begin re-channelling your youngster's energies into self-growth and self-love, by encouraging your child to feel secure enough to let the world in, and to become part of it.

As you will see, there are a number of fundamental principles, which fall (loosely) into ten sections. These are outlined below. A brief, explanatory introduction to each major section is followed by several sub-sections. The sub-sections are also cross-referenced with Part 6: Principles into Practice. **Please allow yourself plenty of time to become familiar with the ideas and underlying philosophy of the fundamental principles before you move on to consider suggestions under specific headings.** It will be worth your while to keep referring back to these fundamental principles from time to time as you work through this book and begin putting the principles into practice. It is also worth repeating that **the more you familiarise yourself with these ideas and the possibilities they open up for you, the more likely they are to spring unbidden into your mind at times when you really need them – when your mind is geared to action, rather than words or reasoned thought.**

1. Positive Parenting Power

I begin with parenting power because, as I have emphasised in previous sections, parents are the most important ingredient in the healing of a child who ***hurts***. Without you there would not be a family! All parents have a responsibility to utilise this power positively, to promote the greater well-being of the child: **the misuse, or abuse, of** the power conferred by age and position can never be condoned. It is up to ALL of us to make sure we use our power well.

1.1 Parents in Charge

Parents need to take charge, to maintain a 'benign autocracy' if they are to provide both love and containment for their child. It is parents with whom a child spends the greatest single part of his day and from whom he learns about the social rules of relationships and family life. If, through repeated challenges from your child who **hurts**, you feel you are losing your power to parent, now is the time to begin reclaiming it for the sake of your whole family.

It is also essential that partners support each other in this powerful role and that the wider network of family, friends and community enables them to be parents to the best of their ability. This includes supporting them when the going gets tough and trusting that they are attempting to do their best for their child.

1.2 Parents as Partners

Parent(s) need to practise their care-taking skills, first on themselves and then on each other. In this way they are laying the foundations for good physical, emotional and spiritual health and are providing a good role model of self-care to their children.

Lone parents may have to bear far more of the responsibility for parenting single-handed than partners who share the parenting role. However sole parents, by definition, will avoid many of the pitfalls of disagreeing about the difficulties they are facing and choosing the best way forward. Nevertheless, it may be very helpful to have someone else to whom you can talk on a regular basis – especially when your view of **reality** is being repeatedly challenged!

1.3 Parents in Partnership

Being a parent, alone or as part of a partnership, is often a very isolating job – after all, we do it in the privacy of our own homes! Partners can and must support each other at all times. If you disagree about how to handle your child, then do so in private – out of sight and hearing of the child(ren). This provides a doubly *secure base* and reinforces the partnership against any tendency on the part of the child to divide and rule.

Inconsistencies between parents can also maintain a child's experience of having separate *parts* (see Part 4: Through the Looking Glass), where the child can be one thing to one parent and another to the other. If you accept the possibility that you may actually be seeing different sides of the same child and act together, you can work towards bringing these different sides of your child closer together.

1.4 Taking a Break

All paid workers are entitled to time away from their work place. Being the parent of a child who *hurts* can be more stressful than any other job, yet, since your work place is also your home, the idea of regular breaks may not come so naturally.

It is imperative that you begin to establish breaks away from home for yourself (and your partner), as a matter of course. If you can possibly find ways of spending time without your child (together), even if it is just a couple of hours a week, you can give yourselves the chance to find out that you are nice people, *really* ! After a short breathing space you may even be glad to see your child(ren) again. (See Staying a Family and Being Apart in Part 7.)

1.5 Making the Break

Taking regular breaks can give you time to talk and help you sort out your own lives more comfortably. This could mean that your relationship does not break up. However, as with any other family, this is a private matter. You will need to take the decision on whether you wish to stay together or to separate, based on a whole range of personal issues. Try to make sure that any decision to split up is wholly your choice and not influenced by your child's ability to come between you or to force you to 'take sides'. (See point 1.3 above.)

2. Taking Care of the Whole Family

It is not just the parents who raise a child. If, as the saying goes, 'it takes a community', then the (nuclear) family forms the 'bridge' between individual and broader **attachment** relationships. Every single member of your home-based family will have special social and emotional connections with you and with each other, giving them a sense of belonging and a sense of who they are. It is vital that you remain aware that, just as they can have a large impact on an additional family member, so the 'home-comer' can have an enormous impact upon existing family members' sense of well-being.

2.1 Don't Forget the Siblings

With so much time and energy being focused on the child who **hurts**, it can become easy to lose sight of the other family members' needs. Birth, adoptive and foster siblings all have their own very special needs and may also have to deal with unique difficulties, such as victimisation, embarrassment, feeling responsible, witnessing violence, and having holidays or treats repeatedly spoilt.

Some of these problems are similar to those faced by siblings of children with physical or learning disabilities, others are particular to families of children who **hurt**. (For a more complete discussion of some of these complex issues, see the section on siblings on pages 91–99 of *First Steps*.) It is essential that you stay aware of your other children's needs, find time to be with them individually, make time for yourselves and avoid collapsing in a heap from exhaustion!

2.2 Diff'rent Strokes

Every child is unique and deserves individual love and attention. When one child is so very demanding of our time and care, others in the family may try to compensate by being extra helpful or undemanding. Even though you are over-stretched and worn out, never lose touch with the ones who don't shout so loud: a meaningful hug, or a simple shared joke, can go a long way to help you all feel that you are on the same side.

2.3 'I' Statements for All

Each member of your family needs to be able to speak out for themselves and feel safe to say what they mean. Practising your own use of 'I' statements can encourage your younger members to do so too. This allows you all to be honest and respectful about how you feel whilst avoiding blaming anyone else. For example, saying 'I feel very angry and upset because my favourite vase has been smashed' can let everyone know the score more openly and non-threateningly than saying 'You make me so angry when you smash my things.'

2.4 Animals Are Family Too

Family pets are frequently the target of the pain and frustration with which children who **hurt** have to struggle. Do make sure that you protect your animals from teasing, tormenting and violence and give them space where they can be safe. You may notice that a family pet is the first in your family to act warily of your child. This could be your first indication that things are not going well: trust them, their animal instincts are often very accurate.

2.5 Being a Family

With all the additional stresses of parenting a child who **hurts** it is easy to forget how to have fun as a family. So when things feel really bad, make sure you arrange something special for all of you – and enjoy it! This can help remind all of you that you deserve good times, just because you are you!

3. Taking Your Time

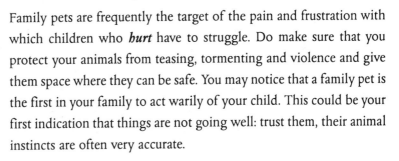

Learning to take your time and not reacting immediately to your child's behaviour can, literally, give you time to think. It can also give you back the initiative, since your child will probably be expecting an instant response. Moreover, not only can you give yourself an opportunity to take some deep breaths, count to ten and calm down, but you will also be modelling a different way of responding than the impulsive over-reactions which your child is used to.

3.1 Choosing your Time

Choosing your time can mean that you can defer dealing with an issue until you are in the right frame of mind (and when you have had time to think through your options!). It can give your child time to begin to think ahead too! This may be a very novel experience for him; it can also be a very salutary one, particularly where you feel your child is trying to wind you up or catch you in the 'anger trap'! (See point 8.12 on page 83.)

3.2 Time to Cool Off

A 'cooling off' period can give you both some time to think. If you take it literally, it can be a chance for either or both of you to breathe some refreshing cool air and to clear your head. Cooling off time is also a wonderful opportunity to bring down levels of emotional and physical *arousal*, to change your pace and to 'get it together again'.

Take care that your cooling off period does not go on too long. You are trying both to avoid your youngster overheating *and* to prevent him from 'freezing you out'!

3.3 Time Out

Sometimes you will benefit from a brief break from your child, so that you can both wind down and begin to get a fresh perspective on what is going on. A school-age child should be able to cope with small periods of separation and use it to good effect. Often, inviting a child to go to his bedroom, or to sit on the stairs, provides just such an opportunity.

Don't worry about what your child is doing during his 'time out', beyond matters of basic safety. Instead think of yourself: make a cup of tea, call a friend, run round the block – anything which can change the way you feel for the better. After the few minutes of 'time out' are up, you may be genuinely surprised at how pleased you are to see each other! If not, maybe you both need a little more breathing space!

3.4 Time In

Some children seem happier excluding us from their lives as much as possible. If your child is like this, you will want to go on respecting his need for some privacy but also to recognise his need to know the comfort he could derive from relationships. In such cases, you can turn 'time out' on its head, and go for 'time in'.

Children who find intimacy a challenge will initially struggle with the closeness of 'time in', so it is essential that you make it as non-confrontational as possible. Perhaps it would be enough, at first, to stay in the same part of the room together. Later, perhaps you could share the same settee or set of stairs. Gradually these short sessions can accustom your child to spending time with you comfortably.

3.5 Thinking Time

You can use time out (or any other special time) as a designated time to think. Once you have established a pattern of taking time out with your child, you can begin to invite your youngster to think about whatever has just gone on, which may have caused a problem. You can give your child as much time as she needs to get into a place where she can 'engage her brain' and reflect on her behaviour and its consequences.

It is vital not to become frustrated and try to hurry your child – since this could be extremely counter-productive! Once she realises that this thinking time is self-limiting, your youngster can make the choice of getting on with thinking right away, or wasting her own time. Mean time, you have some vital time to yourself.

Since thinking is often a 'missing link' for children who **hurt**, giving your child time to stop and think is not only helpful in the short term, it is also an invaluable lesson in the long term. Eventually you will be helping to establish new **neural pathways** in the **brain** and **nervous system**, which will allow your child to develop into a more healthy and competent individual.

3.6 Time to Talk

Talking to an enraged or **distressed** child is unlikely to get you very far. Since a child who **hurts** is easily pushed into **distress** mode, with its associated impulsive action and weakened reasoning abilities, it can be very helpful to wait for a period of calm before you try to talk with your child and help him to make sense of his distressing behaviours. You can then encourage him to make his own connections between what happened in the past, recent *triggering* events, and his current reactions.

Making time to talk to your partner, or to a good friend, is also vital – preferably when the child(ren) are not around. You may feel freer to talk if you are out of the house, away from the scene of so many difficult struggles. Walking whilst you are talking can be especially beneficial, since it seems to 'free you up'.

4. Taking Responsibility

As a reasonable adult you, and your partner if you have one, are ultimately responsible for the management of your family and for each member's well-being. However, a good manager learns to delegate responsibility appropriately and to provide some limited opportunities for the mistakes of inexperience. If you over-protect your child now, the cost of later mistakes could be a good deal greater. (See also Addictive Behaviours and Self-Harm in Part 7.)

4.1 All or Nothing

Your youngster is not responsible for *your* feelings and actions and you cannot always be responsible for *his*. With his 'all or nothing' thinking a child who *hurts* may feel totally powerless in the world and yet believe that he is ultimately responsible for everything which happens. He needs to see that you are actively in control of your own life and that you can safely take charge of his. At the same time he needs to begin to experience some sense of limited control for himself. He will also benefit from being encouraged to make mental links between cause and effect, links which are often very weak in a child who *hurts*. As you will see below, actions speak louder than words here.

4.2 Whose Responsibility?

Be respectful of *all parts* of your child's behaviour, good and bad, and try to help your child accept responsibility for *all* of his actions. It is likely that your child may not 'own up to' some of the things he does. You may have to help him to 'own' the bits he claims are 'not me'. However, whatever your youngster does, and however foul he is being, always remember that there is a beautiful child in there (somewhere) trying to get out! Then you can remind him that he's not *all* bad, as he secretly fears. (Please see Through the Looking Glass on page 37.)

4.3 Denying Responsibility

There may be times when your child denies responsibility for his actions, despite abundant evidence to the contrary. Sometimes this may feel like lying or outright insolence, but to him, for that moment, it may *feel* like the truth. (Again, see Through the Looking Glass.)

At this point, the most important thing may be for you to recognise that there may be *no* point in getting into debate about who did what. Save the discussion until later: then keep it short and matter of fact. Simply state what you *believe* has happened: you don't have to give any reasons. There is nothing to be gained from extracting an admission of guilt, and *much* to be lost. (See also section on Lying and Stealing in Part 7.)

If your youngster has chocolate all over her face and the wrappers are lying under her bed in full view, then the likelihood is that she *did* take your box of chocs. You can let her know that you know this, that you expect her, as you would expect anyone else in your family, to pay for a replacement – perhaps out of next week's pocket money, or by doing extra jobs for you. Then leave it at that *for now*.

It is often difficult for a child who **hurts** to accept responsibility for things he does. The youngster may genuinely be so panic-stricken that he does not remember what he did, at *that* moment, or he does not want to think that he did it (which amounts to the same thing). If you are angry, or are too direct, this may increase the likelihood of this **dissociative denial**. A low-key reminder of his actions later, (when your child is more in touch with **reality**, which includes accepting the consequences of his actions) can give a far more powerful message.

4.4 Units of Concern

Foster Cline introduced the idea of 'units of concern' to illustrate graphically how sometimes, by taking our own responsibilities too seriously, we may deprive our children of opportunities to learn to be responsible themselves.

The concept of one family member 'doing' particular emotions on behalf of other family members may be a familiar one; certainly it has been popularised by many counsellors and therapists. If you do all the worrying about your child's behaviours, it follows that you may be depriving him of an essential 'corrective emotional experience' of the loving kind.

Trying to strike a balance between being the responsible, protective parent and allowing your child to learn from his own mistakes may be difficult but it is vital that you keep working on it! This can be another situation where actions speak louder than words for your child: as long as he is not doing himself or anyone else any actual harm, it is a calculated risk you may need to take.

Your role will then be to act as the 'empathic witness', someone with whom your child can share his difficulties and who can sympathise with him. This is not a time to criticise, for 'I told you so's', or for active interference. A child who *hurts* finds acknowledging mistakes even harder than anyone else: don't knock him when he is down *or* give him someone else to blame. An understanding 'I know', and a comforting arm around his shoulder, may be just what you both need!

4.5 Honesty is the Best Policy

If you 'blew it', if you just don't know what to do, or even if what you have to say is likely to be painful, covering up will not do. First, a child who *hurts* is extremely tuned in to situations and very sensitive to what is going on, however good you think you are at hiding your feelings. Second, it is important that you model honesty since your child may struggle with this issue. (Again, see section on Lying and Stealing in Part 7.) She will probably appreciate your frankness, even if she doesn't show it – and it will certainly give you back the initiative.

However, just occasionally, you may choose to do the opposite! Then a simply stated 'I lied' can have a very powerful effect – at least you are being honest about it and it may get her started on thinking, since you have acted unpredictably for once (and this was deliberate!).

4.6 Owning Your Own Problems

Being ordinary human beings and not superparents, you may have issues of your own to deal with. In fact it is quite likely that these issues have only *really* seemed to be a problem since your child who *hurts* came home: that is because such children can challenge at the deepest levels. It is almost as if your child has 'heat-seeking sensors' which allow him to seek out any potential weaknesses and focus on them! Looking at this positively, children who challenge help us to get in touch with, and face, issues we may have been able to ignore so far but which, in truth, need addressing – for our own greater well-being.

You may feel that you should be perfect, particularly as you have been assessed and 'approved' to be the 'special' parent of a child with 'special emotional needs' – this can make it difficult to ask for help when you need it. It is vital, however, that you do find ways of resolving any personal difficulties you may be having, if you are not to run the risk of 'dumping' them on your family.

If talking things over with your partner, or a close and trusted friend, is not enough, then look for a counsellor or therapist locally who could help you make more sense of your life. Finding one through personal recommendation is a surer way of getting the right help than formal qualifications alone.

5. Taking Issue

As the parent of a child who *hurts*, you are inevitably going to face some intense challenges to your authority and to have to deal with many distressing issues. Remaining loving, containing and respectful can become extremely difficult in such circumstances: it is vital that you learn to conserve your energies and use them well.

5.1 Choosing Your Battles

Whilst this may be a contentious phrase, it expresses the *reality* you experience as parents and can bring some comfort. A good deal of your child's behaviour may be motivated by attempts to feel in control – to escape the overwhelming terror of chaos and powerlessness from the past. She may have come to believe that it is truly a matter of life and death that she controls everybody and everything at all times, and she may have evolved very creative ways of maintaining this illusion of absolute power. (See Part 4: Through the Looking Glass.)

However, this is an illusion which is neither *realistic* to sustain nor valuable to your child's well-being. As caring parents you have to find ways to help your youngster feel safe enough to experience dependency, to feel securely contained and 'in control' (that is secure in the control of a trustworthy adult) instead of feeling totally 'out of control' at a very deep level.

5.2 Win the Battles You Take On

It may often feel as though you are engaging in 'fights unto the death' over even the most insignificant of issues and that you have little choice but to stand your ground or to back down. In fact your most *realistic* and most comfortable choice may be *not* to take issue over a particular situation at all, especially if you are not sure that you can 'win': that is, act in a safe, loving and containing manner for your child.

If you try to take on every issue with a child who *hurts* you would soon be exhausted and you would be unlikely to succeed! It is more likely that you will end up frustrated and angry – feelings with which your child is only too familiar and which may fuel his own high levels of *distress*. Working on the principle that you don't have to struggle on every front simultaneously can free you up in body, mind and spirit to deal with the issues that *really* matter and keep you out of the 'anger trap' (See point 8.12 on page 83).

Beyond matters of personal safety for all the family, it is completely your choice which issues you wish to take a stand on and which you will leave until another time. Dealing with one issue successfully, with a positive outcome for both your child and for you, will begin to strengthen your self-confidence and can help challenge your child's 'all or nothing' thinking. You will both feel better about yourselves and will be establishing a more *functional* blueprint for your child in the future.

5.3 Avoiding Confrontation

Try to find ways to stand your ground without having to back down – your child will feel that she has 'won' because she is in control. She cannot possibly understand that when you lose, she loses too. As the responsible, reasoning adult it is up to you to keep the heat down in family situations and to avoid getting caught in fruitless power struggles. Remember that you do hold the power and can choose to use it to the best effect for all of you.

5.4 Forcing the Issue

There are just some things which you cannot force your child do: like eat, sleep, speak or come in on time. That doesn't mean that you cannot have views on such issues, only that you must be **realistic** in your expectations! You can certainly indicate what you would *like* to happen and show by your own actions what you believe is right but you cannot *make* your child comply – so don't try! The trick is to show that you *care* about your child, and about what she does, without showing you are *upset* or affected by her unwillingness to comply.

5.5 Whose Problem?

When you are faced with a situation involving your child, begin by asking yourself: 'Whose problem is this?' An untidy bedroom can be a pain – but can you **realistically** invite your child to clean it up and expect to see it done willingly or well? If the answer is 'yes', then fortunately your expectations of personal tidiness are reasonable and achievable. If, however, you groan at the thought of entering your child's room, and at the thought of asking him to do something about it, *and* he is of an age to be accepting responsibility for keeping his things tidy, then something needs to change.

God grant me the serenity to accept the things I cannot change;
the courage to change the things I can;
and the wisdom to know the difference.

The Serenity Prayer (Unknown)

The easiest thing to change is your own mind (set). If going into your youngster's room really does make you shudder, and you have tried every reasonable step to encourage him to accept responsibility for his personal tidiness, then don't go in! Shut the door and walk by. If you can get your child to agree to keep his door closed, so much the better, otherwise ask everyone else in the family to operate the 'closed door' system with you. Tell your child that you will be happy to deliver clean clothes and so on to his door and that you wish to retain rights of search and retrieval (for items which go missing, and for issues of health and safety, such as decaying foodstuffs) – then leave it to him!

5.6 What is Really at Issue?

It is easy to find yourself caught in a convoluted discussion with your child with what, on reflection, is a side issue. A child who **hurts** finds it difficult to identify her feelings and may readily externalise blame for things around her. She may genuinely believe that she is upset because you inadvertently walked in front of the TV programme she was half watching: it is up to you, as the competent adult, to use your common sense and gut feelings to work out what is **really** going on.

It will help your child if you can calmly and *uncritically* suggest what you believe is the **real** reason for her distress. By naming the feeling and making the verbal links for her, you are encouraging new connections to become established.

6. Actions Speak Louder than Words

Remember that your child often leaves out the 'thinking piece': you will then have a very strong reason for focusing on actions rather than words. When you do choose words, choose them carefully and keep them brief and simple.

6.1 Being Heard

However good your communication skills are, if you don't gain your child's attention first you are wasting your time and increasing your levels of frustration unnecessarily. Think of it like a telephone call – if the person you are calling doesn't pick up the phone, they are not going to get your message however eloquently it is put (although you could leave a short answerphone message, which would be very helpful if they are resistant to your closeness! – see below).

Paying attention is often a problem for a child who **hurts** – so clearly it is even more vital that you establish contact with your youngster *before* asking her to do something, or trying to have a meaningful dialogue. Often this is more easily achieved through a visual or physical prompt: just touching your child's arm, or making sure you gain eye-contact, can be enough to gain her attention. Sometimes more flamboyant, exaggerated gestures, served with a good dose of humour, will be needed to grab her interest.

6.2 Saying it with Flowers

It is vital to the success of positive parenting that you speak to your child with respect and humanity at all times. Of course, you may not always feel respectful or human and then you, too, have two choices (see point 6.8): you can stay quiet and say nothing until you are feeling in a better frame of mind, or you can speak and act with care, even though you could scream!

If you choose to say nothing, stay very aware of your body language, perhaps focusing on your breathing until you feel more calm and reasonable. If you choose to speak, **say it as if you mean it,** with all your mind. It is surprising how soon the heart can follow!

6.3 Body Language

All children learn to recognise and 'read' gestures and facial expressions before they begin to understand words, (see also Speaking the same language on pages 38–41). Your child has probably become especially adept at interpreting body language: it may well have helped him to stay safe or to feel less powerless in his chaotic world.

We need to be especially careful that our bodies and faces tell the same stories as our mouths – particularly since under stress a youngster may not be able to think or use words well. It could be helpful to think of your youngster as a much younger child and, literally, act accordingly. Make it funny and you will be even more likely to get through!

6.4 Modelling

One of the actions which speak loudest is to show your child, *by your own actions,* what you would like to see your child do. We all know that screaming 'Don't shout at me like that' is farcical – although we have probably all done it at some time! If you don't want your child to do it, don't do it yourself – or at least not where he can see or hear you!

As your youngster is likely to be more responsive to messages through his senses and body feelings, why not go for the quiet touch instead? Reach out and place a gentle hand on your child's shoulder and he will feel you there. He can then begin to learn to calm himself, from tuning into your calmer body rhythms and following your example.

6.5 Going In Where It Hurt

When a youngster has a physical illness, addressing the root cause is usually more effective than merely treating the symptoms. In a similar way, it is frequently more helpful to explore emotional *dis-ease* at a fundamental level. Moreover, since emotional growth is part of an overall developmental process, it is often particularly useful to return to the point of interruption and to 'go in' at that level.

In many cases this means adopting **sensori-motor** (feeling and doing) strategies, which communicate via the emotional, feeling **right brain** and **limbic system**, rather than with the rational **left brain** and **pre-frontal cortex** (which does most of the reasoning and thinking).

6.6 Consequences

These are the good, bad and indifferent things which happen to us all when we act in certain ways. As long as they are not dangerous, they are very powerful aids to learning – especially if we say little and take great care to avoid saying 'I told you so!' Consequences differ from punishments in a very fundamental way. Whilst punishments teach revenge, or allow us to feel angry with, or to blame, other people, consequences are life's natural lessons which allow us to think about our *own* behaviours.

For example, if your child does not eat up his porridge at breakfast time, naturally, he will be hungry later. You can, equally naturally, be very sympathetic about this and tell him that you hope he eats all his cereal right away, tomorrow morning.

6.7 Learning the Hard Way

It is a sad fact of life that we tend to learn the hard way, from our own mistakes. Toddlers struggle to outwit their mothers and explore 'forbidden territory', only to bump their knees and run crying back for comfort. If you try too hard to protect your child from the little **hurts** of life, he misses out on essential, *self-initiated* learning experiences and he may suffer more: when he makes bigger, more costly, and more painful mistakes later on.

Children who *hurt* have suffered a lot already but because their vision of the world is often *distorted* (see Part 4: Through the Looking Glass) – they do not seem to learn the 'right' lessons from their experiences. Hard though it is for all of you, tough love, letting the child find out for themselves what will happen if they choose to act in a certain way, can be the kindest way in the long run. (See also Addictions and Self-Harm and Staying a Family and Being Apart in Part 7.) Then, just like the mother of the toddler, you can be there, ready and sympathetic, to help pick up the pieces and to encourage your youngster to make the 'right' connections.

If you actively try to intervene in your child's choices, this may well be construed as interfering – and can make it 'your fault' (in the *looking glass distortions* of the child's mind). If the child only has herself to be angry with, since she herself was the sole initiator, she may make better connections more quickly.

6.8 Two Choices

When you do talk to your youngster, it can help to keep it simple and to offer limited choices – thus reducing potential conflict, whilst clearly giving her some say in her life. Offering just *two choices* works well as long as you will *truly* be happy with either – because you can be sure that if there is one you don't want the child to make, that's the one she will go for!

A simple example of such a choice is 'Do you want to do this the easy way or the hard way?', thus avoiding a discussion about *whether* it should be done at all and limiting it to two possible options on *how* to do it.

6.9 'Listen Very Carefully … I Will Say This Only Once!'

For a school-age child who has been living in your family for some time, remembering house rules should come quite naturally: this is the way we all try to work out some sort of pattern for living. Simple one-off reminders will usually maintain reasonable order and help to keep you all sane.

You may find yourself reminding your child about accepted rules, over and over again. You may begin to wonder whether you are not being fair, or not being clear enough, or even if your child has hearing or comprehension difficulties. Whilst it is a good idea to check these things out, it may just be that your child doesn't *want* to remember and actually feels in control that way.

So perhaps one of your most basic house rules should be: 'Listen very carefully, I will say this only once!' That way you can remain powerful and allow your actions to speak volumes. If you have said that the car to the swimming pool leaves in five minutes, make sure that it does. Of course, you will need to have made back-up plans the first time, but …

6.10 Headliners

There are a number of 'one-liners' which can be extremely useful in a variety of situations. Keeping it simple will make it memorable to you under stress *and* may make it more intelligible to your child when she, too, is *distressed*. However, they will only be useful if said with respect and with a touch of light humour, or with sincere *empathy*.

'I know' speaks volumes when your child complains that 'it's not fair' or that they wanted to do something else. In just two words you are able to acknowledge how they are feeling, sympathise with them and give them back the problem gently.

'Thank you for telling me that' can have a similar effect and is particularly useful when your child says something outrageous. You also avoid getting sucked into the 'anger trap' (see point 8.12 on page 83), or accepting blame for whatever it is!

'You look as though you could do with a hug', perhaps when your child seems angry or sad, can eloquently sum up that you can see how your child feels and know what to do about it. He may not know what he needs, or may not agree with you, but your wisdom and confident statement can make it feel right.

6.11 Quality Street

Whilst your child may find it difficult to allow you to get close, or to hear your caring words, a couple of sweeties tucked into his school bag, with a very simple message such as 'Thinking of you, Love Mum' may well get through. This can be especially powerful when you have separated after an angry exchange, or there is something particular troubling your child.

Forget ideas about rewarding positive behaviours and ignoring negatives for the moment, your child may be feeling so lost or out of touch that he really needs to see you still care, no matter what. It is also a lot easier to remain loving and respectful at one remove, than it is face to face with a child who is insolent or angry!

7. Promoting Positives

A child who **hurts** is only too familiar with negatives: his whole outlook on life is probably founded on negativity. Being a positive parent and cultivating the positives in these circumstances may be tough but it is *essential* if you are to alter the habits of your child's lifetime.

7.1 Finding your Touch

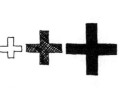

As a parent you may struggle with issues of touch, especially if you know your youngster has been sexually abused. It is vital that you maintain your own trust in the 'rightness' of physical touch, and are able to convey that to your child. You may encounter resistance at first but gentle and gradual insistence on moments of shared contact will eventually pay off for both of you. (See also section on Touch in *First Steps*, pages 49–55.)

7.2 Accentuating the Positives

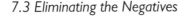

It may feel that there is very little positive behaviour from your child which you can happily reward. In such cases you may have to 'make them an offer they can't refuse' and then you can give praise where praise is due.

Sending an unco-operative child out into the garden to collect stones can provide just such an opportunity. If he comes back right away with two, congratulate him on his good start and encourage him to find some more. If he sulks behind the shed for an hour and comes back empty-handed, that's fine too. After all, you've had a peaceful time without him and can suggest (gently) that he may need more practice on this at another time. After all you didn't **really** want those stones anyway!

7.3 Eliminating the Negatives

It goes without saying that criticism, sarcastic comments, ridicule, put-downs, comparisons with other family members, references to 'bad blood', or implications that you never expect your child to change, are to be avoided at all costs.

Children who **hurt** are uniquely vulnerable to negatives, whether overt, implied or unintended: they believe deep down that they are bad and will perceive confirmation of this at every point. Inevitably, you will slip up on occasion – but if you stay aware of the obvious pitfalls, you stand a better chance of getting through with the positives. If you find that you have **triggered** a **shame reaction**, an immediate gentle word or touch *can* help your child *and* the situation.

7.4 Don't Say Don't

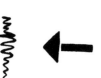

As much as possible you will also want to avoid saying 'Don't' – because, just like with a toddler, you can readily expect stubbornness, refusal and screaming tantrums. Instead you could try making simple, clear statements about the behaviour you would like to see and perhaps model it yourself. Distraction, again just as for toddlers, can work well here.

7.5 Don't Take It Personally

Rebuffs, verbal and physical aggression, running away, preferring to be with anybody or everybody else, can all be very **hurtful**. It is essential that you remember that this 'stuff' is not about *you* but about earlier feelings, which usually belong in the family of origin. Whilst it is *not* helpful to deny them, it does help to put them where they belong.

7.6 Invitation or Ultimatum

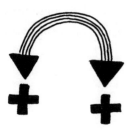

Telling your child that they *must* do something, or trying to impose a time limit on it, can be an invitation to opposition and disaster (see also point 5, Taking Issue above.) Again, this doesn't mean you have to give up your power – just that you have to find ways of using it more effectively. A simple 'You are welcome to watch TV, once you have put your shoes away' is a very positive message, which invites co-operation rather than resistance. You may need to repeat yourself (!) a few times but as long as you remain calm and reasonable, you increase the likelihood that the job will eventually be done.

Another variation on the invitation theme is to begin, 'I'd like you to …' By not *demanding* a response but respectfully *requesting* one, you are increasing the likelihood of co-operation. If the child still does not comply, at least you are not forced into a potential 'win–lose' situation over which you may have little control.

7.7 Saying It Louder

This is one for the child not for you! If your child is screaming obscenities at you, asking her to stop is unlikely to be effective and you will 'lose', in more ways than one. Instead, you can ask her to go on doing what she is doing – *only more so.* This way you both 'win', either way.

If she does continue, or escalates the noise, then she is doing what you have asked and you can congratulate her on her good shouting. If she stops, because the last thing she wants to do is be obedient, then you can congratulate her on becoming calmer – but watch out for a rebound shout. If it occurs, repeat your request as before and ask for some loud movements, for good measure.

7.8 Contingent Praise

Keep your praise linked to a specific task or response, and don't overdo it! Whilst rewards and compliments make children who already feel good about themselves feel better, for children who have little or no **self-esteem**, it can be just too much to take.

Rather than saying 'Well done, you're great!' when your child remembers to clean her teeth, try touching his arm and saying: 'Great job on the teeth-cleaning.' Telling her she is good or wonderful, when she knows deep down inside she is disgusting and useless, will make her feel very uncomfortable, because it doesn't fit with what she knows. It may also make her think you are stupid and even more afraid that, when you find out what she is **really** like, you will not want her around.

7.9 Defusing is Less Confusing

One of the most successful ways of keeping tempers from fraying and avoiding battles is by being aware of potential time bombs. That way, as soon as you begin to see sparks flying, you can step in and cool the situation down *in your own way.* If you are in secure charge, you can take the situation wherever *you* want it to go.

If you can see that your child is getting angry, you may be tempted to ignore the signs and hope it will go away. Sometimes this will be the case, but for many children who *hurt*, once they begin to get angry, their behaviour will escalate – until they get a reaction. This helps them to feel better, because they have probably given their anger to you and because they are doing something which, perversely, feels good because it is familiar.

Instead, use your energy more constructively by responding to your youngster *sooner* rather than later. That way you can help her to learn different ways of dealing with her feelings and can have more choice about the reaction you'd like to give! Make it funny or surprising and you will both feel better – and stand more chance of making a lasting, positive impression.

7.10 Surprise and Rule

A child who **hurts** has learned to expect **abandonment**, rejection, anger and abuse. This becomes so 'hardwired' into his thinking that he will see little else, even if you are being consistently loving and supportive. You can't 'get it right' all the time – but one false move and you are condemned!

If you are to get a different message across, you will have to use some very different strategies. Our brains take most notice of, and remember, things which confirm what we already know, or things which are surprisingly different and yet resemble the familiar, in many respects. They are also recalled more readily if they are **associated** with strong feelings – whether positive or negative. So any ways that you can find which have novel aspects *and* good **associations** will have greater impact *and* greater potential for positive change.

Wearing a big silly hat and balancing your child's breakfast on top may make it far more desirable. Same breakfast, different outcome? You never know, he might even ask for more!

7.11 Humour Can Be Great Fun

It is no accident that some of the best humour comes out of the greatest adversity. It is possible to find something funny in almost every situation and if you are laughing you can't be angry! The same goes for your child – but do make sure you laugh *with* her, not at her! If you can't think of anything to say, *do* something daft instead!

7.12 Playing the Fool

Making an intentional fool of yourself can have your child in stitches but keeps the power with you, because it is *your* choice. It is far more powerful than letting your child run rings round you and make you look a fool.

8. Dealing with Feelings

You may find that you have to work on, and work through, your child's feelings *as well as dealing with your own*. This is not the same as accepting responsibility for *how* he feels but implies that you can act as an essential 'translator', putting unintelligible, and even unacknowledged, feelings into words, which your child can begin to make sense of. (See also Speaking the Same Language on pages 38–41.)

Feelings are often overwhelming and unfathomable to children who **hurt** because they did not have opportunities to experience them safely in their early years. Frequently they learned to **dissociate** elements of their experience from their awareness and may continue to do so, either because they believe it is still unsafe to feel, or because it has helped them in the past and has now become habitual.

8.1 Acknowledging Feelings

This process is fundamental to your youngster's increasing emotional well-being. Having been denied essential emotional experiences, or not having had her feelings accepted or validated, your youngster may need to begin by learning to recognise her feelings and to be given safe and appropriate ways of expressing them. If you are able to validate her powerful emotions, empathise with her and help her make sense of them, you will be giving her one of the most valuable gifts possible.

8.2 Keeping It Simple

To begin with, you may find it helpful to stick to the four most common and readily identifiable emotions: anger, sadness, happiness and fear. These have been termed 'mad, sad, glad and scared' and as such are very easily called to mind. They are also readily depicted graphically!

Try to make the discussion of feelings as commonplace and as matter-of-fact as discussing what you will have for breakfast, or what the weather is doing! They are part of life and need to be treated as such. Of course, your modelling of your own feelings, and how you deal with them, will go a long way towards encouraging your child to acknowledge and handle her own.

8.3 First Guessing/Best Guessing

It is likely that you will have a much clearer idea of what your child is feeling, and why, than she does herself. Do not be afraid to say so. Pretty often you will 'get it right' and if you don't, the likelihood is that she will tell you so, in no uncertain terms! You will not be putting thoughts into her head, or words into her mouth, merely providing her with a vocabulary with which to make sense of what is going on.

8.4 Mixed-Up Feelings

You may see very different emotions in your child within just a few moments. This may make you think you are living with Dr Jekyll and Mr Hyde simultaneously and can make *you* feel crazy. If that's how mixed up *you* feel, try to imagine how it must feel for your youngster. Acknowledging to your child that you are familiar with, and unafraid of, *all* sides of her feelings and behaviour can be very validating and healing. (See also Part 4: Through the Looking Glass.)

Mood and behaviour swings, often from pole to pole, from wanting you close to desperately driving you away, make a lot of sense in terms of a child's deep conflicting needs: for security and containment from a parent figure, on the one hand, and her belief that getting close and being vulnerable is dangerous, on the other. The fundamental conflict which faced your child when she was very young, of seeking protection from the person who was also the source of her pain, is now being replayed in your family. If you can remind yourself of this, you can free yourself from feeling responsible for your child's distress and from taking her attacks personally.

Keep on bearing in mind that there *is* a **part** of your child which remained undamaged by even her worst experiences, although both you and she may struggle to detect even glimpses of this innermost *self*. (See Part 4: Through the Looking Glass.) This knowledge can help you through much of the seeming **unreality** of your daily life together, which in turn may encourage your youngster to try to stay in touch with her **real** feelings.

8.5 Those Crazy Feelings

Parents of a child who **hurts** often end up feeling that they themselves must be crazy. Try to keep asking yourself whether you were like this *before* your youngster came home and remind yourself that you may be picking up just how crazy your child is feeling inside. By **reframing** in this way, you can pat yourself on the back for your sensitivity and commitment to him, instead of beating yourself up for not being able to cope! (See Part 1: Coming Home.)

8.6 Naming Not Shaming

All your child's feelings are O.K., although some of his behaviours may not be acceptable. If you respond negatively to your youngster's feelings, you are invalidating them and making it more likely that they will be pushed away, to resurface out of control. Of course, we would all prefer our children to be happy all the time but a child who **hurts** may have a very dominant angry **part**, with which you will all become very familiar. (See Part 4: Through the Looking Glass.)

In the past, your youngster probably could not afford to feel angry: an expression of anger might well have generated further **abandonment**, abuse or neglect or have been used as an excuse to blame him for an adult's maltreatment. Now, that previously suppressed anger may seem ever present, **triggered** by the most insignificant of events. It will also still carry a good deal of *shame* – although that *shame* may also have been 'split off'. (See also Superkid/Scared kid on pages 48–51.)

Your intention in drawing your child's attention to his feelings is not to *shame* him but to try to *name* his feelings so that he can begin to become aware of them at a more conscious level. Eventually this will allow him to gain more conscious control over his feelings, to make the 'right' *associations*, and to learn to express them more appropriately.

8.7 Doing Feelings

Emotion is, literally, a 'doing word' – being derived from the Latin and meaning to move outward. Unexpressed emotions do not go away, they become locked up in our bodies and may then explode without warning, or cause physical pain or *dis-ease*. It is vital that you give your child repeated opportunities to 'let off steam' in safe, acceptable ways:

this can often involve strenuous physical exercise, making loud noises or laughing like a drain at the silliest things.

8.8 Self-Expression

Effective therapeutic work with children who **hurt** frequently takes account of the lack of **associations** between different **parts of the brain** (see also Part 4: Through the Looking Glass), which underlie their apparent emotional illiteracy and volatility. As parents we too can use musical, dramatic, artistic, play and other creative or expressive strategies, which involve the senses and movement, to communicate with our children. (Many suggestions for such activities can be found amongst the specific strategies in *First Steps*.) It is then that we can begin to add in the words and turn our children's (compartmentalised) areas of knowledge into a more coherent life 'narrative'.

8.9 Role Reversal

One powerful avenue for increasing self-expression is actually to swap roles with your child, temporarily. Not only can it be fun to allow yourself to act out the child's feelings and to allow him to respond as the adult, it can also help you *both* to gain valuable insights: to see what it feels like to have a tantrum and to see how your youngster responds.

8.10 Bringing It On Down

A child in **distress** is a child who is '**in arousal**'. His body is hardwired to respond to perceived dangers: predominantly through *fight or flight* responses. He has not had the essential, early opportunities to learn patterns of self-calming and, frequently, his body gets so used to being stressed that he feels more comfortable like that. Conversely, quiet times can feel very threatening.

Again, reactions which rely on pre-verbal methods of communication, such as stroking, rocking, rhythmic singing and relaxed breathing can get in touch with your child when he is at his most distressed. (See also *First Steps,* pages 57–58.) You are actually setting out to re-write his **distorted brain circuitry** and to lay down healthier, more functional body–mind responses.

Inevitably this will take much time: do not despair, it is never too late to help your child to find a 'comfort zone'.

8.11 Changing the Pace

Activities which change the pace of your interactions can be very effective in altering your child's levels of *arousal*. Speaking in a very quiet, non-challenging voice when your youngster is screaming at you can really encourage him to stop and think. Alternatively, fidgety, over-active behaviour may be cut short by a simple invitation to run up and down the stairs, to dance a jig, or to hop on one leg to the count of fifty. Changing the body's *arousal* levels is one of the most powerful tools in altering emotional, and eventually *cognitive* (thinking), responses.

8.12 Staying Out of the Anger Trap

It is all too easy to fall into the trap of becoming angry; it is far harder to extricate yourself without becoming covered in metaphorical mud! It doesn't help you and it doesn't help your child if you 'lose it': you will probably feel very ashamed of your outburst and regret whatever you said in the heat of the moment.

For your child, seeing your anger can confirm his belief that *all* parents are dangerous and potentially abusive. It also *reinforces* his view that he has to stay on the attack, as the best form of defence. Anything negative that you say or do at the time will be hardwired into his belief and response patterns and 'prove' to him that you don't love him, have never loved him, and never will – because he already thinks that he is unloveable.

Finding different ways of responding to your youngster will be a challenge – but one well worth taking! You will feel better about yourself and, by modelling other ways of being, you will, simultaneously, be helping your child to develop a better view of himself and a healthier *working model* of the world.

8.13 Letting It Go

Once a distressing scene is over you may feel very strung out. It is *essential* that you find ways, which feel right for you, of letting go of that tension: so that you can carry on parenting positively.

This does not mean pretending that it didn't happen. It is important that you acknowledge how bad things have felt and that you choose to let go of the overwhelming negative feelings which threaten to swamp you. Then you can get on with your life and with trying to be a caring, containing parent for your youngster.

8.14 Same Beginning – Different Ending

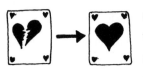

A child who **hurts** has had to adapt to a poor nurturing environment and has probably experienced repeated episodes of **trauma**. One of the ways she tries to deal with these is to re-enact them time after time, in a desperate search for mastery. However, this is often unsuccessful and can actually serve to reinforce your child's worst fears (although frequently bringing some short-lived comfort from an illusory sense of familiarity and of power).

As adoptive or foster parents we are in a unique position to provide *different* endings for these oft-repeated scenes. For a child who experienced the passivity and helplessness of infancy, imagining or playing out, with toys or in **reality**, the possibility of active escape or fighting back is extremely healing. Similarly, for a child who was sexually abused to experience the safety of her own bed, perhaps aided by night lights and a favourite cuddly toy, is a healing emotional experience.

8.15 Equal Intensity – Different Dimension

Sometimes you may *choose* to meet your child's intense emotions with ones of equal intensity. The trick is not to do what she is expecting – to explode into anger, or to retreat in fear – but to reach her through an equally powerful but *positive* response. If she is very worked up, this may be the only way you can show compassion, get in touch and let her know you are there for her. Loud silly singing, feigned wild tantrums, pretend dramatic sobs, flamboyant gestures or even extremely quiet, but meaningful, whispers can be very effective here.

8.16 Meeting the Red Dragon

Anyone can become angry – that is easy. But to be angry with the right person, to the right degree, at the right time, for the right purpose, and in the right way – this is not easy.

Aristotle, *The Nichomachean Ethics,*
quoted in *Emotional Intelligence* by Daniel Goleman (1996).

Modelling positive ways of self-expression, particularly for anger, is essential. Ancient legends depicting the constructive power of the dragon (usually female and frequently red) have been supplanted in more recent times by cautionary tales of the vengeful, destructive nature of 'the beast'. We all need to reclaim our 'red power' at times. A child who *hurts* will need particular help, if she is to accept and harness her rage, with its previous, unhealthy *associations* with pain and violence, and find ways of channelling her energies more usefully – to move from victim, to survivor and eventually to thriver.

9. Calling in the Troops

The old adage that it takes a community to raise a child was never more true than for a child who *hurts*. Sadly, due to the sheer chaos many of us endure, our own expectations and the guilt we feel, we tend to keep our difficulties to ourselves and to suffer in silence.

9.1 Breaking the Silence

Learning to speak out is vital if these children and their families are to receive the help they need and we are to break the desperate cycle of *hurt*, *before* it reaches the next generation. It is also an essential alternative role model for children who were raised to keep unhealthy secrets.

If we do not speak out we are allowing our children to re-enact the silence of their early years and to go on practising their unhealthy behaviours unchallenged. Now is the time to break that silence and to enlist the help of friends, neighbours, family, school, place of worship and anyone else you can think of – as well as looking for professional back-up and specialist resources.

9.2 Getting the Right Help

Having said that, it can be very difficult for outsiders to understand what is going on in your family and to let go of the old myths – that you must be 'doing it wrong' if things are not 'going right' and that it is usually mum's fault! The idea that mothers can cause schizophrenia in their children, for example, is still a common fallacy.

You may find that you will need to start by educating *everyone* about the special emotional needs of your child. If necessary give them some of the material available from Adoption UK (see our publications leaflet for further information) or purchase a copy of *Children Who Shock and Surprise* (Randolph 1994). Give them time to make sense of all this *before* you ask them for their vital support.

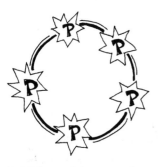

9.3 Networking

Of course, some of the best help can come from 'fellow sufferers': members of Adoption UK who have lived, or are living, with children who *hurt* themselves. You'll find it saves an awful lot of explaining and can begin to make you feel **normal** again! So if you haven't joined Adoption UK yet, now is the time to do so!

Networking can also put you in touch with scarce resources, including financial ones, and suggest supportive child care and mental health practitioners who could help you and your family. A personal recommendation is worth its weight in gold when you are searching for a therapist, or an understanding school environment.

9.4 'Who Ya Gonna Call?'

Remember that you don't always have to cope single-handed! Having someone local you can call on for practical help, *before* the going gets too tough, can make all the difference. The majority of children who *hurt* will act better with people from outside their immediate families: so it doesn't matter whether it's the frail old lady from down the road, or the six foot grown-up son of a friend, just their being there can have a calming effect.

Finding 'industrial strength' babysitters or childminders is not going to be easy – but you need to be able to get out *sometimes*, in the evenings or during the school holidays, and you deserve the break! It can also be very expensive to arrange. Maybe your child could contribute to the additional costs from his pocket money or 'pay you back' by doing jobs for you, at another time? That way you are asking him to accept some responsibility for any special arrangements you need to make to keep him safe. Look within your circle of good friends or fellow adoptive parents for someone who won't be phased by 'difficult' behaviours, not tell you 'he was fine with me', in a tone which implies it must be *your* fault that your child acts up. Then go out, forget about the family for a few hours and enjoy yourself.

You might also like to suss out someone you can call on in an impending crisis. Do make sure that you talk things through with your 'crisis-buster' *before* you call them in and that they **really** do understand what is going on in your family. You may find that just knowing you still have something up your sleeve can boost your confidence and help you to manage things better yourself. Moreover, since you youngster will probably recognise that your back is *not* right up against the wall, he may feel more **contained** and be better able to take control of himself.

9.5 Resource Issues

Whilst *you* remain the most valuable resource(s) for your youngster, locating additional resources can be difficult and may be the last thing you feel like doing when you are in the greatest need. It therefore makes sense to try to cultivate resources *before* you really need them. For example, if when your child is being placed with you, you ask for an adoption allowance to be considered *in principle*, it could be there, should things get tough.

Similarly find out if you, or your child, are eligible for state benefits, such as Disability Living Allowance, can claim Criminal Injuries Compensation, or can apply for trust funding of any sort. This may mean that you are more able to bear the appreciably higher costs of parenting a child who **hurts**. (Contact Adoption UK for information on accessing financial resources.)

9.6 Getting the Specialist Help You Need

Unfortunately, support services can often be hampered by their own resource limitations or by a reluctance for, or a bureaucratic inertia towards, changes in practice. A healthy bank balance can make it easier for you to access specialist child care, educational and mental health resources independently. Whilst this can be invaluable, particularly where you are having difficulty obtaining the support of your local social services or health care team, it can still be problematic for you to locate the 'right sort of help'.

Truly effective intervention services for children who **hurt** are still very few and far between, although progress is certainly being made. Since your child has experienced **traumatic** early **hurts**, appropriate therapeutic work needs to begin at these very early levels (targeting the appropriate parts of the brain developmentally). Hence **expressive therapies** are more likely to get in touch with your child's **real** issues than conventional 'talk therapy'.

Make sure you are clear about what it is you would like and what you wish to avoid, before you begin the search. Be prepared to ask questions and remember *you always have a choice*. If the service you are offered 'doesn't feel right', then decline it gracefully. Ineffective help can be more damaging to your family relationships than no help at all.

10. If at First You Don't Succeed

Life with a child who **hurts** is unlikely *ever* to become 'a piece of cake'. However, if you believe in yourself and trust that you are the 'right' person for this difficult job, it *will* probably become easier and increasingly rewarding. Remember, too, that childhood does not last for ever and that although adulthood brings its own difficulties, it may well *feel* different when your young adult grows up and begins to leave home. (See Staying a Family and Being Apart in Part 7.)

10.1 Ready for a Change?

Right now, you may find that you have tried a strategy which sounded good, or used it well for some time, only to find that it has become ineffective. Now is the time for a change! If it isn't working, and you've given it your best shot: *try something else.*

Carrying on with more of the same is likely to make you feel increasingly demoralised *and* will allow your child to feel 'in control', since you clearly are not. The element of surprise in doing something radically different may also help you to regain your flagging power and 'push' your child into having to think again.

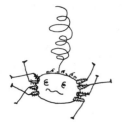

10.2 Enough is Enough?

Sometimes it may feel that you can't take any more: then you take a deep breath and carry on anyway! It is surprising how many times you can do this and how much untapped energy you can find within. At some point, however, you may *really* feel that you and your family have had enough.

This will be a very sad and painful time for all of you; one which is certainly not helped by well-meaning child care practitioners or unwitting comments from friends, neighbours or even grandparents. If you *could* go on, then you would. You owe it to yourself, to your partner, and to your other children, to stand up for yourselves and say that *this is as bad as you will allow it to get.* Then you will still be well enough, sane enough and alive enough to go on being a **good enough** parent for your child who **hurts**, *wherever* she is living.

Currently, positive options for children who can no longer live at home are very limited. This is bound to influence your decision to take a stand – but please do not let it outweigh all other issues. Sadly, it is often the case that children 'don't know what they've got 'til it's gone'. Yes, another separation will be very traumatic, it may well **trigger** memories of other separations and losses, but it can have a different outcome. (See Staying a Family and Being Apart in Part 7.)

10.3 Letting Go

Letting go is *not* giving up! Letting go is having the serenity, the courage and the wisdom* to know your limitations and not to try to exceed them. In fact by letting go you are also encouraging 'keeping in touch' and 'coming back' *and* may be letting some vital hope back into your lives.

You will never stop being a parent, and your adopted youngster will never stop being your son or daughter, wherever they go, whatever they become and despite any claims to the contrary by your child, or from ill-informed support agencies. Think of all the eighteen-year-olds who go off to college. Are they suddenly considered aliens, totally unrelated to you – even if you only speak on the telephone once in a blue moon? So why should an adopted youngster, who bursts out of his family because his experience of previous separations makes this a particularly difficult issue, be judged more harshly?

It is interesting that you may well be deemed financially responsible for your youngster's upkeep, while he is being 'looked after' (though not if this is at Her Majesty's Pleasure), whilst simultaneously feeling excluded from decision-making processes. Rulings about financial responsibilities have been challenged successfully in the past; rulings about accompanying rights, for both your child and yourselves, may also warrant challenging. (See also Adoption UK material on **attachment** issues.)

---

* From The Serenity Prayer (see above).

10.4 Wants and Needs are Not the Same

Even a seriously **hurt** child can learn that what they *want* and what they *need* are two very different things. Being separated from the only people who **really** care for you, and about you, can make that **realisation** very tangible. If you remain there for your child, despite the **hurts** and separations, you are offering her a unique learning experience: that all is not lost and that she *can* come back, either literally or metaphorically. However, it is hoped that the terms of your relationship will have changed and she may come to respect your essential **boundaries**. (Please see also Part 7: Staying a Family and Being Apart.)

10.5 Rights and Responsibilities

There is often confusion between a child's rights and his responsibilities. Recent emphasis on children's rights has indeed been very welcome. However, this concept may be unhelpful to some children who **hurt**: children who already have problems with issues of blame and in linking cause and effect. Suddenly, at eighteen years of age, they may be hit by the full forces of the law and state, from which they have previously been 'protected'. (See Consequences, point 6.6, and Learning the Hard Way, point 6.7, on page 72. Also see Sections on Addictive Behaviours and Self-Harm and Staying a Family and Being Apart in Part 7.)

Conversely, parents' responsibilities have been given far greater weight than their rights – you *do* still have them: use them both wisely!

10.6 Smelling the Roses

However difficult you may find it to hang on through the hard times, and whether or not you are living as a family under the same roof, you deserve to feel good about yourselves. A short walk in the garden each day and a lingering sniff of the roses can go a long way towards restoring your **sense of self**. If you can't do it literally, then do it metaphorically, in any way you like which leaves you feeling good.

Principles into Practice

Spotlight on Aggression

Spotlight on Aggression

For many children who *hurt*, aggression remains a major feature of their lives. Before your youngster came home, he will have experienced serious *hurts* which affected his ability to trust and his ability to feel safe. This, in its turn, may continue to influence his responses to frightening, confusing, conflicting, or even exciting, situations in the present. Aggression is a very common pattern of coping which the child who *hurts* may show, especially within your family, since his original *hurts* were also experienced within a family setting. His original expectations that his parents, and especially his mother, would take care of him, and protect him, have been severely challenged. **This leaves the youngster with seriously ambivalent feelings towards parenting figures: he needs love and security but he does not need the rejection and maltreatment he believes are also part of family life.**

A youngster may openly display his feelings of anger, through threatening or destructive behaviours, or he may have learned to use more indirect expressions of his distress, particularly through '*oppositional*' or 'defiant' responses. It may seem to you that your child is deliberately not listening to you, is avoiding your eye contact, even staying out of your way. Although this may indeed be the case now, as 'taking no notice' can be a very powerful way of 'taking control', it is by no means the whole story. Often this pattern has developed out of an original *terror response*, where the only safe thing for your child to do was *freeze*: to switch off from the terrifying things which were happening to him.

Both direct and indirect *(passive) aggression* may once have been *adaptive* – they helped your child 'get by' in unsafe situations. (See Part 4, section on Getting Real.) Difficulties may be arising currently, in your family, because those survival strategies are being perpetuated, even though circumstances have now changed. So your child remains unable to find out about safe situations, and unable to learn appropriate response patterns, in those safe situations. This may be very hard indeed for you to live with: it is extremely frustrating to feel ignored, rejected or as if you aren't even there. It can be very helpful to remind yourself that **if it is hard for you, it is far harder for your youngster.** Deep down inside, he is also feeling *hurt*, ignored, rejected, as if he doesn't exist – only much more so. Without your help this is unlikely to change; he will continue to feel unsafe, and to act accordingly. (See Part 4: Through the Looking Glass.)

It may be that your child witnessed, or experienced at first hand, terrifying episodes of aggressive behaviour (including sexualised behaviour) from the very adults who should have been taking care of him. Instead of protecting him, he may have seen his parent(s) *hurting* him, his mother or his brothers and sisters, or making repeated threats to do so. In many cases the connection with past experiences and present aggressive behaviours may not be so clear cut: perhaps your child suffered neglect or long-term poor care, experienced the terror of early *abandonment* or was subjected to painful medical procedures and hospitalisation which challenged his trust in his caregivers. Whilst your child cannot feel safe to express the *hurts* and anger at the treatment he received directly in such circumstances, **he may begin to identify with**

the perceived power of this aggressive role, perhaps seeing it as the only way to survive. At the biological level, the original overwhelming feelings become 'hardwired' into his nervous system, especially if his *neural networks*, those vital connections in his brain, are still in the early stages of being established. Any feelings which remind him of his fear, his helplessness, his pain, his confusion may *trigger* a full-blown aggressive response in the present – even though you know that the circumstances are very different.

Some children find less direct, but equally challenging, ways of coping. They may *switch off* from their feelings of sadness, frustration and rage and appear not to care at all. (See Part 4, as above.) This may have been the only choice they had in the past, a choice which did confer some sense of power in a situation of powerlessness. They may shrug their shoulders and look pathetic, or smirk or sneer, or fiddle aimlessly with whatever is to hand, or look back at you with unseeing eyes and a completely blank expression. They are disconnecting from contact with you, and from the intensity of their own feelings, because it feels too dangerous to stay in touch. It will be better for both of you if you can wait until later before attempting to deal with whatever *triggered* this episode originally. **Right now your youngster is in no fit state to hear what it is you have to say.**

This can be a time when even the most patient parent may run the risk of becoming emotionally or physically abusive, since the 'normal' response of the child – to cry, to run away, or to fight or answer back – just does not happen. In most circumstances, an active response would be enough to bring you up short and stop you behaving in an abusive manner. Faced with a passive response, your own natural responses may go awry, with potentially serious consequences. **It is vital that you always stay in control of your own feelings and never use your power as a parent in an abusive manner.** If necessary, take yourself away from this dangerous situation and give yourself time to get back to 'the right place' (see Part 4). If you find that this continues to happen, despite your best efforts, you may need to seek outside help from someone you can trust.

When you feel ready to start 'bringing your child back', begin by acting very slowly and calmly and by talking very quietly. **Sitting down, with your hands open, palms uppermost, will make you appear less threatening.** Do not try to force eye contact just now – that may in itself be too much for your *distressed* child. Instead, stay with your youngster until he is able to feel secure enough, and in touch enough, to respond more appropriately. It may help to keep on repeating quietly, 'I'm here; you are safe' over and over, especially when you feel that even a soft touch would be too much.

For many adoptive parents aggression, in both its active and passive forms, is one of the hardest things they ever have to face. Often committed to peaceful co-existence and liberal democracy, prone to being reasonable, thinking and talking things through, meeting violent responses from a child, or within themselves, can challenge their fundamental assumptions about humanity. They are keen to give, although deep down they may also be expecting something in return – perhaps that warm glow inside, as they face and meet a challenge. Moreover, they used to believe that *all* children are innocent, loveable, responsive to nurture and eager for their reassurance, understanding and support!

A child who **hurts** *is* all of these childlike things and *does* need your commitment, love and empathy *but* he may well not show it – most of the time anyway. (See Part 4: Through the Looking Glass.) What *you* may see is an angry, **hurtful**, controlling, insolent or destructive whirlwind which leaves you, by turns, feeling helpless, scared, desperate or increasingly angry. These are often feelings you may not have experienced frequently as an adult, or may have no conscious memory of ever experiencing at this magnitude – although you probably will have done so as a young child. Consequently you may have very few tried and tested strategies for dealing either with the aggressive behaviours themselves, or the way you begin to feel inside. **What is more, you cannot believe that you feel this way: it is as if your child has brought out a completely alien** *part* **of you which you did not know existed and of which you are deeply ashamed.** (Again, see Part 4: Through the Looking Glass.)

Things to remember at this point:

- We all have 'good' and 'bad' **parts** in us, that is what makes us uniquely human.

- Feeling this way is not in itself 'bad', although acting punitively or violently on these feelings should be avoided at all costs.

- You are **reflecting** how your child feels, deep inside. Use this knowledge as a guide to managing the situation.

- You don't have to get 'hooked' by your child's feelings. Avoid the 'anger trap' at all costs! (See point 8.12 on page 83.)

- Your child also has 'good' and 'bad' **parts** in him. Whilst you may only see an angry destructive tyrant, there is a small, very lost and scared child hiding in there somewhere. (See Part 4: Through the Looking Glass.)

- Blaming yourself and feeling guilty will only tie you up in knots. You need to stay free for positive action. (See Promoting Positives on pages 75–79.)

- It *is* possible to get through to your child, to go *beyond* the rage to the distressed child hiding away inside.

- Take time to think before you act. Just counting up to ten slowly can give you the time you need to start thinking reasonably.

Below are short descriptions of two typical scenarios involving aggressive behaviour from children who **hurt**. They are followed by some **realistic** examples (although they are by no means exhaustive) of how parents could have dealt with these situations, and how they may have worked out. They are intended to illustrate the great variety of choice you have in facing a particular situation and to open up the possibility of you becoming more creative in your responses – as you become more familiar with these choices, and as you regain your confidence in yourself as a **good enough** parent. Beneath each vignette I have indicated some of the particular strategies from the fundamental principles which were used. In time you can learn to 'mix and match' your own strategies, in your own unique way, to suit your individual situation.

Through the Looking Glass – Anger

<table>
<tr><td>

Child

</td><td>

Mother

</td></tr>
<tr><td>

I am bad, I am so bad –
I could kill someone!

</td><td>

Sometimes I really hate her.
This is killing me!

</td></tr>
<tr><td>

They hurt me when I was little.
So why shouldn't I hurt them
and their little children?

</td><td>

I feel so bad when she hurts other children.
They're only little.

</td></tr>
<tr><td>

I can wind her up!
It makes me feel good and powerful.

</td><td>

I get so upset when she's like this.
It feels awful to be so helpless.

</td></tr>
<tr><td>

Why doesn't she go away and leave
me alone.

</td><td>

I try so hard to get close to her – but
she won't let me.

</td></tr>
<tr><td>

I know she's going to get rid of me,
so why doesn't she just get on with
it?

</td><td>

Maybe she would be better off
with another family?

</td></tr>
</table>

Occasionally I have tried to point out why some of the approaches which were used by the parents were unhelpful. I have deliberately included these examples to alert you to some of the possible pitfalls of responses that are not respectful, loving and supportive. **However bad you may be feeling, being *hurtful*, rejecting or punitive will only serve to make the situation more intolerable and will leave you feeling bad about yourself.** Your child will seize on these negative messages as absolute confirmation that you are not to be trusted and that families *really* are unsafe. It will also *reinforce* his belief that his aggressive behaviour is acceptable, even justified, whilst deep down he will continue to feel worthless and that he deserves to be treated badly.

You may notice that some of the suggestions are quite different from each other, perhaps even contradictory, and yet each may still be very effective for a particular child, in a particular situation, at a particular time. **It is not so much what you do but the way that you do it. If you act with love and respect and BELIEVE that what you are doing will help the child, it probably will.** For everybody's sake, try the most '*normal*', most comfortable and least challenging first — you may find that you don't need to do anything else just now. You can always keep some of the other suggestions up your sleeve for later, or just have a chuckle about the crazy thing you might do in your dreams! Paradoxically that can actually help to keep you sane and acting reasonably and responsibly.

Scenario 1

Jack is ten years old. He came home to Lindy and Sam five years ago after being received into care following allegations of maltreatment in his birth family. Jack continues to have some contact with his birth parents, through phone calls, letters and the occasional short visit.

Lindy has reminded Jack to put his shoes away under the stairs when he comes in from school and before watching TV. Jack erupts (as he frequently does when he has been asked to do even little things by his adoptive mum) hurling his shoes and verbal abuse at Lindy, kicking the TV, spitting at his older adoptive brother, Simon, and running out of the room, slamming the door loudly on the way.

Possible Outcome 1

Lindy first checks out with Jack's older brother, Simon, that he is O.K. and tells him she is sorry this has happened again. She goes to find Jack and asks him why he is upset. She is understanding when he tells her about his bad day at school and gives him a big hug. She tells him it's O.K. to feel angry but it is *not* O.K. to act like that. Lindy then goes with him and encourages him to pick up his shoes and to apologise to his brother, before getting him a drink and a biscuit and sitting down with him to watch TV.

✔ **POSITIVE PRINCIPLES ILLUSTRATED:**

Don't Forget the Siblings	2.1
Modelling	6.4
Finding Your Touch	7.1
Acknowledging Feelings	8.1
Keeping It Simple	8.2
Bringing It On Down	8.10
Letting It Go	8.13

NOTE: Asking a child directly what is the matter with them will often elicit a defensive response such as 'I don't know', or sullen mutterings. It is very probable that your child will *not* know why he is upset, since he has remained '*switched off*' from many of his feelings in order to survive. It can be very helpful to make an informed guess (8.3) as to the root of the *distress*; if you are wrong, you can be fairly sure your child will let you know! Some children may also use this opportunity to complain about something else, which to them may seem vital but is in fact an incidental issue (5.6).

Possible Outcome 2

Lindy checks out with Simon that he is O.K. and tells him she is sorry this has happened again. She fetches a special video out of the cupboard and offers it to Simon. She then goes into the hall and Jack throws a book down the stairs at her. He calls her a 'F****** B****' and then glares at her with eyes of hate. Lindy puts her hands up to her head to make 'ears' and begins to bark loudly. She carries on barking until she hears Jack laughing (or at least making non-confrontational noises). She then goes upstairs with him and sits with him on his bed. She can feel that his body is hard and tense.

She remembers that it is this weekend that Jack is to hear from his birth mother, and talks to him about how he may be feeling about that. Although he ignores her at first she knows by the way his body gradually softens that he is listening and making sense of what she says. She stays with him for perhaps half an hour, resisting the temptation to worry about the dinner, allowing him to let out some of his anxiety, anger and excitement over the impending visit. Some time later she goes downstairs, leaving Jack to come down when he is ready. Lindy has a cup of tea and puts her feet up for ten minutes before getting on with preparing the evening meal.

✔ **POSITIVE PRINCIPLES ILLUSTRATED:**

Taking a Break	1.4
Don't Forget the Siblings	2.1
Diff'rent Strokes	2.2
What is Really at Issue?	5.6
Finding Your Touch	7.1
Humour Can Be Great Fun	7.11
Playing the Fool	7.12
First Guessing/Best Guessing	8.3
Letting It Go	8.13

Possible Outcome 3

Lindy checks out with Simon that he is O.K. and tells him she is sorry this has happened again. She tells Simon that she will deal with the situation and asks him to remain in the sitting room, or to go· out to call for one of his friends. She goes into the hall, where Jack jumps on her, pulling her to the ground. He is screaming, 'I hate you, you can't make me. Why should I do women's jobs? You're not my real mother anyway!' He tries to bite and pinch her. Lindy rolls over and manages to sit up, whilst keeping hold of Jack. Jack resists and struggles with what seems to be superhuman energy.

Lindy holds his arms and secures his legs with her legs, so that he cannot hurt her or himself. She tells him that he is safe and that she can take care of them both. She says that she can see he is feeling very angry and that feeling angry is O.K. but that hurting people is not. She wonders whether his anger has anything to do with the anticipated visit from his birth family and tells him she can understand how he could be feeling. She acknowledges how much he must miss them *and* how angry he must feel that he can't live with them. She reminds him that it is never a child's fault if things don't work out in a family and tries to reassure him that she will look after him and keep him safe now. Minutes pass.

After some time she senses he is close to crying and lets him know that it O.K. to cry – even for big boys and daddies. She strokes his hair and wipes his eyes gently. Gradually his body moulds into hers. They remain in this position for some time and she reminds him that there can be an easier way of letting her know how he is feeling. She hopes he will 'get it' one day. Eventually she suggests he must be hungry after all that hard work and takes him into the kitchen to get both of them a snack.

✔ **POSITIVE PRINCIPLES ILLUSTRATED:**

Don't Forget the Siblings	2.1
All or Nothing	4.1
Finding Your Touch	7.1
Acknowledging Feelings	8.1
Mixed-Up Feelings	8.4
Bringing It On Down	8.10
Letting It Go	8.13

Possible Outcome 4

Lindy checks out with Simon that he is O.K. and tells him she is sorry this has happened again. She tells Simon that she will deal with the situation and asks him to remain in the sitting room, or to go out to call for one of his friends. Lindy asks Jack to go outside and run round the garden shouting as loudly as he can. She opens the front door and guides him outside (handing him his wellies on the way out). Since she knows he will be safe in the garden, she watches from the window and grins encouragement as he stomps, screams and makes rude gestures at the world. Once Jack has used up some of his energy and the movement has 'moved him on', out of his anger, Lindy invites him in, congratulates him on working hard on his feelings and gives him a big hug. Jack is then encouraged to think about what has upset him, to apologise to Simon for making him upset too, to put his wellies and his shoes away and to sit down with some refreshments to enjoy children's TV. Lindy stays with the two boys for a while before getting on with the cooking.

✔ **POSITIVE PRINCIPLES ILLUSTRATED:**

As above PLUS:

Don't Forget the Siblings	2.1
Time to Cool Off	3.2
Accentuating the Positives	7.2
Contingent Praise	7.8
Humour Can Be Great Fun	7.11
Doing Feelings	8.7
Changing the Pace	8.11
Letting It Go	8.13

Possible Outcome 5

Lindy knows that Jack may be feeling upset when he comes in from school – that as a child who *hurts*, his '*hurting* other people' part may walk through the door – and she is ready for it. She walks up the road to meet him, throws her arms wildly around him and begins to tickle him insanely. She suggests a game of football in the park before going home, leaving Simon to turn the oven on for the evening meal she prepared earlier before meeting them in the park. They all make a lot of noise and have some fun in the park before returning home tired but relatively peaceful.

✔ **POSITIVE PRINCIPLES ILLUSTRATED:**

Being a Family	2.5
Humour Can Be Great Fun	7.11
First Guessing/Best Guessing	8.3
Changing the Pace	8.11
Staying Out of the Anger Trap	8.12

Possible Outcome 6

Lindy decides to ignore Jack's outburst and carries on preparing the dinner. She can hear that he has gone upstairs and leaves him time to calm down on his own, knowing that anything he breaks will be Jack's own – and that he possesses little of value since he has destroyed so much already. She does not intend to replace any broken items, although she will be happy to help Jack to save up to pay for replacements himself.

When he comes down she is ready for him and congratulates him sincerely on his good work on his feelings. She reminds him his shoes are still in the sitting room and tells him he is welcome to have a snack and to watch TV, once he has put them away and said he is sorry to Simon.

✔ **POSITIVE PRINCIPLES ILLUSTRATED:**

Choosing Your Time	3.1
Whose Problem?	5.5
Learning the Hard Way	6.7
Eliminating the Negatives	7.3
Don't Say Don't	7.4
Don't Take It Personally	7.5
Invitation or Ultimatum	7.6
Contingent Praise	7.8

Possible Outcome 7

Lindy picks up the signs of underlying anger in Jack's behaviour. She knows that it could escalate into something which would be dangerous for herself and for Simon and she feels that Jack is becoming too big for her to handle on her own. She quietly asks Simon to put his coat on and go round to her neighbour's house right away. She tells him to ask Mr and Mrs Smith to give her a hand. Only last week she had spoken to them about the possibility of them helping her out in just such a situation. Jack continues to prowl round the house shouting and banging doors and furniture.

When Mr Smith arrives Lindy puts him in the picture before getting her own coat and going to join Simon for a cup of tea at Mrs Smith's. Mr Smith, who is over six foot tall and used to play rugby in his youth, goes upstairs and finds Jack in his mother's bedroom. There are belongings scattered all over the floor. The bathroom and Jack's own bedroom are in a similar mess. Mr Smith calmly suggests to Jack that he should put the rooms back into order and offers to give him a hand. Jack, after an initial reluctance, makes quite a good job of tidying up. He even tells Mr Smith how stupid he has just been to get angry with his Mum, when he had been upset about something else. A few minutes later, Jack and Mr Smith set off for Mr Smith's house. Jack appears quite calm and is able to apologise gruffly for his earlier behaviour. Lindy gives him a hug and offers him some tea.

✔ **POSITIVE PRINCIPLES ILLUSTRATED:**

Taking a Break	1.4
Diff'rent Strokes	2.2
Finding Your Touch	7.1
Defusing is Less Confusing	7.9
Letting It Go	8.13
'Who Ya Gonna Call?'	9.4

Possible Outcome 8

Lindy tries to ignore Jack's loud swearing and threats, although she is clearly distressed by his behaviour. She takes him some juice and biscuits into the sitting room, as he watches TV. She glares at Simon who is trying to change the channel back to the programme he had been watching before Jack came in. She tells Jack she is sorry she upset him and asks what is wrong. He tells her he hates his shoes, they are so old and falling apart. Lindy tells Jack she will buy him a new pair in the morning; meanwhile, she puts the old ones away herself. She feels it is somehow her fault for annoying Jack and for not realising his shoes are so shabby.

Lindy tells Simon that he cannot have a new pair as well because his are still in good condition (although both pairs were bought at the same time). She goes into the kitchen to prepare the meal, having changed her plans to include Jack's favourite. Jack does not eat his dinner, telling Lindy 'it stinks' and is 'not like what my *real* Mum makes'. When Lindy's husband comes home she shouts at him. By this time Jack is busy upstairs and Sam cannot see what all the fuss is about. He suggests Lindy goes to see their GP to get some pills if she can't cope.

✗ NEGATIVE PRINCIPLES ILLUSTRATED (BOTH BY OMISSION AND COMMISSION):

Parents in Partnership	1.3
Making the Break	1.5
Diff'rent Strokes	2.2
What is Really at Issue?	5.6
Eliminating the Negatives	7.3
Don't Take It Personally	7.5
Defusing is Less Confusing	7.9
Acknowledging Feelings	8.1
Letting It Go	8.13
Wants and Needs are Not the Same	10.4

Possible Outcome 9

Lindy takes no notice of Jack's outburst and carries on with her housework. She doesn't want to have to face another upset and hopes that he will settle himself down. Jack returns to the living room and demands that his mother brings him a drink because he's thirsty and he's too tired to move. Lindy takes him a drink and some biscuits. After a few minutes Simon calls her. He tells her that Jack is flicking juice at him and has stuffed biscuit crumbs behind the curtain. She tells Simon to take no notice and asks him to let her get on. Some minutes later she can hear more loud voices, so she calls to the boys and tells them to stop messing about. Moments later Simon runs into the kitchen holding his head. He says that Jack has hit him with the television remote control unit and that he won't give it back.

Lindy suggests that Simon goes upstairs to do his homework instead of winding Jack up. Jack then goes into the kitchen and demands more juice. He is angry because the carton is empty and throws it on the floor, knocking a dish off the kitchen unit. Lindy sighs and mutters under her breath as she picks up the pieces. Jack watches her bend over and then kicks her hard in the lower back; he laughs as she struggles to get up. Lindy tries to pretend she is not *hurt* but Jack taunts her, calling her weak and useless. She screams: 'Go away, leave me alone! Get out of my house, I've had enough. And don't come back!' At this Jack rushes out of the house, shouting: 'Well, I knew you never wanted me anyway. Just you wait. It'll be your fault when I die of starvation in a cardboard box!'

✗ **NEGATIVE PRINCIPLES ILLUSTRATED (BOTH BY OMISSION AND COMMISSION):**

Possible Outcome 10

Lindy feels very angry that her routine and her once peaceful house is being upset again by this child. She shouts back at Jack, glaring at him and saying, 'Don't you speak to me like that young man!' She tries to force Jack to pick up his shoes, grasping his wrist tightly and pushing him across the room. She is fed up of this and she isn't going to stand for it any more. Jack resists and spits at her. She slaps him and calls him dirty, lazy and no good and says he has always been trouble. She grounds him for a week and threatens him with: 'Wait until I tell your Dad and your social worker.' Jack kicks her and tells her he doesn't care. He says he is going to tell the social worker that she has hit him and then he is going to get his *real* dad to smash her face in! He sneers at her and rubs his hands in gleeful anticipation.

Lindy feels terrible. She knows she shouldn't have lost her temper and she is terrified that Jack will tell someone what she has done. She begins to feel that she isn't fit to look after children and to blame herself for all the family's difficulties. This isn't what she wanted when she answered an advertisement in her local paper to consider being an adoptive parent of a desperate child. She resolves to make it up to Jack and lets him have his own way repeatedly over the next few days, to try to make amends. She is devastated when she finds that her favourite ornament has gone missing and discovers fragments of it stuffed behind the bookcase in the living room. Jack denies that it has anything to do with him and blames their old labrador. Lindy desperately searches for proof and tries to talk Jack into admitting what she suspects *really* happened. She feels she must be going mad but is afraid to talk to anyone about how she feels, in case they take Jack away.

✗ NEGATIVE PRINCIPLES ILLUSTRATED (BOTH BY OMISSION AND COMMISSION):

Scenario 2

Josie is now thirteen. She is small for her age, attractive and wiry. She came home to Sue and Jim five years ago, after experiencing years of inconsistent and neglectful parenting, and several moves in and out of the care system. Sue works from home part-time, whilst Jim works full-time in the local town. They have been together for twelve years. The family also has two cats and a tortoise.

Sue and Jim have planned an evening out at the cinema for themselves. They have spent days worrying about leaving Josie: sometimes it seems like ages before Josie will sit in the same room as them, after they have been out without her. They are also concerned about whether their neighbour, who is to 'baby-sit', will be able to handle Josie's behaviour. They have agreed to go ahead and do it anyway!

Possible Outcome 1

It is 5 p.m. and Sue has just discovered that Josie has poured cold tea all over her bedding. She knows that Josie is upset that she and Jim are going out without her. She reminds herself that they both deserve a night out and that there is no point in both of them becoming upset too.

Sue goes to find Josie and says to her: 'I hate it when you try to destroy our things. I know that you are upset that we're going out and I also know you'll enjoy having Maxine here and watching the video we chose earlier. We will be back by 11 p.m. – you know that.' Sue adds: 'Maybe one day you'll be able to tell us how you're feeling right away, instead of doing *hurtful* things like this.'

✔ **POSITIVE PRINCIPLES ILLUSTRATED:**

Parents as Partners	1.2
'I' Statements for all	2.3
First Guessing/Best Guessing	8.3
Naming Not Shaming	8.6
Staying Out of the Anger Trap	8.11

Possible Outcome 2

As above. When Jim comes home and hears what has happened, he backs Sue up but begins to feel very guilty about 'abandoning' Josie. Sue reminds him that Josie is thirteen years old, that they are only going to be out for about three hours and that it is O.K. for Josie to feel upset; she will handle it. Jim reminds himself that his own childhood experiences of his parents' separation and divorce may be colouring his perceptions and that both he and Sue have been looking forward to this break.

Jim and Sue agree that they will ask Josie to strip the bed and put on clean sheets before they go out. They will sit down together and tell Josie very quietly and simply that she can take her time doing it and will remind her that it will be Josie who will have to sleep in uncomfortable, wet sheets if she 'forgets'. When Josie complains that she is too tired to strip the bed, they both nod sympathetically and say, 'I know.' They give her a hug and tell her they hope she will have a good evening.

Sue and Jim have already put the clean bedding ready, with a note wishing her luck and reminding her that they will be back by 11 p.m. Alongside it is a bag of chocolates in the shape of little stars.

✔ **POSITIVE PRINCIPLES ILLUSTRATED:**

Parents in Charge	1.1
Parents in Partnership	1.3
Owning Your Own Problems	4.6
Avoiding Confrontation	5.3
Being Heard	6.1
Consequences	6.6
Headliners	6.10
Quality Street	6.11

Possible Outcome 3

Josie is in her room, lying on the floor, staring at the ceiling. Her stereo is blaring away beside her. She does not respond when Sue knocks on her door, or when she calls her name. Sue can see that Josie is upset because she and Jim are going out. She sits down with Josie, and takes her hand, as she tells her that she knows how hard she finds it to feel O.K. about them going out and leaving her.

When Sue is sure she is able to listen, she quietly offers Josie two choices: Josie can spend ten minutes with Sue now, thinking about what has just happened and working out what she is going to do about it, *or* she can stay where she is and then sit down with Sue and Jim before they go out and try to work out together what is going on. When Josie chooses the first option, Sue congratulates her on a good choice, and continues to stroke her hair, until she senses that Josie is ready to talk.

They discuss what might be upsetting Josie and what Josie can do to put things right. Before they finish, Sue lets Josie know that what she has just done is not acceptable behaviour for a thirteen-year-old and reminds her that she does know other ways to be. She then gives her a hug and reminds her that dinner will be on the table in thirty minutes, saying: 'You're welcome to join us as soon as the mess is cleared up.'

✔ **POSITIVE PRINCIPLES ILLUSTRATED:**

Time In	3.4
Thinking Time	3.5
Whose Responsibility?	4.2
Being Heard	6.1
Body Language	6.3
Two Choices	6.8
'Listen Very Carefully…'	6.9
Headliners	6.10
Finding your Touch	7.1

Possible Outcome 4

Sue decides to delay any response, other than continuing to give Josie the message that they are both still planning to go out, until Jim comes in from work. Sue then shares with her the events of the day; Jim suggests that he goes upstairs and pretend to find the wet bed. He carries the sodden bedding downstairs to the room in which Josie is watching TV and 'throws a tantrum'. As previously agreed, Sue retires to the bathroom to wash her hair.

Jim kicks, screams and rolls around all over the wet linen, shouting out: 'I'm so angry! It's not fair! Why doesn't anyone take any notice of me?' He feels surprisingly powerful at being able to lose control in this way. Josie watches him in dumb amazement. After a few minutes, Josie goes and makes a cup of tea for Jim 'because he's upset'. They sit down together and start to chat about the film Jim and Sue are going to see later. Jim 'apologises' to Josie for his 'outburst' and wonders aloud whether Josie ever feels like that. Jim also says he wishes he had punched one of the pillows, *before* he came downstairs to talk to Josie about the mess that this might have stopped him from throwing a 'wobbly'.

Before they go out, Josie brings down the soaked bedding and asks Jim to help her reach down the clean linen. Together they remake the bed. Whilst they do this, Jim talks about Josie's early childhood, about how she was left on her own for long periods, and about how that would have made her feel. He tells Josie it wasn't her fault that these awful things happened, she was only a small child. Now that she is older Josie may, understandably, still feel scared of being left. Jim tells her that when he was little and felt afraid, he would cuddle his teddy 'Bert' until he fell asleep. Then Jim fetches his old battered teddy and tucks him into Josie's bed, along with her night-clothes.

✔ POSITIVE PRINCIPLES ILLUSTRATED:

Parents in Partnership	1.3
Choosing your Time	3.1
Time to Talk	3.6
Modelling	6.4
Saying It with Flowers	6.2
Mixed-Up Feelings	8.4
Naming Not Shaming	8.6
Doing Feelings	8.7
Self-Expression	8.8
Role Reversal	8.9

Possible Outcome 5

Sue and Jim recognise that Josie is having a particularly bad day. First of all they shut the cats up in the warm basement out of harm's way (the tortoise has hibernated recently). They then call a friend on the After Adoption Network and have a good moan together. The friend offers to come round later as 'back-up' for the baby-sitter – or at least to give her a ring during the evening. She reassures Sue and Jim that they shouldn't change their plans – that Josie and the baby-sitter will be fine. She also suggests that they might use a little of Josie's pocket money (due next day) to pay for the cost of cleaning the sodden duvet.

The next day, Jim and Sue decide to call their social worker to request a meeting to discuss Josie's continuing difficulties and to see if they can access the respite service locally, for very short breaks, using a regular, trained carer. They also agree to make enquiries about grant money and benefits which could help them pay for more help around the house, so that Sue can spend more time with Josie, when she is at home.

✔ **POSITIVE PRINCIPLES ILLUSTRATED:**

Animals are Family Too	2.4
Acknowledging Feelings	8.1
Meeting the Red Dragon	8.16
Getting the Right Help	9.2
Networking	9.3
Resource Issues	9.4
Getting the Specialist Help You Need	9.5

Possible Outcome 6

Sue and Jim feel knocked out by the constant challenges to their parenting. They feel they have tried everything to manage Josie's behaviour, including behaviour modification – but nothing seems to be changing. They feel they are letting Josie down. They have also explored outside resources, including child and family therapy and respite care, without success. They are beginning to dread Josie being around and feel their health is beginning to suffer.

Sue and Jim decide to try something 'completely different'. On the suggestion of another adoptive parent they enrol in Adoption UK's parent empowerment course, 'It's a Piece of Cake?' based on *Parenting the Child Who Hurts*. They feel it is worth a try, as nothing else is working!

They also agree that, if things do not improve considerably, they will consider looking for a residential school place, or small therapeutic residential unit, for Josie. That way they feel they will be able to go on being Josie's parents in the best way they can. They find out all they can about these options and agree that they will only accept a placement where staff are fully committed to supporting them as Josie's parents. In the meantime, to cheer themselves up, they buy themselves some flowers, then order a take-away and a bottle of wine!

✔ **POSITIVE PRINCIPLES ILLUSTRATED:**

Ready for a Change?	10.1
Enough is Enough?	10.2
Letting Go	10.3
Rights and Responsibilities	10.5
Smelling the Roses	10.6

Possible Outcome 7

Sue gets really upset when she finds the wet bed. She has been expecting Josie to do something to try to stop Jim and her going out together. She feels it is not fair and becomes more angry the more she thinks about it. She runs down the stairs and stands with her hands on her hips, confronting Josie with the evidence. She seems to lose control and screams at Josie that she has just about had enough of this behaviour.

She thrusts the wet linen in Josie's face and tries to drag her towards the utility room and the washing machine. Josie resists and a physical struggle begins, during which Josie's dress gets ripped and Sue sustains a black eye. Sue goes to her room, crying.

When Jim returns home, Josie meets her at the door and tells her that Sue had attacked her and deliberately tried to tear off her dress. She calls Sue a 'weirdo' and makes sneering remarks about her sexuality. Jim is at first speechless, then he rushes off to find Sue and begins to scream at her, claiming that he always knew she was volatile but now she's becoming really unstable. He tells her she should go and see a doctor and get herself sorted out. Jim then finishes making tea for himself and for Josie and leaves Sue to sob alone in their room. He cancels the baby-sitting arrangements and goes out to the pub on his own for the evening.

✗ **NEGATIVE PRINCIPLES ILLUSTRATED (BOTH BY OMISSION AND COMMISSION):**

Parents as Partners	1.2
Parents in Partnership	1.3
Taking a Break	1.4
Avoiding Confrontation	5.3
Forcing the Issue	5.4
Body Language	6.3
Keeping It Simple	8.2
Naming Not Shaming	8.6
Bringing It On Down	8.10
Staying Out of the Anger Trap	8.12

Possible Outcome 8

Sue goes to look for Josie and asks her angrily what she thinks she's been doing. Josie says: 'It wasn't me.' When Sue asks 'Why?' she does not reply; this incenses Sue further. She moves in close to Josie's face and scowls as she shouts, 'Don't try to be clever! Answer me when I ask you a question. Are you stupid?' Josie remains silent and just stares blankly at her. 'Just you wait until Jim gets home, then you'll be sorry,' she says. Sue then tells Josie to get out of her sight until then, or else!

Still very upset, Sue picks up the phone and dials the adoption agency and asks to speak to her social worker, who is in a meeting. Sue demands that she be brought immediately to the phone and then hurls abuse at the receptionist when she explains that this is not possible. Finally, she grabs her coat and, without saying anything to Josie, leaves the house.

When Josie realises she has been left on her own, she starts to panic – she hasn't really recovered from the earlier upsets and it also *triggers* memories of being left alone for long periods in her birth family. She feels devastated: very *hurt* and very scared. She goes downstairs and pours cooking oil all over the sitting room carpet and then sprinkles flour on top. She grabs one of the cats and holds it down in the mess, so that its fur becomes very matted. She then runs out of the house, leaving the front door open.

When Jim comes in from work a few minutes later, he finds the scene of devastation and an empty house. He doesn't know what to do and, in panic, he calls the police. He makes up his mind that when Sue comes back, he will ask her to leave.

✗ **NEGATIVE PRINCIPLES ILLUSTRATED (BOTH BY OMISSION AND COMMISSION):**

Parents in Partnership	1.3
Making the Break	1.5
Denying Responsibility	4.3
What is Really at Issue?	5.6
Body Language	6.3
Don't Take It Personally	7.5
Defusing is Less Confusing	7.9
Those Crazy Feelings	8.5
Naming Not Shaming	8.6
Meeting the Red Dragon	8.16

NOTE: This vignette also exemplifies Sue's boundary problems, her failure to take care of herself, her struggles to provide nurture and containment (the 'Twin Pillars' of *good enough* parenting) and her failure to check out where she herself is coming from before acting ('Starting from the Right Place'). **It is in just such circumstances as this family's that parents need to pay especially close attention to these issues – since when you are under stress you are more likely to 'lose it' (decompensate), and act in unhelpful or damaging ways.**

Sensitive Situations

I have deliberately spent a great deal of time looking at foundations: the foundations of adoptive families, the foundations of children's lives in *attachment*, *development* and *trauma*, and the fundamental principles of parenting a child who *hurts*. Without all this 'foundation work' it would be difficult, if not potentially dangerous, to build up a coherent structure of effective strategies which would allow you to remain respectful, responsible, nurturing and protective, or for our children to learn basic trusts: trust of care, trust of control and trust of self. Having beavered away at putting sustainable foundations in place, now is the time to take the next leap in faith, as sure as you can be of yourselves and of the direction you need to take.

Like buildings in general, you can choose (theoretically) to construct a magnificent diversity of structures on top of your foundations, using the basic building blocks. These structures may look very different on the outside but fundamentally their function – to provide you with comfortable living and working space – remains the same. Similarly, once you have laid down the fundamental principles for family living, you are relatively free to go about your 'construction' in your own particular ways. Most of you will feel comfortable following a reasonably well-defined plan, yet each 'plot of land' will vary and each person's 'dream home' will be influenced by their own experiences, their available resources, the community within which they live, and 'the state of the art' in terms of technical knowledge – over and above their unique dream within the 'grand design'! By building in a number of structural and safety factors, within your own individual plan, you can retain the confidence you need to do an effective job – even if what you are trying to do feels very different from the approaches of your friends and neighbours.

The ideal way of approaching family life, with a child who *hurts*, is from a basis of sound ground work, with an outline framework drawn up, a selection of building blocks and cements, and a 'yellow pages' list of useful crafts-persons on whom you might call if specific difficulties should arise. The likelihood is, then, that you can do what *you* want in the way that *you* want, staying open to any alterations in the original design which may become necessary, and keeping some of your options open. You will need to be sure that you are able to maintain acceptable health and safety standards (including fire regulations) as you build and maintain your family home. The essential difference here is that **a family is a living, growing structure** made up of very unique individuals, so that you will always be constructing a one-off, vital family system in your own unique way.

The section below (the selection of building materials if you like), is intended to supplement the fundamental principles in Part 5, as working guidelines only. Rather than overwhelming you with suggestions for every conceivable eventuality, I have tried to concentrate on a small selection of situations which often prove particularly sensitive or challenging to adoptive parents. (For a canny child who *hurts* it may be only too easy to work out what parents' strategies are, if you follow a rigid formula which does not allow for individual situations and personal creativity.) I have then tried to provide a fuller, but by no means comprehensive, outline of strategies which have been used effectively by parents in the past. Consider them as 'living, working examples' of the fundamental principles and consult them not as 'the oracle' but as possibilities for you and your family.

At the risk of repeating myself, **you *really* do know your family best and only you can *realistically* judge which suggestions will suit you and your child, at any given time.** If you are able to consider each situation, trusting that you have viable options, then your lives will feel freer and potentially more comfortable. Feeling that your back is being pushed up against a wall is no fun and tends to leave you responding under pressure. Knowing that you have choices, even if it seems you are choosing between the lesser of several evils, does confer a feeling of control and responsibility. It also provides a better model of living for children who *hurt*!

> *I seek the freedom to be all of who I am*
>
> *Daybreak*, Maureen Brady (1991)

These words of Maureen Brady's are particularly apt in the context of parenting a child who *hurts*, both for you as adopters and for the child herself. Often during the course of a day you may find yourself thinking or feeling things you did not imagine you had in you – most of them pretty challenging and uncomfortable to a positive *sense of self*. In a similar way, the child's poor expectations of herself, part of the *internal working model* born of past experience, influence not only her current thoughts and behaviours but also her continuing perception of herself as bad, tainted, untouchable, unloveable. If you are not to *reinforce* these mis-perceptions with mis-responses, that is to match her *hurtful* actions with equally *hurtful* reactions, it is up to you, as the adult, to make the first, essential changes of 'step'. (See also Part 4: Through the Looking Glass.)

You all deserve to be free to choose any and all of who you are. The best place to start in this seemingly complex 'dance of poor expectations' is with yourself. Your greatest freedom is to choose to get away from the role of 'bad parent', in which you can feel cast by circumstance and the *looking glass* of your child's *distorted* beliefs. These beliefs can be so powerful that you begin to lose sight of your 'better side' altogether. That is why it is so important that you act 'Mr or Mrs Nice Guy', even when you don't feel that way, just so that you can start finding out about your pleasant side again. Then you will be much better placed to be loving, containing, patient and supportive over and over again, until you can begin to change the steps of your child: your partner in this crazy 'dance'.

Similarly, you will be looking for ways to alter your child's deepest *perceptions* of herself as worthless, or beyond repair. **Regaining a healthy perspective on your own self-worth should be your first step. This should be closely followed by a determination to help your child see those undamaged *parts* of herself she cannot see, or keep in mind.** You can only genuinely do this if you, yourself, *really* believe that your child already has something good and loveable about them – which can be a tall order if you are faced with an almost permanently *hurtful* onslaught from your youngster. So try to find *something*, however small, which makes you feel good about her: that is the seed from which you can both nurture something even better. **Then the final step in this new dance-sequence is to have FUN!**

Fun has probably not been at the fore-front of your mind for some time – but as fun is more likely than not to be found somewhere in your *mid brain* and *limbic system*, that needn't be a problem! You probably have a great number of memories of having fun to get in touch with, if you allow yourself the chance, whilst your child may have very few. She therefore needs to have plenty of practice at having fun to fill in the gaps. **Often you will have to side-step the prevailing** *dance of anger* **completely in order to provide opportunities for fun – not as a reward for 'good behaviour' (or you might wait for ever) but just for the fun of it!**

Isn't it wonderful to think that one of the best ways to help your child out of the *looking glass*, and to feel good about herself, is to enjoy *yourself*: wholeheartedly and without restraint! It doesn't have to be justified, or sensible or pre-planned or hardwork or cost lots of money – although at first you might find this helps. However, it does have to push your child's emotional *arousal* levels up in positive ways – so take care not to overdo it at first, in order to avoid an unwanted 'blow-out'. Repeat the pleasing experiences often enough and they will begin to be hardwired and can eventually replace, to some degree at least, the negative hardwiring you are seeing right now.

Make a list of all the different ways you can think of to have fun. Do this on a 'good day', when you are not stressed out, and just write down anything that comes into your head, however silly. This gives you better access to your intuitive, emotional *right brain*, where your best 'warm, fuzzy' memories from childhood are tucked away. Keep on adding to the list whenever a fun idea crops up and pin it on your notice board or fridge, to help you keep it in mind. Perhaps you could decide to do at least one 'warm, funny' thing each day with your youngster(s). Even adolescents can be tempted to join you, if you choose carefully and pick your moment. I find that a quick trip to the local Italian ice cream parlour invites least resistance all round!

On the *biological* level you are working on structural rewiring (yet another house-building metaphor) through fun-filled, corrective, physical and emotional experiences, whilst on the *psychological* level you are trying to change your child's *distorted* expectations of the world and re-establish trust in others. On a more intangible, *spiritual* level you are seeking to reawaken that indestructible spark of life with which your child was born and which has remained at least partially hidden for so long. **A child needs your faith in her and in this process of reawakening if she is to heal from her hidden *hurts* and learn to trust in herself. Only then will she, too, have the freedom to be ALL of who she is.**

Bedwetting and Daytime Incontinence

Some children take longer to gain full control over their bodies, and their 'outgoings' than others. However, we do tend to expect most youngsters to have 'got to grips with' taking themselves to the loo relatively well by the time they start school. In fact these days many schools, even at nursery level, appear reluctant to accept young children who have not acquired basic self-toileting skills – although occasional 'accidents' are tolerated. Night-time bedwetting tends also to have become a thing of the past by this time, give or take the occasional 'leak', as bladder control continues to strengthen and mature.

The stresses of beginning a new school, going down with an illness such as chickenpox, or going away on holiday may cause a temporary relapse but, with a little understanding, time and encouragement, dampness usually fades to a distant memory. Children who *hurt* have to cope with many more *(dis)stresses* than most children: making the transition into their new family will be just one of many. Consequently you might expect that the process of gaining effective bladder control could take longer and could be more susceptible to new stresses, which other children would take in their stride.

For some children the problem seems to carry on regardless, way beyond school age and despite your best efforts at following the conventional wisdoms. In this case, it is vital that you give yourself time to think through the possible hidden motivations in your child's continuing bedwetting, before you consider trying out some of the less conventional approaches which parents have successfully used to help their child.

What You May See (The 'Presenting Problem')

You may see a child of eight, nine, ten years or more who repeatedly wets (or soils) the bed, or wets in other inappropriate places, and who seems totally unmoved by the whole thing. He may make no attempt to remedy the situation, may conceal wet bedding or night-wear, or openly leave it in the middle of the sitting room for all to see. He may take no notice of your requests that wet clothing be put ready for washing, or that he wash himself to avoid the pervasive, tell-tale smell of urine. Overnight stays with friends, school trips and family holidays may have become increasingly difficult to manage. Your washing machine may be threatening to break down and you may feel that you are not far behind. You may have reached the point where open confrontation seems unavoidable and you are torn between feeling sympathy for your growing youngster and intense frustration at the continuing difficulties.

Beyond the Looking Glass (or What May Lie Beneath)

- An older child may continue to bedwet because it reminds him, unconsciously, of his previous family. The smell, in particular, can be a very potent reminder of what he has lost, even though there may have been a good deal of suffering involved too.

- Some children seem oblivious to their bodies and the feelings they produce. This is particularly likely to be the case where a child has suffered repeated, early ***traumatic*** experiences and has not learned to make appropriate connections (***associations***) with his body sensations.

- Children who have experienced overwhelming helplessness may feel that the only control they can exert is over their own bodies – what goes in and what comes out. It is therefore vital that you find other, more acceptable, ways of enabling your child to feel in control and avoid being sucked into unproductive control battles.

- Animals often use urine and faeces as territorial markers. Could this be an attempt by your child, at some primitive, unconscious level to mark out or claim space in your home? This could be a positive ***reframing*** (for you) of an otherwise difficult issue.

- Some youngsters appear to sleep so deeply that they do not wake up in time to take themselves to the loo, often wrapping themselves up completely in their bedding, so that absolutely everything becomes wet. This may be a result of the child having been left alone repeatedly, or abused in their own beds, especially during the hours of darkness – with all the terror which that evokes.

- Nightmares, often an expression of deep-seated childhood fears, may make your youngster so ***distressed*** that he loses conscious control of bodily functions. In some cases, he may appear to be awake, and to be moving around the room, before 'peeing' in a chosen spot. This may, in fact, be part of a ***night terror*** pattern, over which the child has no conscious control and no subsequent recall.

- For some children, being wet and smelly is a metaphor for how they feel. If a child has not been well cared for, she comes to believe she does not deserve good care: she is in fact too bad, or too dirty, to be treated well by others. She may well begin to accord herself the same sort of treatment.

- Occasionally a child may *associate* the attention she gets after wetting her bed with a degree of care she could not otherwise expect. Perhaps, in her birth family, her mother would come to her to change her bed after her father had abused her, hence making her feel 'loved'. This has implications for your strategy of choice – deciding to make it your child's personal responsibility may give her the unconscious message that you do not, in fact, care about her and cannot love her.

- **There are children for whom the sense of control gained from wetting their beds seems to far outweigh the usual social or physical discomforts. For these children, the only way is out! That is, you need to get out of the control battle and give your child enough space to make a better choice, based on personal comfort rather than humiliation, or on *distorted* beliefs about who is in control.**

First Choices

Your first choice can always be to do nothing: sometimes that can be the very best choice of all, **as long as you feel comfortable with it and you feel that it is the most respectful and responsible thing you are able to do.** Few children continue to wet the bed into adulthood, so time could be your greatest ally.

Your local health visitor or Continence Advice Service may be able to provide you with useful suggestions, or guidance, on what incontinence aids are currently available, including the latest 'drug' treatments. **However, when it comes to the crunch, remember that you cannot make your child become dry: even the most sophisticated gadgets and drugs may be of no avail if the sense of security or control your child derives from his behaviour gives him a bigger short-term pay-off.**

Find out about alternative therapies which other parents have found successful with their children's bedwetting – including homoeopathy, aromatherapy massage and cranial osteopathy. Contact other parents on the After Adoption Network in your local area, or call Adoption UK at Lower Boddington for guidance.

Since bedwetting often has connotations of babyishness, dirtiness, humiliation, embarrassment and *shame*, in society as a whole if not in your own family, a child may need repeated assurances from you that she is O.K. – and that you expect she will get a hold on the problem pretty soon. She will also benefit from being offered, in a supportive, non-critical way, some practical strategies to handle wet bedding, clothing, bodies, etc., at home and elsewhere.

These could include: providing copious spare pants, along with wipes or easily accessible washing facilities, and encouraging regular toileting before going to bed. You could also try star charts and small reward incentives, if you feel these might work and will not become arduous or counter-productive. Some of the more 'obvious' ways of dealing with bedwetting may not, in fact, be effective. For example, reducing liquid intake in the evening, and 'lifting' a sleeping youngster, may deprive a child of experiencing a full bladder and of learning to do something about it.

Finding ways of encouraging your child to take more personal, age-appropriate responsibility for her actions, such as stripping the wet bed and putting the sheets out to be washed, may often be enough to get you all through this. Above all, a calm and matter-of-fact approach from *all* the family is essential.

Building a child's *self-esteem* and confidence in himself is *not easy* and your youngster may readily become discouraged, or even appear to 'sabotage' his own achievements. For some children it is just too scary and uncomfortable to be seen to be doing well, either because it doesn't fit with what they 'know' about themselves or because, in the past, good things were inevitably followed by bad. At least this way the child feels he is in some sort of control.

You cannot give your child that much-sought-after sense of feeling good about themselves, by talking, however hard you try! The youngster has to work it out for himself – and one of the best ways he can do this is by 'getting it right', whether he wants to or not. **This means that you will not only have to make it as easy as possible for him to succeed, you will also have to try to take away any of the factors which are currently getting in the way of his changing.**

This could include such seemingly supportive acts as changing all the bedding for your child whilst she is in school. Your motivation in doing this may be to help your child feel cared for and to avoid her experiencing embarrassment, which would further damage her *self-esteem*. In her *looking glass* world, she may instead experience this as not needing to be responsible for her own actions, or that it doesn't matter if she goes on making a mess, since someone will always be there to clean it up. Not quite the message you really wanted to give!

A child who feels somehow comforted by consistently wetting has to be helped to find other ways of obtaining more appropriate relief. Perhaps you could set aside a 'comfort' time each evening, when you can provide cuddles, strokes, whispers, songs and all the other acceptable, *soothing* things (perhaps including opportunities to suck on a bottle containing warm milk) which you might ordinarily reserve for a much younger child.

Your youngster will almost certainly have missed out on such vital comforts as an infant – **the bedwetting may, in one sense, be seen as trying to return to those early years, to get what she didn't the first time round.** By choosing to provide regular times for comfort you are setting more appropriate *boundaries* and expectations and are likely to see a reduction in the incidence of wet beds.

If Things Still Don't Change …

If it feels like a more 'upfront' challenge, as if your child is deliberately wetting his bed, or in an inappropriate place, this may indeed be part of the problem. It is certainly your *reality*! Whilst you will want to look beneath the surface, it can be refreshingly simple to step aside from the hassles which are preventing your child moving on. It is, in any event, counter-productive, if not potentially dangerous, to engage in lengthy 'reminder' sessions about washing or trying, forcibly, to get a child under the shower 'for his own good'. Although well-intentioned, you are more likely to crank up his stress levels and render him even less able to think or act responsibly.

If you've tried unsuccessfully to persuade your youngster to wash, you may find that making *no* references at all to personal freshness can lighten your day considerably. Unwanted comments from other children at school may be painful to witness but may be a far more effective force for change. After all, your words of encouragement seem to have fallen on deaf ears so far – doing more of the same is hardly likely to work any better *and* you run the grave risk of becoming frustrated, or even punitive.

Similarly, leaving your youngster's bed exactly as he himself left it may evoke a more healthy response (especially if everything else you've tried so far hasn't worked). Discarded, wet clothing could be returned to the bedroom too. Try leaving a little message on the bed saying 'I love you', along with a note asking your child to let you know if he wants to change his bed, or wash his clothes – and that you'll be only too happy to help him. **Do and say nothing more.** It is very unlikely that your child will choose to sleep in the damp bedding for many subsequent nights, although he may resort to the floor rather than 'do the right thing' in the short term!

Again, do and say nothing about the bedwetting, other than showing a genuine, generalised concern for your child's well-being. Be prepared to respond swiftly and respectfully to any approaches she makes to you for help in resolving the problem. A single, matter-of-fact reminder of the 'house rules' regarding wet things wouldn't go amiss. It is really a matter of time and patience on your part, in the hope of getting your child to acknowledge the active part she can play in her own greater comfort. A genuine increase in *self-esteem* can be the lasting result, once the penny drops (in the right place!).

If the problem still persists, then it is very likely to intrude into the broader context of family life. You may find yourself sharing the sofa with a very unsavoury body: it could become very tempting to drop increasing hints about washing, or to begin spraying the area, in an exaggerated way, with an altogether sweeter odour (or if you don't, one of your other children may!). **Not only is this likely to *reinforce* the child's negative self-image, it is also unlikely to be effective and may be all the reward your youngster needs to cling to her smelly habit.**

You could decide, instead, to set some limits on a child's participation in shared activities, as a consequence of her unpleasant smell. Couched in a very positive manner, such as 'I'll be really happy to give you a cuddle, once you've had a quick shower' or 'I'll be ready to give you a lift to basketball practice when you're washed and ready to go,' you can make it very clear to your youngster what is needed and what the consequences of 'doing it her way' really are.

Keep any sarcastic, critical or threatening thoughts to yourself and allow plenty of time for your message to be received, understood and acted upon – **the habit didn't come into being overnight and it is unlikely to recede swiftly either.** And, as with any other suggestions, do bear in mind that progress may slip at times of increasing general stress, or as part of 'an anniversary reaction' (see *Sensitive Situations* on page 131).

'The Phantom Piddler' or Smearing of Faeces

Finding puddles, stains and smelly messes around the house, time and time again, is not only irritating and unpleasant, it can become very embarrassing *and* it can drive you mad! Your youngster, on the other hand, may well deny all knowledge of the incidents and seem indifferent to the upsets it generates. Too right – who needs to feel frustrated, angry or sad when you can get someone else to do the hard (and painful) work for you?

So a vital part of your approach must be to give every appearance of calm, and to find other outlets (if and when necessary!) for your understandably strong reactions. **Staying in control of your emotions will enable you to stay in control of a challenging situation and will help your child find better ways of controlling his life** – and more acceptable ways of expressing his own (e)motions. Again, this does not necessarily mean ignoring or tolerating the behaviour, rather that you will need to find innovative, and preferably amusing, ways of encouraging the child to become responsible for his own actions, to be respectful of other people's property and feelings *and* become more fun to live with!

Begin by showing that you expect your youngster to clean up after himself: provide the essential equipment, stand back and don't hold your breath (even if the stench is overpowering!). It is likely that your child will resist your request initially – perhaps pleading innocence (and remember that it *is* possible that he has **dissociated** the memory of the act from his **conscious awareness**) or refusing to co-operate in the clean-up. If you are sure that your perception of the situation is correct, then you can act confidently, quietly but firmly insisting that he should clear up the mess – without getting into pointless and time-consuming debates about 'whodunnit'.

Consider teaching your child to clean the bathroom: it is a job he will eventually have to learn anyway. Amazingly, children can begin to take a pride in, and feel proprietorial about, things they have taken care of themselves. If this becomes the case they are much more likely to feel comfortable with, and to use, the bathroom appropriately themselves.

Remember to give appropriate praise for a completed job, however long it has taken! A quick hug to give the message 'that it's all over and done with now' can be very powerful here.

Make sure that you allow masses of time for the first few requests, and, preferably, that you have something diverting and enjoyable to take your mind off the 'will he/won't he?' scenario. Whilst you *cannot make* your child co-operate, you *can make* it not worth his while to resist – and worth his while to do so. 'I'll be happy to play dominoes with you, once the job's done' or 'Feel free to take your time, I'm enjoying this book' may be all the invitation a 'stuck' child needs to do what you *really* want him to do anyway!

Alternatively you might choose to confirm your child's choice of 'dumping ground' as a regular bathroom area. If you can get your head round the fun element in this, and **leave sarcasm and vindictiveness out of it,** giving permission to your child to do what he is doing already may be the quickest way for him to stop! Maybe you could erect a sign in the target area, saying something along the lines of 'nearest public convenience this way' or 'now wash your hands'. Any *oppositional* child worth his salt will avoid such invitations like the plague – which may mean he will begin to use the *real* bathroom more frequently!

Then again, you could compliment your youngster on trying to claim his rightful place in your house, like your pet dog 'peeing' on every lamp-post in the neighbourhood. (Tongue in cheek maybe, but you must sound genuine!) Then perhaps you could suggest more acceptable ways of 'making his mark' – such as having his own corner, with his own bean bag and a notice board (for leaving messages and being noticed).

See if you can also come up with lots of opportunities for being *really* messy – perhaps working with clay or paints in the shed in the garden. With plenty of baggy old clothes for protection, you could have *real* fun together!

If you decide that you would prefer to undertake the 'toilet attendant's' job yourself – for whatever reason – and are happy to do so, you might consider asking your child to do something else for you in return. This could be anything – preferably something you are fairly confident he may do acceptably well – which can give you a little breathing space to recover your own sense of well-being.

Conversely, you may actively choose to give your child the cuddle you know he *really* **needs right away and have done with all the hassles.** A comforting 'I can see that you must be feeling pretty shitty/pissed off at the moment', accompanied by a genuinely loving touch, may produce a much more meaningful response and, eventually, resolve this difficult and frustrating situation more readily. Since the child will most likely be expecting a telling-off or a scene, this can be a very effective method of establishing who is in control and sharing your youngster's underlying (and *distorted*) *hurts*, which leaves you both feeling less fraught and more connected.

Finally, and whatever else you choose to do, be gentle with, and kind to, yourself. Perhaps you could buy yourself some sweet-smelling flowers, or arrange to have an aromatherapy massage, in recognition of the repeated assaults on your senses – or just pick up the telephone and have a good moan to someone you know will listen and understand. Then get back on track and get on with living your own life the best way you can, so that you can help your child to begin to live hers!

Sleep Problems

Children who have been *hurt* in the past expect on-going *hurts* in the present, remaining constantly 'on watch' for hidden dangers. This can make sleep particularly problematic since, by definition, it requires the ability to 'let go' and relax watch over the external world – something which the youngster has rarely had the opportunity to do. When sleep may also bring repeated nightmares or ***night terrors*** and has strong links with the fears of darkness and of night-time abuse it is no wonder that sleep disturbances are so common.

Since wakefulness is rarely suffered in absolute silence it can also have very powerful effects on all members of the family. As parents we want to 'be there' for a ***distressed*** child, yet repeated disturbed nights can take their toll on our ability to remain ***empathetic*** and to maintain our own sense of well-being.

What You May See (The 'Presenting Problem')

You may see a pre-teen or teenager who actively resists going to bed, or who is wakeful and disruptive throughout the night and may not seem to need much sleep at all. She may have developed a variety of tactics to delay bedtime, or to keep you around through the night. She may cry out repeatedly or prowl silently around the house at night, raid the fridge or flick from channel to channel on TV. Sometimes 'things happen', your possessions mysteriously vanish or are broken; other children in the family are becoming anxious or frightened too. You are increasingly worn out from endless nights of wakefulness. Your temper is beginning to fray and you, too, are finding it difficult to go to sleep, to stay that way or to awake refreshed.

Beyond The Looking Glass (or What May Lie Beneath)

- Sleep, by definition, requires a fall in levels of **arousal**. A child who **hurts** may have perpetually raised levels of **arousal** and is unlikely to have learned healthy patterns of self-soothing. Hence she is in double jeopardy in the sleep stakes.

- Many children born to disorganised parents will have a disorganised pattern of waking and sleeping. This could partly be an inherited characteristic, and partly a pattern learned from early experience – even in the womb. Either way, this can make your child's sleep rhythms very different from your own – and potentially problematic.

- Children who have suffered separation, neglect, have been cared for inconsistently or abandoned (even temporarily) become hardwired to avoid subsequent separations and **abandonments**. Even a very young infant will continue to fight sleep in a vain attempt to make sure that 'mum' stays around. Once established, this pattern can become hard to break, as it is at such a fundamental and unconscious level of being.

- Parents often row at night – perhaps after an evening's drinking. Young children are very sensitive to such upsets, will come to feel responsible for the difficulties, and will struggle to find ways of distracting sparring adults even by entering the fray themselves. Again, this pattern, established in a previous family, may be anticipated in yours – and your family's sleep may suffer as a result.

- The sexual exploitation of children frequently takes place during the hours of darkness. Whether it is through witnessing the sexual activities of adults, or through being used themselves by abusive carers, the child's devastating experiences of terror and **shame** are very likely to become **associated** with night-time and the vulnerability of sleep. For some children this will also become the time when they will attempt to master their own pain by similarly abusing other, more vulnerable, individuals.

- **There are a small number of children who *hurt* who see night-time as yet another battlefield for control and who have evolved a sophisticated pattern of wakefulness in which to act out their *hurts* in a seemingly hostile world. This is the pattern which they have adopted, from an early age, to survive their *dysfunctional* families and which, unfortunately, they believe is the only way to get by. Sadly, it then becomes the parents, and frequently siblings and pets too, who are forced to become eternally vigilant and to experience the vulnerability and isolation of the dark hours.**

First Choices

It is hard to ignore a child's distress at night: there are no distractions, other than sleep itself, and that seems to become impossible! Ignoring the problem may also exacerbate the situation since, for many children, it is the feeling of helplessness and isolation which underlies their distress. Giving calm reassurances, with a brief cuddle, a small drink and a night-light can help – as can all the pre-bed routines recommended for babies and young children. (See also *First Steps*, pages 72–74)

Since time itself can be a great healer, you may choose to allow nature to bring about a resolution to this one, bearing in mind the above. As long as you, your child and your partner can cope well with interrupted nights and can *still* be on song the next day, this could be just the 'right thing to do'!

If there is a Sleep Clinic in your area, it could be worth checking this out. Although the service may be aimed at much younger, or more physically or learning disabled, children the staff may be able to listen sympathetically and offer some handy hints.

Be very accepting and understanding of your child's difficulty. By acknowledging what you believe is the underlying reason for his poor sleep pattern, you are validating his life experiences and helping him to make *associations* between cause and effect. Your child may have never realised that it is *normal* for a child who has been frightened of going to sleep as an infant to go on struggling as he does – he may feel that he is 'wrong', is 'going mad' or is 'acting like a baby'. **This does not mean that you don't want to work towards change – your child will probably want this even more than you do!**

Remember that you cannot make a child sleep – however, like the proverbial horse, you can take him to bed and try to show him the comforts of relaxation and oblivion. It may turn out to be enough to establish a *bed*time, rather than a *sleep*-time, and to accept that how much of that time your youngster stays asleep is irrelevant, as long as he stays quiet and is sensitive to the sleep needs of other family members. Why not maintain a supply of good books, tapes, pens, felt-tips and paper for such 'night-owls', so that they don't become restless and start disturbing the household? (See also *First Steps,* pages 72–74)

Where fear of the dark itself is a problem, leaving a landing light switched on or fitting a 'plug-light' can go far in dispelling fears of the shadows of the night. Forget about fossil fuels and world ecology, this is the lasting survival of your family you are talking about!

Some children will find it difficult to sleep on their own, perhaps never having experienced being on their own at night. Others are disturbed by having to share a bedroom with anyone. Do a little bit of detective work when your youngster first arrives to establish past experiences and present preferences – and keep working on it until you feel things are 'right', as far as you can make them. If space is really limited, partitioning or strategically placed curtains can give some sense of separateness. An enlarged photo of you, a cuddly teddy or the pet dog/cat on the bed, or tapes of your voice (all *transitional objects*, or reminders of belonging and comfort) may give your child enough additional security to settle into a healthy sleeping pattern.

A child who has been locked into his room and left for extended periods is going to feel anxious whenever he is left alone again. His level of *arousal* may go sky-high, so that he loses some measure of control over his actions. He may try to create a lot of noise, to attract attention, or to destroy the room or its contents. In this case (and hopefully you will have been forewarned!), be ready to ensure doors are kept at least ajar and that other *transitional objects* are in place, to provide adequate, additional security.

Where food has been scarce or deliberately withheld, a child may have learned to forage at night, when the coast is relatively clear. Hopefully you will have been informed, if this has been the case, so that you can get across to your youngster that she can help herself during the day (within some reasonable limits). You could also provide some 'essential night-time supplies', for reassurance rather than consumption if possible. (See also notes on pages 126 below.)

Older children often feel that they should be allowed to stay up later – and this is true as far as it goes! Parents also have rights – including the right to a peaceful evening in their own company, or with friends. Again, if you make the youngster's bedroom a comfortable place to be and do not try to *impose* 'lights out' or sleep, this could be an acceptable compromise which gives you both the personal space you need.

Your child may be especially sensitive to 'atmosphere' in you home – in the past her life may have depended on this skill. So, if you or your partner have been irritable, or angry, or over-excited, or depressed whilst your youngster has been around, try to sort things out and reach a comfortable state of agreement before bedtime. This way the child does not go to bed feeling to blame for whatever went on, or anxious that ill-feeling may escalate once she is in bed.

Similarly, if you are going to have a row (however friendly), do it somewhere else – especially once your child has said 'good night'. To a youngster who was brought up in an atmosphere of fear and **hurt**, the slightest raised voice can **trigger** great anxiety and may lead to a (**dissociative**) panic response. Even the sound of an exciting video may be enough to cause major **distress** – so be selective, keep the volume down or invest in a pair (or two) of earphones.

More positively, you may wish to create a particularly relaxing atmosphere, in the widest sense. Soothing music and selected aromatherapy oils in a burner or diffuser can alter levels of arousal and improve *all* your chances of a good night's rest. I find Mozart, cello music, Winnie the Pooh tapes and lavender oil especially conducive to relaxation!

If Things Still Don't Change…

It is vital that you seek help from sympathetic professionals in such circumstances. Psychotherapeutic work with your child may help to uncover and resolve some of the **distorted** patterns of thinking which underlie their distressing behaviours. Some prescribed medications may also be effective, in the short term, although long-term use is likely to have adverse effects, especially when the drugs are used in isolation. Many parents have found that complementary medicine has more to offer here, so find out what is available locally and talk to your friends and other Adoption UK members about their positive experiences.

Every member of your household has a right to feel safe in their own bed. If you, or one of your other children or pets are being subjected to abusive or frightening situations at night, **then you must try to make yourselves safe.** In a minority of cases this may involve buying a good padlock or two and applying them to *your* bedroom doors. Younger and older siblings may wish to feel in control of their own security – in which case providing them with their own lock and key (on the inside) may work well.

Always ensure that pets have a 'safe place' of their own, to which they have free access, especially at night. Cat flaps will deter *most* youngsters! (For suggestions on managing night-time 'absconders', who leave via windows, drainpipes or even catflaps, see section on Running Away, pages 162–164.)

Encourage each family member to speak out openly about any fears s/he has – especially of being frightened or hurt by a sibling. **Breaking the cycle of abuse HAS to involve breaking the conspiracy of silence,** which your child who *hurts* has already become a party to. Don't let embarrassment, or a wish not to speak ill of a child, get in the way of openness and security here – and when your child visits other houses overnight, make sure you alert the adults to potential difficulties *before* they happen. (See also section on Anger, Aggression and Violence starting on page 127.)

Lying awake, waiting for the first footsteps of a night prowler can mean that you get very little sleep at all – even when your youngster is actually tucked up safely, asleep in his own bed. If this has been your experience, you could consider fitting some sort of alarm to the door of your youngster's room (or even installing a video (CCTV) system). Although this can be more disturbing to all of you in the short term, it may help your child become more aware of his anti-social behaviour and to stop himself sooner.

Be aware that you will need to choose a system that is sophisticated enough to withstand a child's natural desire to suppress it (in many varied, and often inconceivable, ways!). Batteries and plugs are easily removed by small fingers, especially if the equipment is fitted at child height. An effective system can give you and your family that feeling of security you need to get a good night's sleep, in readiness for another interesting day!

If your youngster is a hamster/guinea pig – that is, she stuffs herself silly at night – then locking away the food may be less effective (and feel much more uncomfortable and punitive) than providing a plentiful supply of victuals in the child's bedroom. That way you remain in control, your child is less likely to feel deprived and is more likely to remain quietly in her room. She may even eat less, eventually!

Some children thrive on the 'buzz' they get in trying to out-think and outwit you: it may feel that whatever you do, your child is soon one step ahead. It may then be time to backtrack! This is not the same as giving in or giving up, it is a matter of taking on only what you can *realistically* 'win' (for *all* of you). In this case, an open invitation to 'feel free to wander round and help yourself to what you need' might be more effective, as long as there are no personal safety implications.

Oppositional **children seem to prefer to do just the opposite of what they think you want** – and if they *think* you want them to potter about, then staying in bed may seem a more pleasing option. Do make sure you are comfortable with your own boundaries first (perhaps sleeping with your valuables under the pillow) and be prepared to be patient.

Leaving loving little messages in strategic places around the house can be caring, fun *and* effective. 'Hi! How are you doing? See you in the morning!' or 'I'm sorry you can't sleep, help yourself to some biscuits and milk' can make the steeliest child feel warmer and put him in mind for sleep.

Try, as a short-term measure, working a shift system with your partner (or a willing friend or two!). One of you could sleep during the night, the other can catch up on lost sleep during the day (if paid work doesn't interfere!). **You don't all have to suffer at once, and it may be all your child needs to begin to learn that he is safe and can afford to sleep at night himself.**

Consider requesting respite care facilities in *really* persistent cases – preferably before you can take no more! You may have to be very assertive to get what you need – and be prepared to insist that *all* relevant information is shared with other carers from the outset. They, too, will need thorough preparation and training if they are to do a good job and be truly supportive. (See also section on Staying a Family and Being Apart starting on page 186.)

Make sure that you apply for all available allowances, such as Disability Living Allowance and Invalid Care Allowance, for non-sleepers of more than six months' duration. You can obtain information and application forms at your local main post office. At least you can feel recompensed in some small way for your difficulties – save it up and take yourselves away for occasional short holidays, preferably without the sleepless one. It can make all the difference!

Remember to keep on taking care of yourself in the best ways you can!

Anger, Aggression and Violence

Whilst these three issues are closely linked, they are not synonymous, as many therapists and writers seem to believe. **Anger is an emotion, a feeling which motivates an individual to action** – whether that is to change the world for the better or to destroy it! **Aggression and violence, on the other hand, are the 'doing words', the acting-out of angry feelings in threatening or hurtful ways.** Understanding this distinction is essential if we are to enable our children to grow into healthy and caring human beings.

In terms of primitive survival, anger evolved as the driving force which made physically possible the choices for *flight or fight*. It came to involve the release of a complex array of *neuro-chemicals* and the altering of normal bodily functioning to concentrate resources where they were most needed, for running away or standing one's ground to defend oneself. Whilst the underlying *physiological* responses have not changed over the millennia, our environment certainly has. This means that the natural response to any perceived danger is *still* for the body to prime itself for *flight or fight*, as if life itself depended on it, although this is unlikely to be the case! Clearly too, some element of human *choice* in anger has always been possible and, as we have developed increasing insights into humanity, these choices have broadened to include possibilities for positive, constructive action and for compromise.

However, in many of our own childhoods, there were strong social pressures to deny the feelings of anger, particularly for girls and women. Probably most of us grew up believing that anger itself was bad and that we must *dissociate* ourselves from such an animal, inhuman feeling. More recently, an equally strong counter-trend has encouraged young people, in particular, to 'let it all out', claiming that anger is natural and therefore to act out our anger is also natural and health promoting. **Sadly, few people have appeared to explore the middle ground, or to differentiate between the *healthy acknowledgement* of angry feelings and the *unhealthy acting out* of aggressive and violent tendencies – for both victim and perpetrator.**

There is growing evidence that denying or suppressing our anger leaves us with our own potential internal time-bomb of chronic ill-health – physical, psychological and spiritual. This is particularly the case when we are put under further stress: either through excessive demands on our time, through fatigue or illness, or because we, often mistakenly, perceive a major level of personal threat where none exists. **Sadly, it is at precisely at these times that we have least access to our 'thinking' brain and tend to rely on our 'emotional' and automatic responses:** the least 'humanised' part of our being. As a result we frequently say or do things which are *hurtful* to others, or to ourselves, and which we may later regret. The on-going guilt and *shame* which is generated can contribute to increased attempts at denying and suppressing subsequent angry feelings – but may in fact make it *more* likely that we will again lose control and act out our *hurts*.

If we think of this in terms of *trauma* and *dissociation*, not acknowledging anger directly means that our angry *part* can become separated from the *self* we wish ourselves to be – it therefore becomes *less* under our conscious control and can burst out on us unawares, with potentially harmful results. For children who have been *hurt* early in their lives, the tendency is for them repeatedly to inflict emotional or physical *hurts* on people close to them, or conversely to inflict pain on themselves, through picking, cutting, burning or engaging in dangerous activities.

In order to be able to live with themselves, children who *hurt* need, increasingly, to separate themselves from the *part* which does the *hurting* (to feel as if it was 'not me'). So the *dissociative* response becomes reinforced (they frequently develop a 'look' at this time, which you will increasingly come to recognise – see also page 132). **This inner separation of thoughts and behaviours means that the young person has ever-decreasing conscious control over his own angry behaviours.** In 'extreme' cases the seemingly separate identities of *Dissociative Identity Disorder* may result.

On the other hand, the beliefs that all *feelings* are O.K., so *being* angry is O.K., or that it is essential to 'let your anger *out*' in order to 'let it *go*', are equally unhelpful. This can be destructive both to relationships within society and to the individual *sense of self.* **What you must encourage is a healthy recognition and acknowledgement of angry emotions – whilst actively promoting alternatives to anger's destructive acting-out.** This is especially the case for children who have experienced repeated, early threats to their well-being, who may never have been enabled to make connections between external events and internal feelings and who may have witnessed poor anger management first hand.

Remember, too, that despite all human 'progress', our *bodies* still respond in the same underlying way they did thousands of years ago, when faced with threat. You all know how uncomfortable you feel when, for example, someone sneezes behind you – you jump a mile and your heart pounds, as if a bomb has just exploded. **The build up of *neuro-chemicals* such as *adrenalin* make you feel jumpy, but you have nowhere to jump and seemingly no reason to:** though it is hoped that this uncomfortable sensation passes within a few minutes. **This is emotion with nowhere to go.**

Increasingly, *psychotherapists* and '*body-work*' *therapists*, are beginning to recognise that *repeatedly* unexpressed emotion (which is literally, after all, the outward movement of feeling) can become stuck in our bodies, bequeathing us a legacy of restricted movement or chronic body pain, as well as becoming stuck in our minds and our behaviours. Returning to that 'sneeze', if you had jumped, run a mile or made a lot of noise, you would have immediately felt better, since you would have acted in the ways your body had primed you to act. Assuming that you had looked where you were going, you need not have distressed or *hurt* anyone else and would soon have recovered from your exertions, ready to carry on with life. Furthermore, if you had been able to recognise what had frightened you, made sense of why you had responded in that way, even laughed at your melodramatic reactions, this would indeed have been an entirely *adaptive* response to an otherwise unpredictable world.

This in itself is a gift – a wonderful cue to the most health-giving release of anger! You do not necessarily need to beat pillows, or shout obscenities at an image of an abuser, to experience relief from your feelings – although these are becoming time-honoured ways of working out anger. **What is needed is to allow a natural process to take place: from the recognition and validation of a feeling, through brief but strenuous physical movement of any safe kind, towards comfortable completion, free from guilt or doubt.**

Any kind of non-competitive 'aerobic' activity, such as running, jumping, throwing, swimming, dancing, cycling, climbing, wood-chopping, cake-mixing, bed-making, football-watching, choral-singing, laughing, even vigorous showering, can allow you to work through an angry feeling constructively and leave you feeling good. (A 'good workout' has been shown to alter the **neuro-biochemical** balance. In particular the **neurotransmitter serotonin**, a totally natural antidepressant which makes one 'feel good', is released in increased amounts. At the same time, the excess of ***adrenalin-related compounds,*** which prime for ***fight or flight***, is burnt off through exercise.)

For children who ***dissociate***, all this will naturally take some time as well as a good deal of supported practice – but it sure beats being beaten up or called 'a f****** cow' time after time! You could try to build on your youngster's existing interests and encourage her to throw herself into these wholeheartedly (although you should beware of overdoing the encouragement and provoking a backlash of resistance or sabotage – see page 118). In encouraging these 'displacement' activities, you will be helping to establish a more ***functional psycho-biological*** response, as well as establishing healthier social and recreational habits.

Furthermore, once a ***dissociated part*** of the ***self*** (in this case an 'angry ***part***') is given recognition, and accepted for the protective task for which it originally evolved, it can be developed into a real and powerful *positive* force for your youngster. If a child's anger is validated, there is less need for the repetition of angry behaviours and a greater likelihood that she can make conscious choices about, and accept greater responsibility for, her own life.

What You May See (The 'Presenting Problem')

You may see a youngster who is impulsive, who 'throws tantrums', hurls abuse, destroys property (especially yours) blames other people for 'winding him up', engages in repeated control battles, victimises others (especially younger and more vulnerable individuals), and who often seems unmoved by, and unrepentant of, his misdeeds. (Other children tend to turn their anger in upon themselves in repeated acts of ***self-harm***. Please see section on Addictive Behaviour and Self-Harm, beginning on page 165.)

Your attempts at closeness are frequently perceived as a threat and any moves you make to calm or soothe a situation are strongly resisted. You may feel that you are living on the front line of a war zone, fighting an unequal battle against a relentless and incomprehensible enemy: it's like walking on eggshells. Your ***self-esteem*** is probably at rock bottom – since sticks and stones of the verbal kind can ***hurt*** even more than the physical ones. You have most probably blamed yourself for the intense tensions in your family, especially if siblings are also being ***hurt***, and have been too ashamed to speak out about the situation, or to ask for appropriate help.

Scared Kid

It wasn't *me*.
I didn't do anything!

I'm bad. I deserve to get hurt.

Nobody loves me.

Don't leave me on my own.
Help me!

She is going to kill me –
I'm going!

This is scary.
Get me out of here!

I feel so messed up!

Superkid

I don't care.
She's not my **real** mother.

She deserved it, so I hurt her!

It doesn't matter. I hate her anyway!

I'm not scared!
I can manage on my own!

I'm going to kill her!
I'm stronger than anyone.

She's scared!
It's a good job I'm in control round here!

This family is just a mess!

Beyond the Looking Glass (or What May Lie Beneath)

- By definition, children who **hurt** have been severely traumatised and tend to perceive the world, especially families, as inherently threatening. They have hardwired responses to even limited distress, which are often violent or aggressive and they tend to act before they think.

- Some children find it difficult to discriminate between feelings in their bodies. Some come to **associate** almost *any* uncomfortable feeling with anger and act out accordingly.

- Anniversaries, such as birthdays, Christmas, or the day your child came home, may **trigger** aggressive outbursts. Although your child may not even be aware of the date, let alone the meaning of such events, you may be able to see a clear pattern emerging.

- There is growing evidence that some tendencies to impulsive, aggressive and violent behaviours may have a genetic component. Since the tiniest infants are born with in-built fear responses – to loud noises, to falling and to **abandonment** – even the most apparently 'insignificant' stressor can 'hardwire' these inherited tendencies.

- Exposure to even small amounts of drugs (including tobacco) or alcohol in the womb can have serious effects on an infant's developing nervous system. This can render him excessively irritable and hard to settle – and set him up for a potential lifetime of impulsive or explosive reactions. Research is also showing that such children are more likely to attempt to 'self-medicate' such **dysregulation** as they approach their teens. However, the use of such substances is also known to increase volatility and to reduce normal social inhibitions.

- Anger can readily become established as a **dissociative** response, meaning that even less conscious will may be involved. It may take only a minor **trigger**, or *part* of the **physiological** pattern of anger to be felt, to bring about a total switch into 'anger mode'. A child may seem very flushed or sweaty, his eyes very piercing or glazed, and a familiar, threatening posture may be adopted. His ability to listen to reason, or to rationalise, is greatly reduced as **neurological** energy is relocated from thought to action.

- Anger is an emotional response to perceived threat, which is mediated predominantly by the **limbic system** and the **autonomic nervous system**. The thinking brain, the **pre-frontal cortex**, tends to be bypassed. Once this **physiological** response becomes hardwired, new lessons addressed to the conscious mind can be difficult to learn and the old 'feeling' ones *very* resistant to change.

- A child who lives with violence may learn to respond with violence, since that is what he knows. This may also lead him to go on expecting violence, to adopt attack as the best form of defence, or even to provoke violence: that is, to re-create what is most familiar.

- A child who has been **hurt** has little choice but to blame herself for the maltreatment she received from 'caring' adults. This inevitably **distorts** her perceptions of cause and effect – in particular the part she herself can play in her own life. She is likely to **project** intolerable feelings of blame from herself onto others.

- Violent and aggressive behaviours can become addictive. A child raised under severe stress becomes habituated to 'stress mode' and may only feel truly alive when he is experiencing the '**adrenalin** buzz'. Even the longest tantrum or anger jag does come to experiencing the '*adrenalin* buzz'. Even the longest tantrum or anger jag does come to an end eventually, at which point there may be a release of *endorphins* (internally produced *opioids*) as the body attempts to manage the inner turmoil. Unfortunately, the comforting feelings that the *endorphins* (just like their relatives morphine and heroin) produce may actually help to perpetuate the youngster's initial, violent behaviour.

- With time a youngster may derive an over-riding sense of control from an anger state: for whilst anger is mainly about loss of conscious control it is also about domination and the abuse of power. For a child who has experienced absolute powerlessness and vulnerability the mantle of anger can provide an invaluable sense of power and invulnerability. (See Superkid/Scared kid on pages 46–50.)

- Anger tends to breed anger, along with fear. An intensely angry child may bring out the worst in any of us (under threat) and cause us, momentarily, to become the irrational, unpredictable monsters the child has always believed us to be. This need only happen very occasionally to perpetuate the child's *distorted* beliefs and to confirm his own aggressive actions as truly necessary for survival.

- When anger becomes habitual it becomes part of the child's *self-identity*, of his perception of who and what he is. Other people's expectations and reactions may also feed this one-sided view of himself: **it is easy to lose sight of the fact that inside this angry child there is a terrified, lonely child trying to stay alive.** (See also illustration on pages 47.)

First Choices

Since anger, violence and aggression are very difficult issues which many adoptive parents will have to face daily, I make no apologies for the fact that many aspects of this complex problem area are also covered in other sections of this book – see particularly Spotlight on Aggression, pages 91–110, and the bulk of the middle section of Fundamental Principle). **Please do make sure that you re-read these alongside this current piece.** A toddler who is in the middle of a tantrum is like a whirlwind, and can seem equally dangerous and unstoppable – to both child and parent. In *First Steps* I suggest that ignoring tantrums is unhelpful and can result in the young child feeling even more terrified and out of control: two feelings which probably played a large part in triggering his initial rage reaction. I suggest, instead, that *holding* a youngster through his distress allows him, perhaps for the first time, to feel 'contained', both physically and emotionally.

Like most other things, feelings tend to appear more manageable when given boundaries: the infinite becomes finite. In this case, the apparently overwhelming feelings of anger, frustration and pain can seem so unbearable to a child who *hurts* that they are experienced as life-threatening (which, indeed, they were to the developing infant). Being held securely and carefully through his 'worst' feelings can help a youngster feel safe enough to get things into proportion and to learn to deal with situations more responsibly. (Please see *First Steps*, page 114.)

If Things Still Don't Change ...

If the toddler tantrum feels 'dangerous and unstoppable', an older child's outbursts may literally become so, as his physical size and strength combine with his *adrenalin*-stimulated anger to pose an increasing threat to others. The child himself may feel less out of control and terrified, since he has probably *switched off* from much of his *real* feeling. Conversely, those close to the youngster may experience these feelings, magnified, for him.

One of the first things to do, in this kind of situation, is to keep faith and build up your own inner strengths: this is so that you can convey to your child that you are not afraid, that you can handle whatever he throws at you (metaphorically and literally) and that you believe he can begin to handle himself too. **It can be very easy to try to absorb a youngster's anger, hoping that by being accepting you are demonstrating your continuing love. Sadly, this message tends to become** *distorted*, **through the** *looking glass*, **so that the child perceives you as a vulnerable victim** (and probably deserving of his ill-treatment). (See illustration on page 41.)

You will also, tacitly, be giving your child lots of practice in becoming a partner- or child-abuser, so that the inter-generational cycle of *hurt* you are struggling so hard to interrupt will, instead, be perpetuated. To repeat, **to be truly loving is to be both nurturing and containing and you can only achieve this for your child if you first achieve it for yourself**.

Living with anger is extremely exhausting, it tests each of us to the limit and can show us *parts* of ourselves we may not wish to recognise. **Try to see this as a gift:** a positive challenge to help you learn and grow, just as you wish your child to learn and grow. You really do deserve to have the best, so do absolutely everything you need (even if it means spending time and money on yourself) to make sure you can feel good about yourself through the worst times. It's a good model for your youngster too!

Practise breathing. Yes, I know we do it all the time or we'd be dead, but under stress, or with other people who are stressed, we tend to hold our breath, or to breathe very quickly and shallowly. Taking conscious control of our breathing, paying particular attention to the out-breath, reduces *arousal*, slows down emotional responses, and gets more oxygen to the 'thinking' brain. It can also set the rhythm for your child, unconsciously offering him a more comfortable pattern of breathing. **The closer you are to the youngster physically, the more likely he is to be able to pick up your slower breathing rhythm and take it up himself.**

Thus, a firm and friendly hand on the child's shoulder, an arm on his arm, or a quick hug, can do so much to defuse an angry situation – especially if you can see it coming! Even a full-blown violent outburst can be contained and dispelled by touch, although you will need to be more vigorous with your *holding*, to protect both your child and yourself. **It is vital that you find out about** *safe holding* **and become confident in its use before you try it out with your child,**

on your own, at home. Adoption UK has produced several information sheets about *holding*, which are obtainable, from Lower Boddington, on request. (Please include a large SAE.)

A further essential part of the *holding* process is 'active listening': listening to your child and responding, without judgement, to what he has to say. There is nothing more infuriating to anyone than being ignored when they are in a high state of *arousal* – positive or negative! Don't try to tell a child to 'calm down' or to argue that he doesn't *really* feel the way he says he does – unless you want to push up his *arousal* levels even more!

That does *not* mean, however, that you have to accept everything he says at face value. In fact you are likely to do him a *dis*service if you do so, since he is very unlikely to be able to see what is *really* going on. He will be reacting to *something*, but will often lack the *associations* to make sense of what that is. Instead, he will have developed a pattern of behaviour to cope with his confusing feelings as best he can.

Some children 'do anger' when faced with fear, sadness, pain, confusion or even fun and excitement: they have never learned to discriminate between feelings, or to handle even small amounts of stimulation well. **It is essential that you keep in mind that there are other sides to your child, that she is not just the seething cesspit of rage that she seems.** If you can hold on to this, then she is much more likely to be able to get in touch with *all* of herself, to dare to believe in other possibilities about her *self*, including the fact that she is loveable.

You will need to learn to interpret body language, to read between the lines, and to use any clues you can, to get an idea of what the situation *really* is and what has *triggered* the angry outburst. Only then can you begin to help your child to do the same thing, so that she can learn to recognise and manage her own thoughts, feelings and behaviours in a more healthy way.

You may find that you can work out what has upset your child quite easily and even begin to anticipate potential *distress*, perhaps at or around the time of a personal anniversary, or after an exciting day out. **When this happens let your child know right away!** Just be matter-of-fact about it and **stay clear of sarcasm, implied criticism and being patronising.** A child can only learn to make connections (*associations*) between events, body sensations and emotions if she is helped to recognise and name them, over and over again, without feeling ashamed of them. This is, after all, just how the *good enough* parent would help an infant or toddler.

Try putting both hands firmly on your youngster's shoulders, looking him squarely in the eyes, and saying: 'I can see you are upset. I think you are feeling [angry/sad] because […]. You must be feeling *really* bad inside. Let's see what we can do.' **This way you are combining active listening with physical touch, naming feelings and bringing some *reality* into the situation. You are also implying that you can work together and that a violent outburst is not inevitable.**

Whilst often you cannot, or would not wish to, change what has happened, you can show appropriate *empathy* and you can offer some short-term suggestions to help your child get back in control of his feelings. These could include running up and downstairs whilst singing at the top of his voice, dancing the conga, munching an enormous crisp apple (very cathartic and you can't shout obscenities whilst you crunch), using the '*slow-motion*' response, or 'chilling out' outside in the fresh air.

Once the child's level of *arousal* begins to come under control, you can begin to think about talking together about what went on. There is little point trying to do so when the youngster is so intensely primed for action, not thought. The temptation, once the worst is over, could be to let sleeping dogs lie – but do so at your peril. Sleeping dogs tend to wake up again at regular intervals, unless they are made a fuss of and exercised well! The same applies to children who *hurt*.

Remember that your child *really* has a great deal about which to feel *hurt* and angry. Tell her so: it can be very affirming. **Beware of showing too much anger or *distress* though, or you may push her into having to defend her birth family.** Try to encourage her, instead, to see that staying angry or vengeful keeps her in the past and keeps her *hurting*. Remind her that her present circumstances *are* quite different and she *can* feel the good things more if she lets go of the *hurts*.

Writing about, or painting scenes from, a *hurtful* time can reach *parts* merely talking cannot. Getting things down on paper tends to make the whole thing more *real* and poetry, drawing, painting, drama and even singing all use the *right part of the brain,* whilst talking is a *left brain function*. A letter to an abuser, expressing all the *hurt* or rage or muddle in the child's heart, does not have to be sent. **In fact, a symbolic burning of the paper can be an extremely effective way of speaking out, of 'letting go' and allowing a child to move on.**

Try to find something to laugh about! **Laughter** is good for our spirits and good (aerobic) exercise for our bodies. **It is also a very powerful antidote to anger,** and it tends to be contagious, as long as you laugh with, and not at, your child. If your child is throwing a wobbly and calling you 'a f****** cow', try being a cow and mooing merrily about the house. It can be lots of fun!

Even if you can't see the funny side of life at first, act as if you can and you soon will. A child who *hurts* needs and deserves to have fun too, although his rage may often get in the way, so if you can find funny things to do which include all the family, so much the better. Why not keep some simple, humorous cartoons pinned up in your kitchen and living rooms, to remind you that funny things are possible when things are not going well?

Remember that these angry feelings, however awful, are not *yours* and should not be. Most of your youngster's rage comes from the past although, as his 'now' parents, you will get most of it thrown in your face. **Don't let it get to you. It is important to accept responsibility for your own mistakes and equally important that you don't become a dumping ground for your child's, or for circumstances beyond your control.** Otherwise you may find that you are tacitly legitimising a violent or aggressive episode. For children with poor cause and effect thinking it is vital that you remain very clear on this one!

Practise adopting a non-threatening posture: since you are dealing with primitive emotions, why not employ primitive (animal) forms of communication? Your stance, your speed and tone of voice and your eye contact can all communicate fear and anger, or give a message of calm and self-assuredness (even if you don't *really* feel that way!). Keep an open, non-challenging posture, or sit down with hands on your knees, palms uppermost. Keep you eye contact steady but neither overpowering nor submissive. Breathe deeply and speak slowly and clearly. This will also give you more time to think through what you are going to do next.

Stay aware that the 'feel' of your home environment can play a vital part in altering your child's level of *arousal*. Check out the smell, the noises, the look the feel of your home and try to introduce aromas, sounds, colours and textures which tend to soothe rather than stimulate.

There may be things you have overlooked, or taken for granted, which negatively affect your youngster, which you can introduce, or alter, to have a more beneficial, calming influence.

Whilst I would not claim that television is responsible for making a child aggressive, it does provide a background of legitimised violence, which has become commonplace, even 'normal'. It also provides vicarious excitement and can *arouse* powerful emotions, especially in children who are already hardwired to respond to *any* stimulation with aggression. Television, films and videos, can also be a source of fresh and increasingly gruesome ideas, which can attract these same children and lead to them practising some of the more bizarre ones on you!

Swearing is also commonplace in the media but a child who *hurts* seems to have an unbeatable turn of unpleasant phrase. You will probably hear expressions you have never heard or dreamt of before. Don't let it get to you! **Take a good look in a big mirror and reassure yourself that you haven't grown horns or cloven hooves: in fact, you are beautiful!** Repeat as often as necessary.

It is often worth appearing to ignore the swear words, since you can't actually stop them – short of using unacceptable brute force! However, the next time your youngster asks you for a favour, such as a lift to town, you can gently remind him, in all honesty, that 'f****** bitches don't drive cars'. There's no arguing with that.

Humour can be particularly powerful in many ways here. You can try to find something to laugh about in the words themselves, as well as in the bizarre and impossible images they can conjure up. Try encouraging your youngster to use a thesaurus to improve his range of vocabulary: some of the alternatives are just so funny, and if you're laughing you can't get caught in the 'anger trap'! (See page 83.)

Try asking your youngster for more! An invitation to 'say it louder' (or longer or ruder), or to consider the true meaning of the words he is using (and helping him to find substitutes – 'haemorrhagia' sounds good where bloody is merely offensive), can put you back in charge and will certainly challenge a kid's *perceptions* of 'normality'. Remember, too, that any *oppositional* child worth his salt is likely to avoid doing whatever you ask him to do (which in this case is the last thing you want him to do), so either way you win!

Opening the window and suggesting that the neighbours might like to listen to your young person's skills in self-expression can be helpful, especially if you do it tongue-in-cheek. It can stop a tirade in midstream *and* provide some necessary fresh air simultaneously.

Once in a while you could try shocking him with a foul-mouthed outburst of your own (perfectly timed and controlled of course). Acting unpredictably, *just occasionally*, can help your child to start thinking; hopefully some of his friends will see the funny side of this too!

Make sure that you protect yourself, and all other family members, from tormenting, threats, destructive behaviour and violence. Many siblings suffer *hurts* in silence, unless you give them permission to speak out and to take care of themselves (see pages 60–61). You will need to set a powerful example here.

Encourage your children to let you know what is going on. It may feel like tale-telling but it is essential if the *hurting*, which tends so much to rely on secrecy, is to stop. Give your little ones, or children made more vulnerable through disability, referee-style whistles and let them be *real* 'whistle blowers'. Just the knowledge that they have something up their sleeves can alter a child's demeanour and render them less vulnerable!

Teach siblings, both older and younger, to fight back. In an ideal world pacifism works well; in the non-ideal world of a child who *hurts*, each of you has to have a bottom line and have ways of defending yourselves from *un*reasonable attack. Children cannot be expected to rationalise and 'take' another child's repeated anger as adults often do. **You can make it quite clear to everyone that this is an exception and that normal rules of peaceful co-existence must hold elsewhere.**

You may find that your youngster tones down his bullying in the family, if he knows he may be found out or may 'get thumped' in his turn. Remember that this would be a common natural consequence if he were to go on acting like this in the *real* world beyond the family!

If you know, or suspect, that bullying is also taking place in school, or at youth groups your child attends, talk to the teachers or youth leaders. Try to get across to them your child's problem, without sounding unloving or hateful yourself, and encourage them to work with you, to help your child give up his *hurtful* behaviours. **Keep in regular touch, since these things can go underground and then re-surface at any time.**

This can introduce you to one way of using your 'angry energy' positively, to fight for your child. Contact prominent members of the child care and mental health professions and let them have some material about children who *hurt*. Ask them what services they currently provide and encourage them to develop an effective system of support for families like yours. You are not the only one!

Set up a 'safe house' to which your other children, or you yourself, can run if you feel the situation is getting out of hand. This could be somewhere in your own house, or at a neighbours', or it could be a favourite ice cream parlour, so that you give yourselves a treat to help make up for your distress. Make sure that pets are safe, too.

Establish a house rule that all damage to property should be repaired or paid for by the child himself and that YOU set the value on damaged articles. If you know that it was an accident you can set a very low figure, if you are sure it was deliberate be more *realistic*! If, as is likely, the offender has no money, then you can ask for time or labour in lieu, or deduct the value from an imminent birthday present (but don't drag out the repayments or they will become meaningless). Operate the same rules for the child's own property, so that you are seen to be fair – but remember that you are the judge of who did what and how!

If damage or *distress* becomes unmanageable you will *all* suffer, including the child who *hurts*. **Do not shy away from asking for outside help, from friends or neighbours, or from calling in the police if threat of, or actual, injury or damage occurs.** Although none of us likes to involve the police in family matters, or would willingly choose to give a youngster a criminal record, allowing her to continue to act out of control is potentially much more damaging to her sense of *self*.

In particular, it is establishing a pattern of behaviour, and *distorted* thinking ('I can do anything. They deserve it. No-one can stop me.') which will be very hard to break (and faced with the *real* world, when she leaves home, she may be in for a very nasty shock indeed!). Unfortunately this also tends to become consolidated into the child's self-perception (see Superkid/Scared kid on page 47), that 'this is who I am – the angry/violent me', which has then perpetually to be lived up to, at the expense of the pleasanter or more vulnerable sides. In other words, **the more a child is permitted to act in anti-social ways, the more it will become ingrained (as *neural pathways* become consolidated) and the more likely she is to continue doing so into adulthood.** At eighteen she will be legally deemed an adult and will be expected to accept full responsibility for all her actions, so the sooner you start helping her to act (and think) responsibly the better.

Today's police force is being trained to treat 'domestics' with more respect and understanding. They are also very adept at verbally 'laying down the law' and firmly spelling out what will happen if aggressive behaviour persists. **It may be very worth your while getting to know your 'local bobby' before things escalate, to check out how to get hold of them quickly, and what they are likely to do.** Explanations are difficult when feelings are running high – and more often than not it will be *you* who is feeling aggrieved or upset by the time they arrive, whilst your youngster will be able to act with nonchalance!

You may wish to keep a record of violent incidents, including photographs of damage or injury. Most law-abiding people, and many professionals, find it difficult to imagine that a child can *hurt* full-grown adults. You too, in your quieter moments, may doubt your own memory – and **disconnecting (*dissociating*) from *traumatic* events doesn't just happen to small children! If it happens to you, it then becomes harder to decide on an effective course of action and to stick with it,** especially if you can see the vulnerable side of your youngster, in between the violent episodes.

Allegations of abuse often come out of a violent incident. Your child may *really* believe that you *hurt* her, in the *distorted* thinking of her emotional *distress*, or she may make an accusation to get her own back, or as part of a fundamental control issue. You cannot *realistically* live with a child who *hurts* and protect yourself absolutely from such allegations. You can, however, be vigilant to the potential dangers and strengthen your own weak spots, so that your youngster has no excuse on which to build. Contact Adoption UK for information about current literature on *attachment* issues and for support should you need it.

If you have experienced *real* injury at the hands of your child, you may wish to consider applying for Criminal Injuries Compensation for yourself. This does not entail criminal proceedings, although evidence (such as photographs and reports to the police) will be required. Although any money you receive will not compensate fully for your suffering, it does at least acknowledge your pain and provide you with a financial resource, so that you can make wider choices as to how to help yourself and your family heal. **Personal therapy, house redecoration and relaxing holidays, for example, are all costly but may be very necessary to your continued health and well-being**.

Lying and Stealing

There are lies, white lies and 'barefaced' lies. Whilst you can expect and accept children's 'bending of the truth' of the lesser varieties relatively easily, 'barefaced' (or Superkid, see pages 47–50) lies are a different thing altogether. Children may try to cover up for their own mistakes or deficiencies, or because they can't *really* remember what happened in the first place. You can usually tell when they are 'telling porkies' because they may not sound too sure of themselves and they won't want to look you in the eye.

Although Superkid lying may start off for the same reasons, for self-protection or because of genuinely confused recall, it is done with much more audacity: the child may be extremely convincing and will almost certainly look you straight in the eye as she speaks. Such 'terminological inexactitudes' can make you doubt your own senses, can convince you hot is cold, can make you feel in the wrong, or leave you arguing the toss at great length. You may set out to establish 'the truth' at all costs and expend inordinate amounts of energy in doing so – and then the youngster may laugh and say, 'So what?' She may be enjoying the whole process, you certainly will not!

Superkids have a *distorted* view of the world, fuelled by their own experiences of being *hurt* as young children. Their current *distortions of reality* therefore make as much sense to them as the '*real*' world they are trying desperately to survive. Deep down they may argue (although this is probably an unconscious process) that they have been lied to, misled, brought up in a secret world of fantasy, guilt or blame, so why shouldn't they try to cope with the world in the same way?

If they have developed a strong tendency to disconnect their thoughts from the pain, the terror and the *shame* of past *abandonment* and maltreatment, then they will probably use the same set of strategies to handle similar feelings in the present (and since they will become 'hardwired' to respond in this way, even minor similarities of feeling can *trigger* a full-blown reaction). The result in this case can, understandably, become **the 'barefaced' lie. It is so convincing because, at that moment, the child believes, or chooses to believe, that she is telling herself and you the whole truth.**

Lying and stealing often go hand in hand: a child who takes (or deliberately damages) your possessions has to feel O.K. about doing it and has to feel that he is not *really* responsible. So the same internal process of disconnecting themselves from what *really* happened has to take place and the deceits become easier. Often, with a younger child, items taken may have little cash value, to you or the child – but magpie-like he picks them up and stashes the remains around his bedroom nest, often in full view. Small sums of money also tend to go missing on a regular basis, although comestibles, especially refined, carbohydrate-rich 'junk foods', can be a primary, or secondary, target.

As children approach their teens the problem of stealing often intensifies – if not in frequency then in quality and quantity. As social pressures to spend, to dress just right, to smoke, to drink or to try out drugs grow, your freedom to leave your purse or valuables around your own house diminishes. Though all adolescents may take small sums sometimes, this feels very different and the youngster's responses are also very different.

What You May See (The 'Presenting Problem')

A youngster who can be caught with the evidence in his hot little hand will swear blind: 'It wasn't me!' Your possessions, especially money, may be regularly going missing and you start blaming yourself for leaving them lying around. In some cases you wish that he would just ask you for things – you wouldn't mind in the least giving them to him! You may also begin to feel that your home is not *really* your own and find that you become permanently glued to your handbag.

Your child may be adept at turning up the emotional heat, seeming upset to make you feel guilty for blaming him, playing the 'it's not fair' card, or coming up with long and incredible explanations of what *really* happened. Blame will invariably be pushed onto someone, or something, else – even the goldfish could be guilty! You end up feeling like Perry Mason, without his expert team of investigators to help you uncover all the evidence, or like a vengeful judge intent on giving the maximum sentence for the offence. You need the Wisdom of Solomon to resolve disputes between siblings and nerves of steel to withstand the emotional pressure from your youngster – and you are running out of both!

Through the Looking Glass – The Lie

Child	Parent
I am a mistake.	Maybe I'm mistaken.
All the time they lied to me. So who cares?	I can never trust anything she says. It makes me feel so upset.
It's a secret. They'll kill me if I tell!	Why can't she just tell the truth? I don't believe this is happening!
She's so stupid. She won't know anyway.	Does she think I'm stupid? I catch her red-handed and she still denies it was her!
I don't *really* remember. It was *not me*.	Nothing she does or says feels real.
She's mad at me. Help!	Am I going mad? Help!
She's not my *real* mother anyway!	I really love her.

Beyond the Looking Glass (or What May Lie Beneath)

- Children who have experienced *trauma* may suffer *developmental delays*, including many subtle intellectual ones. They may have a weakly formed sense of conscience and of cause and effect. Their thinking also tends to remain concrete and their 'thinking about thinking' – the way they think that *we* think – is also that of a child of a much younger age. It's rather like a toddler who hides her face and believes that you cannot see her at all: the child may lie because she cannot envisage that you can work it out for yourself from what you can *really* see!

- Parents who are inconsistent, or neglect or abuse their children, usually try to conceal the evidence of their maltreatment from society. They fear that they will lose their offspring if they are witnessed acting in such *hurtful* ways. So, either by default or deliberately, they encourage their children to collude with them in their denial. This is often their first, very powerful, lesson in the art of the lie.

- Parents who maltreat their own children tend to justify their own actions by projecting their 'badness' and guilt onto their vulnerable and impressionable victims. The innocent child feels intense *shame* and *distorts* her own perceptions to free the abusers of the responsibility for their shameful actions. She also infers that she does not deserve to be treated well – that she is in fact worthless. These, too, are very pernicious lies perpetuated by the adults in children's young lives.

- Feelings of *shame* and worthlessness are unbearable. A child may not be able to live with herself and such powerful feelings. The choice she has relates to her very existence: to die with the truth, or to live with lies.

- Most children are treated reasonably well *some* of the time. This strengthens their view of the 'caring' adults as good, a view which tends to be reinforced by society. The adults often present an acceptable face to the outside world, keeping the truth hidden within the family. The child cannot tolerate the glaring inconsistencies in her experience and so she learns to deny (*dissociate*) the secret and acquiesce with the public version. She has to learn to lie, convincingly, to herself.

- Other children are able to find ways of speaking out, yet the perpetrators of their pain may continue to claim their innocence. Lying is seen as a way of life. The child may also feel that they are being punished for telling the truth – by being taken away from all that is familiar to them. Maybe, they may unconsciously argue, lying would have been a better bet!

- Children reared on *shame* are extremely sensitive to it. They know how deep it can go and they try to resist it with all their minds. Even a neutral 'innocent' question can *trigger* a *shame reaction*, from which a child may try to escape by concealment or *distortion*. To do this well, they have to learn to conceal 'the truth' from themselves, so the *dissociative* response becomes hardwired and instinctive.

- Any mistake, or shortcoming, may be seen as confirmation of the absolute badness which a child who *hurts* may feel, and fear others will see in her. Again, this is unbearable: the only way to resist is to deny all mistakes, all weaknesses, all transgressions. The internal denial has to be externalised and the 'barefaced lie' becomes an old friend.

- Many adults in the child's life have been 'economical with the truth', believing that they are sparing him from suffering. They feel that if they paint a less damning picture of his family, or soft-pedal on the painful facts, the child will not be so upset. In fact, the child was there and experienced all the *hurts*, at some level, and if he thinks he remembers what happened, he is left to assume that he must be making it up or exaggerating. Someone, somewhere, is still lying.

- Some children believe that their adopters are looking for a certain sort of child. This may in fact be so, or it may be a false assumption on which the child tries to rebuild his life. He struggles not to be himself, to be someone else more acceptable: to live a lie.

- There is some research evidence that there may be a hereditary component to stealing. Whether this is carried in the genes or may be better explained by the mediation of *trauma* (or both) is not yet clear. Either way, it should *not* mean that we can expect 'bad blood' *or* make excuses for our children's unacceptable behaviours.

- Adopted children commonly feel that they have been 'stolen away' from their birth parents. Even when children were 'given up' at birth and 'have always known about their adoption', they may still have an enduring fantasy that they were dragged away kicking and screaming and that one day their *real* parents will come back to claim them.

- For children who have been *hurt*, their innocence, their innate joy in life, their trust, their sense of self, their childhood, have all been taken from them, or severely damaged. 'So what's wrong with me taking a little here and there?'

- Often children who are accommodated are moved around seemingly at will. Frequently their few precious possessions are left behind, or become mislaid en route. A child's interpretation may be that possessions are arbitrary and impermanent: yours as well as his.

- If a child has been neglected or nurtured very inconsistently she may have had to learn early on that to survive she will have to help herself. She may have had to forage for scraps of food; there may never have been anyone to ask for, or give her, what she needed. This behaviour then becomes a hardwired habit, kept in place by her continuing feelings of neediness.

- Some *dysfunctional* adults use their youngsters as part of the stealing habit. They may use them as cover for their own dishonest activities, or teach the child to do the stealing for them (presumably on the assumption that, if caught, the child will get away with it). In a youngster's *distorted* reasoning this may become a more than adequate justification for continuing to steal. Any concept of remorse may seem totally alien to him.

- As the urge (and opportunity) to self-medicate, using drugs, alcohol or sugary foods, intensifies when a child approaches adolescence, stealing may become more 'vital'. The adolescent may use all the strategies he has developed over the years to help him survive – lying and stealing may just seem like two very necessary choices.

Through the Looking Glass – Stealing

Child	Adult
She's too mean to give me anything.	If only she would ask! I'd gladly give it to her!
She didn't see me. She won't know it's me.	I saw her doing it! Does she think I don't know it was her?
Who cares? They don't love me anyway!	I get so upset when she takes things.
If I have lots of things – then I will be somebody.	I feel like she is stealing my life away. I've got nothing precious left!
I want it. I need it – I have to have it!	She doesn't even use the things she takes. She breaks them or throws them away!
She took me away from my *real* Mum. So why shouldn't I take things from her?	If only she would let me give her what she *really* needs. She doesn't seem to care!

First Choices

logo

If your child is telling 'little white lies', or takes the odd fifty pence piece, and you feel that this is a normal part of her growing up, then you will probably be quite right. In that case you will *not* find it difficult to stay calm and objective. You will automatically point out the discrepancies and talk to your child briefly about how it makes you both feel. You may well settle for an admission or an apology, give a short explanation of why it is not a good idea to tell fibs, and then let it go.

Obviously you will wish to keep in mind the understandable reasons why a child may go on lying or stealing and provide lots of love and encouragement for him to try to 'get it right'. However, as long as you feel that your child is showing some remorse for his actions, you may not be overly concerned.

If you are more concerned you could ask your class teacher, or Cub, Brownie, Scout, Guide, or woodcraft leader, or your church, synagogue or mosque leader, to have a little word with your youngster, at a low-key level. All these organisations place high value on honesty in any case and, through stories, rules or role-play, can emphasise the difficulties of 'telling porkies' or 'nicking fings'.

Should you feel that facts or items from your youngster's early life have been concealed, overlooked or 'lost', you could go back to the placing agency and talk to the social workers who were involved with his family. Getting in touch with previous foster parents can be particularly helpful, as you tend to get a more personal touch and memories seem to last longer. Case workers may not have written everything they knew down in the official records, or they may have learned new information at a later date.

Ask your current social worker to help you to talk to your child about his painful experiences and to help him make sense of the inevitable muddles in his thinking. If s/he does not feel they have the expertise to do this, get in touch with your nearest after adoption agency for advice and support, or contact Adoption UK directly.

If Things Still Don't Change ...

Don't let other people make you feel you are over-reacting, when they say something along the lines of: 'But *all* children do that!' You and your family are the ones who are **hurting** and only you really know how bad it is. If 'they' were in your position 'they' wouldn't be making placatory remarks, 'they' would be screaming for help too!

Whatever else happens, you will still want to remain sensitive to the reasons why your child may lie or steal. **However, even if you are certain she uses *dissociation* as a survival and defence mechanism, a youngster still needs to accept responsibility for her own actions and to learn to recognise when she has 'switched' into unacceptable behaviour.** Your long-term aim will be to help your child to choose honesty, as part of a 'growing up healthy' plan – but this may take quite some time, so be prepared to be patient! **Make sure you are 'squeaky clean' yourself when it comes to being honest.** If you cheat on car parking fees (which is technically stealing revenue from the council), or even lie about your age, your child may feel justified in carrying on lying and stealing himself. Most Superkids don't need much encouragement in that direction!

If you choose to involve other people in dealing with the issue, you may find it helps to 'reframe' your description of your child. Many adults fight shy of calling any child a liar or a thief, however inveterate and 'barefaced' they may seem. **You could try saying 'my child has difficulty distinguishing fantasy from** *reality'* – **but remember that you do not**, however hard others may try to convince you that you do!

There is absolutely no mileage in trying to prove to your child that they did what you know they did, they will still deny it and you will only exhaust yourself unnecessarily. It is actually very liberating to say to your child, 'I believe in all probability that you did … and I am going to ask you to make good the loss/damage. If I find out that I have made a mistake, then I will be only too willing to apologise and put things right.' It is highly unlikely that you will have to polish up your apology speech but if you do, **do it with good grace** – and remind yourself that you are *modelling* for your child how to acknowledge and deal with *your own* mistakes.

If money goes missing, you can let your youngster know that you expect him to repay you the full amount he 'borrowed', with as much interest as you think fair. An unsecured loan, or an overdraft without prior arrangement, attracts large fees and high rates of interest these days. It will help to prepare your child for the difficulties and dangers of the money market place if you operate on similar principles.

Use the 'interest' to treat yourself in small ways, or to invest in a stronger padlock for your room. **Having things stolen or damaged and being lied to as if you are an idiot can make a huge dent in YOUR** *self-esteem.* You need and deserve to find ways of making yourself feel better.

Keep a list of suitable jobs by which a youngster can repay you, since he will rarely have any money to hand. Although it can be very hard to persuade a child to do something for you initially, if you can be persistent and can establish a pattern of 'wages for housework', you will always be able to get something back from a penniless offender. Although he may not do the job as well as you would like at first, perhaps deliberately, you can always begin by paying according to standard and output.

As long as you do not pressurise your youngster with critical comments, or reminders about the time, you can comfort yourself that at least you know where she is and what she's doing. **If the job is done poorly, you can accept it and suggest that she probably needs a lot more practice at the same job** to improve her performance. Eventually there may come a point where jobs are accepted as part of life and you can relax and enjoy the fact that *you* are not doing them yourself. Young adults who have begun living on their own, have even been known to thank their parents for giving them essential survival skills – such as knowing how to use the washing machine and clean the bathroom – so keep up the good work!

Some older kids will, of course, continue to resist our attempts to grow into useful adults and may do such things as disappearing out of the house for hours, when a task needs doing. Fine. Relax and put your feet up whilst you have the house to yourself, your teen will be back some time! **Why not wake him up at seven o'clock the next morning, as you get up, and remind him quietly that the job is still waiting for him?** If he's looking forward to a hearty breakfast or a lift to football, you can re-emphasise your willingness to co-operate, as soon as the original task is completed. (In fact you could point out that waking him up early is giving him extra time to do what is necessary – and shows what a loving parent you *really* are!)

Take care that you keep your word, especially when it comes to consequences, **and that you always mean what you say.** If you are careless with your words, why should your youngster try to be careful with hers? Moreover, a child with weak connections between cause and effect *must* experience great consistency if she is to 'get it' and 'get it right'.

On the other hand a very occasional, and clearly intentional, 'whopper' can be fun. It also carries the message that you are not stupidly predictable and may encourage a child to think. The let-down she may feel may be salutary in helping her to learn what it feels like to be intentionally set up and lied to. **Treat this one, as you should your child, with great respect.** Do it only out of love, not as a punishment or 'for her own good'.

Help other people in the family, especially younger children, to be as responsible for their own things as their maturity will allow. This may mean alerting them to the fact that a sibling steals – but reframe any extra safety measures they may need to take as good practice for when they leave home. This also beats having to intervene in eternal arguments about who did what to whose things, or to keep on replacing lost or damaged items.

You could act as 'banker' for smaller children's cash and permit bigger ones to show the offender what they think of them, or to choose the consequence of the theft: it may help the child who *hurts* work out what life is *really* like!

Be prepared to alert friends, relatives, visitors, teachers and youth group leaders to your child's difficulties with the truth. A child may swear blind that you haven't given him any breakfast or lunch and play on the sympathies of peers and adults to scrounge an extra snack – they're the sort that taste best! It might sound like a feeble excuse, or even sour grapes, if you try to explain *after* the event – so speak up before it happens. It could be that people won't believe you until it they see it for themselves – but then again they may and at least you're covered.

The same goes for children who repeatedly help themselves to other people's possessions. It doesn't feel good to have to tell your friends and relatives to hold on to their handbags, or to ask the teacher to frisk your child's pockets every lunch time, but it's better than an embarrassing cover-up or an upsetting scene later. It won't stop the problem but it makes sure it is dealt with consistently and gives your child the message that he can't play one adult off against another.

Challenging a child in a straightforward way about what he has said or done is often necessary. You do, however, have to be sensitive to his feelings and his tendency to be thrown into a *dissociative* state (of panic, *shame*, anger) by a penetrating look, or even a sharp tone of voice. **The plain truth is the last thing you are likely to get, if your child becomes fearful, ashamed or angry,** and you will have to deal with another distressing scene before you get any further.

Always choose your time and place carefully to begin talking about such things. You need to be quite calm and unhurried and your child does not need other distractions, such as a friend waiting to play hide and seek. However, for a much older child you could 'go public' and speak openly in front of his peers about his activities. Sometimes this can have a very powerful effect, since an adolescent places enormous value on what his associates think.

The message you try to get across at these times is all important: that you expect honesty, that you believe your child can achieve this, and that, although you care greatly about him, you are nobody's fool. Allowing consequences to happen naturally, if he lies or steals, should help him recognise cause and effect and give him some practice at conscience-building. **Long lectures on right and wrong, or the evils of deceit, are both inappropriate and ineffective here.**

I do not believe that telling the child that you love HIM but not HIS BEHAVIOUR is helpful here. For a child who is familiar with disconnecting himself from his feelings and actions, this could be interpreted as a continuing invitation to deny responsibility for some of his actions and act 'as if' they are 'not me'. If you can love only his 'good *parts*', then he may have to work even harder to *dissociate* himself from his 'bad *parts*', in order to be acceptable. Some children feel so bad inside that this message will just reinforce what they already believe – that they are fundamentally unloveable.

Coming face to face with a youngster who shows no remorse for his stealing or lying can be very distressing. It may feel like being thrown up against a brick wall time and time again. You may also feel that his lack of remorse indicates that your child is in some way irretrievably evil. Whilst this can be understandable, **it is essential that you keep on reminding yourself that no child is all bad.** Even the prickliest hedgehog is more than just a ball of spikes!

If your youngster behaves in an extreme manner – by compulsively taking valuable things and trying to take you all for a ride – you can reassure yourself that there is an equally extreme *part* of her character which feels blame and shame intensely. You may not see it (and she may deny its existence vehemently) but it is *real* and one day it can become a *reality*! Hold on to that thought as your face hits the 'brick wall' again.

Keep working on the underlying issues which have shaped your youngster's *perceptions* of the world and her *distorted* responses to it. A well-chosen therapist, who has a good understanding of *dissociation,* can help all of you to work through some of these difficulties and enable your child to begin to make sense of her own behaviours. For all of us it is a question of balance. Your child was certainly a victim in the past; now she needs to grow beyond that into the present. She needs to be discouraged from becoming a victimiser, of any sort, in the future and to learn to accept her vulnerability as a *real part* of herself.

If you uncover a lie, or that something has been stolen from home, whilst your child is at school (which is often the case for mothers) don't let it rankle inside – but don't forget it either. Make a mental (or literal) note to remind yourself to talk to your youngster later – but don't waste time fretting about how you will 'bring it up'.

For most eight-year-olds 'a little bird told me' or 'guess what I found today', said in a light and humorous way, can start the ball rolling. Sometimes a brief, funny note to an older culprit – such as: 'Someone ate all my chocolates last night. Do we have a phantom gobbler in the house?' – can let her know that *you know* she probably ate them. If the wrappers are still under the bed (and they usually are, 'just to wind you up!') you could include a message about putting them in the bin.

When you do see your adolescent, you could ask her which chocolate she liked best – she may let slip her complicity. A knowing smile from you, and an exaggerated Inspector Clouseau or Colombo 'light-dawning' reaction, could show her that you've noticed *but* you are not going to be caught in the 'anger trap' or stereotyped as the punitive mother!

Your aim here is to get across that you know, or can make a good guess at, what really happened and that you are not a helpless sucker. It is NOT to catch her out. You can then take your time to choose how you want a child to make good any loss. Continued fabrications can be dismissed as a tedious but amusing waste of time.

Later, you may wish to give your child 'time to think' (see point 3.5 on page 63) and to reflect on what she has said (or done). If you would like a more truthful version, you can ask for it matter-of-factly, saying something like: 'You're welcome to help me eat this bar of chocolate when you can remember more clearly what happened.' Begin eating anyway and if you don't get any change from the child this time, at least you get all the chocolate!

An uncomfortable side-effect of living with a young person who finds the truth difficult is that you may end up doubting everything she says. A youngster may play on this and say: 'It's not fair, you never believe me.' Possibly quite true – but you don't need to point out why. A good response can be to say that you would love to be able to trust her and to remind her that trust has to be earned.

Even a young person's hopes and ambitions for the future can become jaundiced in your mind by your past experiences and her tendency to be *unrealistic*. There is a delicate line to be drawn between getting sucked into unlikely expectations and appearing to weaken her already low self-image. Try to bear in mind that there is almost certainly a part of your youngster who does want to achieve something good and an equally strong part which does not believe this is possible. So, although it may feel like you are just being bull-shitted, there is frequently more to it than that. It is up to you, as the reasonable adult, to find the balance.

Check out whether the young person is just saying what she thinks you want to hear (and that you do *not* actually hold expectations which are inappropriate right now). If this is not the case, you could respond with something along the lines of: 'If that's what you *really* want, then go for it! Good luck – and let me know if you find you need some help' – and *mean* it! All of us learn through experience. **Mistakes**, with someone there to support us and have faith in us but *not* to rescue us, **can make *really* powerful teachers.**

Sadly, difficulties with *reality*, along with an ability to sound utterly convincing, can lead to unfounded allegations of abuse, particularly for youngsters who have actually experienced abuses in the past. **Whilst it is helpful to stay aware of this, do not allow it to affect your responses to your child which are truly nurturing and boundary-setting.** If you know, or suspect, that a child has suffered past abuse, seek out a child psychotherapist with experience in this area *and* ask for help from your adoption agency in counselling your family.

Talk to other people about your concerns regarding allegations, before it becomes a *real* issue for your family, and keep some sort of record of incidents which you feel could be misinterpreted. (Further advice relating to allegations of abuse is available from Adoption UK.) Talk to other parents who have faced this situation (through the After Adoption Network) and **think through a coherent strategy to avoid and survive such allegations: the *distress* and disruption they cause can *hurt* you, the child who makes the allegation and other family members very deeply.**

Only *you* can know when petty pilfering at home becomes criminal theft or damage. It is tempting to go on giving your adolescent 'another chance' in the hope that he gets the message and changes his ways, or to feel that at least you are keeping his behaviour within the family. If this is clearly not the case and you feel that you've done what you can, or amounts are clearly escalating, it may be time to call in reinforcements, in the shape of the 'long arm of the law'.

No-one wants their child to have a criminal record – getting a job is hard enough without one – let alone to implicate a member of their own family in crime. You are probably a very law-abiding citizen and the thought of being associated with an offender may be alien or an anathema to you. However, there are many steps on the way to a court sentence and the fact that this is a 'domestic' offence can slow procedures down further (you can choose not to press charges, for example). What usually happens, if you proceed with a complaint, is that a youngster will receive an unofficial 'talking to' and an official caution from the police. As long as no further offence occurs, that should be the end of it.

If your youngster responds positively to this, then all well and good. If not, then sadly he is clearly in need of more help in controlling his impulses and becoming a responsible citizen. **Trying to protect your child from the rigours of the law is commendable but it is likely only to make him feel above and beyond the law.** The sooner the lessons of honesty and responsibility are learned, the lower the cost to the young person, to you and to society.

You may wish to encourage other people, such a local shopkeepers, to get tough too. If you've done the rounds of taking your youngster to apologise for taking stuff from shops and he remains unrepentant and hell-bent on continuing to 'nick' things, it may be more loving, in the long run, to 'shop him' rather than to turn a blind eye. Again, your messages of loving concern and your desire to protect can become *distorted* in the young person's mind and may be seen instead as weakness, or as tacitly condoning the behaviour.

Tough love is not easy but it HAS been shown to be effective. Some young adults have actually said that if their adoptive parents had *not* involved the police at an early stage, they would have gone on to commit more serious crimes and would have spent long periods in prison.

Other parents have taken comfort in the respite from distressing scenes that a custodial sentence brings and have been able to work at establishing a different, more comfortable relationship once the young adult is living away from home. (See also Staying a Family and Being Apart in Part 7.) If you still have any doubts, do get in touch with the After Adoption Network and speak to parents who have already used these strategies successfully.

Sadly, for some young adults, it is only when it *hurts* far more to carry on doing something than to stop it that they are going to want to change – at its extreme, it is like an alcoholic who hits rock-bottom and then determines to give up the booze. The young person may have to spend time in prison before he is ready to face up to his life. Then, as for the recovering alcoholic, it can be a long hard grind back to emotional health – and he will need all the positive support and encouragement you can give.

Even if the situation does not get this far, all this is still going to take its toll on your peace of mind and on your well-being. By this time, parents are often becoming chronically exhausted and ill; as they approach retirement age they should be looking forward to winding down their exertions, not cranking them up. **It is part of your commitment to your family that you should take effective care of yourself – and that includes drawing lines in the sand for yourself, your partner and your children.** Be gentle with yourselves and give yourselves the time and space you deserve to put enjoyment back into your lives, in the knowledge that you have done the very best you can.

Staying Out Late and Running Away

The issue of keeping late hours can bring a good deal of conflict into any family. Social expectations and norms have changed so much since we were in our teens (in the dark ages of course!) that it can be very difficult to work out what is 'right'. Simultaneously, perceived social dangers are on the increase (although I'm not so sure about the safety of 'the good old days'), leaving us with very *real* concerns for a youngster out on the streets – especially at night. We know that we are legally responsible for the actions of our under-sixteens, and often feel morally responsible for our young adults, whilst the new legal emphasis is upon children's rights and freedoms, rather than on their personal responsibilities.

This situation can be magnified for all young people who have been adopted, for whom issues of belonging and identity are far more immediate, and for whom the developmental task of separation at adolescence brings particular challenges. An adoptee experienced the *primal wound* of separation at a very vulnerable age. Current attempts at moving away from a family, at this time of teenage emotional turmoil, can bring up many unresolved issues. A youngster may need a good deal of help in making sense of, and working through, these conflicts and confusions.

Children who *hurt* may also bring with them many ambiguities about families, about trust, about sexuality, about power and control, and may also have poor reasoning skills, lack *self-awareness* and have a history of impulsive, thrill-seeking or *oppositional* behaviours. This is not a case of 'giving a dog a bad name'; there are genuine reasons why you may be justifiably concerned for your son or daughter's emotional or physical safety at this time.

What You May See (The 'Presenting Problem')

Youngsters of perhaps eleven upwards start to test their strength against house rules with increasing confidence and frequency. At first it may just be a little push beyond the curfew at weekends (*whatever* time you set). Then it may escalate into nightly battles about who, what, when and where. You try to be reasonable, to balance concerns for homework and personal safety with a willingness to be flexible. The youngster responds by increasing challenges to your deadlines and to your authority in general. You stay up well into the night, or lie in bed waiting to hear signs of the young person's return. Then she comes in, goes straight to bed and sleeps the night through, as if she hasn't a care in the world. You do not!

You worry about what your youngster is getting up to and you may start looking for tell-tale hints of tobacco, alcohol, drugs or sexual activity on or about her person. You feel concerned that she may be mixing with the 'wrong crowd' (the ones most likely to be out late and also the ones to whom your youngster is most likely to feel attracted) and about your responsibilities as a parent (given the current social and political climate). If you go out to search you may meet with jeers and obscenities from your adolescent (and her mates). You may end up trying to bribe her into coming home, or into making threats which you later regret. You may feel confused and helpless and approach each evening with dread. In the mornings you get up exhausted and angry because the young person can lie in bed and recover, whilst you cannot. For some, the night-time summons from your teen to 'come and fetch me', or from the police station (with more or less the same message), becomes a depressingly regular occurrence. You wonder what more you can do.

There are also some children, of as young as eight or nine years, who run away and place themselves at grave risk, and still others who make *realistic* or *unrealistic* threats, which they may follow through to a greater or lesser degree. Some youngsters' behaviour can have an almost pathetic quality; for a small number their behaviour may seem deadly serious.

However, the problem becomes very much more common in youngsters of secondary school age. Your teenager may pack her bags at the slightest upset and make a dramatic exit, during which she hurls abuse and tries to blame you for the risks she is about to run. She may claim that she doesn't belong in your family any way and knows when she is not wanted. She will often hint at plans to search for members of her birth family ('her *real* family') and make exaggerated statements about how much money she has, what her plans are, and how she hopes she will never see you again.

Running away may build up into a pattern, each 'run' going a bit further, or lasting a little longer, as the young person gains in confidence and practises survival skills. Adolescents may also steal increasing sums of money, or valuable items, from you to fund their absences, although they still tend to continue to leave painfully unprepared for the hardships of sleeping rough. You may get into a pattern of spending hours searching the streets for the runaway, or in making telephone calls to anyone you can think of who may know her whereabouts. You may call in social services or the police for help – with varied amounts of success, depending on many factors, other than the age of your youngster. Sleep can become impossible and you may begin to lose time from work as well. Your health can start to suffer and your confidence as a parent can hit rock-bottom.

Beyond the Looking Glass (or What May Lie Beneath)

- In their *distorted* thinking, children who *hurt* often believe that their adoptive parents are the source of all their problems. They fantasise that if they could only get away from us, their troubles would be over. Often this is combined with an over-idealised image of a 'rescuing' birth family – if only they could find them!

- For children who have been moved around, either with their birth families as they struggle to get away from their problems, or within the 'care' system, packing their bags and making a getaway can become a way of life.

- Some adopted youngsters believe they are no good, that they came from a 'bad' family and they will end up just the same as their parents. Sadly, in an illusory quest for control, they often follow in much the same footsteps, however much they have vowed to be different.

- Running away plays a big part in the *flight or fight* response. Unfortunately the child is often trying to run away at the *wrong* time, from the *wrong* family and the *wrong* dangers.

- The proneness to impulsive or thrill-seeking behaviours, which often typifies *traumatised* children, strengthens this common mis-perception and can make the teenage years a very dangerous time.

- Making threats to run away can give a great sense of power; everyone seems to jump when you start packing your bag! For a child who has experienced helplessness and powerlessness, this can feel particularly good.

- A child who has learned to be *oppositional* in order to survive is likely to become intensely defiant of his parents as he approaches adolescence. He has been practising the skills and now his hormones are coming into play – just as the opportunities for the greater freedoms of approaching adulthood loom into view.

- Youngsters with a *physiological* tendency to *self-medicate* or *self-harm* (see also section on Self Harm, on pages 165–179) are most likely to seek the freedom to do so away from home, often during the secrecy of the night hours. These activities are often addictive and will therefore be sought with increasing frequency, so the staying out or running away is likely to escalate.

- Many children and young people seize on the popular culture of children's rights and fail, as many in society fail, to recognise the accompanying responsibilities of growing maturity. They have more time, more money and more expectations than ever we did and some (especially youngsters who have been *hurt*) believe they are entitled to it all NOW!

- Most adolescents seem to have an inverted daily *biorhythm*: they sleep by day and are full of energy by night. Adolescents who *hurt* have often had night-time anxieties and difficulties sleeping. Again, they are coming into their own: they need not be on their own in the dark any more. They have lots of friends who are willing to join them in exciting escapades which defy the darkness.

- Responsible parents naturally have concerns for their children's welfare. If they were reasonably law-abiding in adolescence themselves they may have '*unrealistic* expectations' of teenagers' conduct. If, on the other hand, they sailed close to the wind themselves, they are only too aware of the dangers and *hurts* to which a youngster can be exposed. Either way, they may appear over-protective – to both the youngster and to well-meaning outsiders. The youngster is likely to respond with an increasingly direct challenge.

First Choices

A parent can, and should, try to wrap her vulnerable new-born in cotton wool, to protect him from the rigours of the outside world. As the child grows older the caring adult will still do her/his utmost to ensure that he remains safe but s/he also recognises that **learning to handle risk is part of the process of growing up.**
Eventually s/he will expect the youngster to have acquired sufficient self-help skills to take care of himself in most situations and only occasionally to need to intervene. Easier said than done – especially if you can see the continuing vulnerability of your child and you have

concerns over his self-care skills! **You still have to try,** however painful the process seems: the growing youngster will probably demand this anyway!

You could begin by suggesting to your youngster that she is welcome to go out once her homework/the dishes/the tidying up is done. You may also feel happy to offer her a lift to her destination, once you are both ready, or to fetch her home at an agreed time. This has the added attraction of giving you some idea of where she is going and more control over when she comes back. If she declines a lift *with no strings*, then it may be that she has something to hide.

Talk with your partner and your child about her need to run away. A youngster may need a good deal of help in finding other ways to let you know how she is feeling. Constant reassurances that you will always be there, and that you hope she will too, may be necessary at first. You could set aside informal 'active listening' or ***holding time***, when you spend time close together and can talk comfortably about anything which is upsetting either of you (see *First Steps*, pages 69–70).

Suggest to a youngster that if she feels the need to 'take off' she goes to someone you both know and trust. Encourage her to leave a message telling you where she is going, or to telephone you to let you know she is safe. BT 'phone home' cards are very handy and are available for just your home number, if you are anxious about large telephone bills!

Stay as calm as you can and be matter-of-fact with your child about your worries and the risks she is taking, in either running away or staying out late. You don't have to be swayed by a youngster's claims that 'all my friends stay out until…'. Try networking with his friends' parents and you'll probably find they are having the same struggles! Together you can stand firmer and feel more confident in your decisions; sometimes you may even be able to work out what your young people are getting up to.

Check out your expectations and motives, for evening house rules, with a good friend. You may find that you can become more flexible or more ***realistic*** when you have looked at the situation more closely. Don't blame yourself and think that you 'got it wrong' – instead congratulate yourself on being courageous enough to consider changing to 'get it right'.

It is also worth bearing in mind that the only person in whom you can ***realistically*** bring about change is yourself. However much you may feel that your youngster needs to change his behaviour, there may be little you can, in ***reality***, do about it. Nevertheless, it is amazing how much better you can feel, just by looking at something in a different light: that's part of how humour works too!

If Things Still Don't Change …

Part of your motivation to adopt may well have been your wish to nurture, encourage and protect a child who has suffered great **hurts**, long before his time. You probably feel that *no* child should have to bear such pain and you are certainly committed to helping him heal and to making sure he never suffers like that again. However, the plain fact is that **even if we could give twenty-four hours a day to supervising a growing child, we could not protect him from all the dangers and challenges in this world. He is designed to be a living, moving, exploring, challenging human being** and nothing we can do could, or should, change that.

Moreover the very fact that such a child is now living with you is a measure of his capacity to survive, even when he was *developmentally* at his most vulnerable. He has developed, though certainly at a price, a great *resilience* to adversity and has acquired many coping strategies which have served him well so far (albeit with inevitable *distortions* to his perceptions of himself and the world). It is very *unlikely* that your youngster will *ever* have to live through anything as *traumatically* life-threatening as in his early years, or that he will fail to come through, somehow. **For all his palpable weaknesses your youngster has acquired many strengths; try to remind yourself of this when he seems determined to put himself at risk, time after time.**

Remember, too, that *good enough* parents do what they can to keep their growing youngsters safe *and* accept that there is only so much they can do. They have to find faith enough to believe that the child will get by, and resist pressures from others who may make them feel culpable for their young person's personal choices. Again, this could be called 'tough love' (see page 152 above) and should be seen as your having *realistic* expectations for yourselves – something that the same critics often suggest are lacking.

Parents and society often have differing perceptions of, and concerns about, girls and boys, young women and men. We tend to believe that the world is particularly unsafe for females, despite statistical evidence that more violence is experienced by young men in public places than by young women. These beliefs are not, in fact, mutually exclusive and they may be very *real* concerns. It is probably not in the least reassuring either to know that more children and young people are at risk from sexual molestation (or even violence) in their own homes than on the streets.

However, if you believe that your home is a safe place, then YOU have done all you can to establish a *secure base* from which your children can explore the world. This *must* stand them in good stead, reducing their present vulnerability to *some* degree and providing a safe place to which they can eventually return. Even though a child's very earliest experiences may have been extremely *traumatic* **you will almost certainly have made some *real* difference.**

The youngster who stays out on the streets into the early hours, or who runs away, is communicating, by his challenging behaviour, that he has a problem. Metaphorically he may be saying that his life is running away out of control, or that he is trying to stay out of family life, and all the hidden dangers he believes that entails. We cannot change this alone: the youngster may need some very skilled therapeutic work, and a good deal of support from you, to sort out the muddles in his head and begin to see what it is he is trying to get away from.

Be as certain as you can be of where you stand on protecting a vulnerable child, versus allowing her to take some risks – and to what degree. Even if your youngster is emotionally immature, chronologically and *physiologically* she stands alongside her peers. Take on only the battles your feel you can and must win – and make sure that you do! (See pages 67–68.) Once you recognise your position you can stand tall and firm, better able to resist implied or *real* criticisms, from both the young person and wider society.

This may be a time when you will wish to look again at the self-care skills your child brought with her and those you have tried to instil in her yourselves. A crash course in self-defence, or a visit to the drug and alcohol abuse centre, or the family planning clinic, may be better if it comes sooner rather than later for a young person. **Even if you feel your youngster is still too young to do any of these things, she probably believes she is old enough and may have friends who are already doing it.** (For more on these sensitive issues, see section on Addictive Behaviours in Part 7.)

The fact that the information and guidance comes from someone other than you, though with your implicit approval, may make it more acceptable. Again, you cannot force these issues, you can only offer opportunities and demonstrate that you are not going to throw up your hands in shock and horror, whatever happens. That way you are 'keeping open the doors' for your young person to come back to you for help, as and when she realises she needs it. (See Staying a Family and Being Apart, page 201.) Remind yourself that most young adults do come back eventually!

It is well worth thinking through what your responses would be in such difficult circumstances, although you can be pretty sure that a youngster will come up with the one thing you haven't thought of, or have deliberately avoided thinking about. **Keep on reminding yourself that this isn't your problem and that you are there to give *empathy*, ideas and support and not to 'sort it all out' for her.**

Some parents have found that allowing a young person to suggest a suitable time to come home is more effective than bargaining and constantly conceding ground. It allows him to practise decision making and to accept more responsibility for the outcome. This can be very effective in helping the youngster to become more *realistic* but does assume a certain level of maturity of thinking, which may not be appropriate for your youngster.

You may wish to consider imposing consequences for lateness, if they do not occur naturally. One to avoid like the plague is grounding, as in: 'After this, you're staying in all week!' Not only is it likely to be seen as punitive, it is unenforceable in many cases *and* you will suffer as well. A grounded youngster is not a happy youngster and a whole week can feel like a lifetime to both 'prisoner and warder'.

Sometimes you might wish, instead, to suggest that he is 'grounded out' for a short period of time: that is, you do not want to see him for a while. That way you don't have to suffer *and* you are asking him to do what he was going to do anyway!

I have already hinted at waking a young person early the following morning, as a consequence of not having completed jobs the previous day. You may also choose the breakfast hours as *your* best time to talk about your concerns over lateness, or other behaviours. **It is hardly ever a good time to talk in the dead of night, when the young person has just come in**. However, some youngsters may be at their least defensive when awoken from sleep and you may stand a better chance of getting your message across then. Whenever you choose, keep it brief and to the point, with 'I' statements, not blame or anger (see page 61). Then you can get on with your day, or go back to bed yourself, depending on the circumstances.

Offering lifts to or from wherever your youngster is going, if you feel genuinely comfortable about giving them, can give you some knowledge and control over 'where, when and with whom'. It beats being nagged for a lift, or rung up in the small hours, when you'd actually like to say 'no'. It also removes the temptation for a young person to think about 'borrowing' your car keys, or your cash to pay for a taxi home. You may, additionally, be able to use the time you spend together in the car *talking* to each other – an opportunity which may not come up very often otherwise!

However, you don't have to if you don't want to. It is your choice. I personally do not 'do' nights. I like to go to bed early and I don't get out of bed for anyone, any time, unless it is a life-threatening emergency – and then I may send my husband instead!

If you live in a rural area, miles from anywhere, your services as a chauffeur may be more in demand than if you live on a good bus route – but it can also give you more control over whether your youngster does go out or not. Even the most awkward teenager will think twice about going to the disco if it is a ten mile walk each way (and it is raining). This holds, too, for running away. It is just harder to make it on your own, especially with the suitcase full of useless odds and sods that kids always seem to pack.

If you set a return time, the chances are that your youngster will get back just a little bit later than you agreed. If this is regularly more than a few minutes, you may feel you are being deliberately challenged. You could try openly adding on an extra fifteen minutes beyond the agreed time, so that she knows she has 'no excuse' for further lateness. If this doesn't work after one or two tries think again (see also point 10.1 Ready for a Change on page 88).

You may decide that your time limits are more than fair and that you intend to take a determined stand. You *could* decide that you are going to go out every night for as many nights as it takes to show your youngster that you are not giving up on her, that you care enough to go on putting yourself out until she gets the message. **This will only be possible if you can remain truly patient and not become frustrated and 'blow it'. However, it can work!**

Initially, your youngster is likely to resist your attempts to look after her interests and may be verbally or physically abusive, or keep on running away from you. **Be tenacious.** You may also need to enlist the help of a group of good friends who will go with you, for physical and moral support. Or you could try using humour – perhaps taking the stop-out a flask of hot soup and some rolls 'because I don't want you to get hungry', or an extra woolly 'because it's so cold'. If you can see the funny side of it, your teen, and her mates, may do too!

You cannot MAKE your young person arrive home on time, although you can make it more uncomfortable for him if he does not. Locking the door may seem harsh but if you have a shed or an old caravan in the garden, you could leave a sleeping bag and torch in there and a note for the late-homecomer on the front door. Of course, you are likely to be woken up by pathetic pleas, angry shouts or persistent banging at first; you must be ready to stand firm – and make sure *all* family members understand that they are *not* to open the door before seven o'clock in the morning (or whenever).

It is against the law to deny a youngster under sixteen years access to their own home, so do make sure that you are offering reasonable alternatives if you intend to lock outer doors. This could be a friend or relative, with whom you have an agreement and who will support you in your struggle. Make sure they don't make it too easy or comfortable for your youngster and undermine all your good work. If they operate a 'drive-you-home' service next day, they may also wish to charge for petrol or for their time.

Once the young person realises that you are not going to weaken he may accept your way, or go off and spend the night elsewhere and pretend he doesn't care. Then you should both get some sleep. He may later make a big fuss about how mean you are, or even threaten to go to the police or social services to report you. In all likelihood he won't but if he does, **remain calm and certain in your choice of strategy.** Try to ascertain from the authorities what they would suggest you do and to enrol them in helping you with this difficult problem.

The police in particular are keen to keep young people off the streets, in the interests of crime prevention. They may be only too willing to 'read the riot act' to a 'stop-out' – and to see your side of it too. Social workers are trained to be more 'child-centred' and may find it harder to see beyond the youngster's particular version of events. You could ask the duty social worker whether she would be willing to remain on standby for future episodes, so that she can gain a better picture of what is going on. The police are also required to inform them of a youngster's presence at the police station, if an overnight stay appears necessary.

You may feel that you are not prepared to, or are not in a position to, go and collect your child from the police station, should this situation arise. An officer is likely to be very understanding if you say that you are not willing to risk losing your licence by driving when you have had a couple of glasses of wine earlier in the evening. You can say that you will collect your offspring as soon as you can the following morning (either from the police station or from emergency accommodation, if that is being arranged). **Try to sound as sympathetic as you can about your youngster's short stay away from home, although it is reasonable to carry the secret hope that this experience will have some deterrent value.**

There may be times when you wish actively to involve the police in the search for your child, because you are concerned about her whereabouts, or for her safety. It can help if you have already found the time to speak with officers at your local police station about the difficulties you are having. You may wish to ask for a designated person, who is more familiar with your family's circumstances, to be available to respond, although frequently this is not possible. Here the law should work with you, in terms of your youngster's age, but responses do seem to vary geographically, and over time.

If you believe that, in addition to being out late at night, your youngster is having under-age sex, drinking or taking drugs, do say so. Police officers have a duty to investigate such activities and if you can provide addresses or supporting evidence you will be making their task easier for them. Again, cultivating a friendly working relationship can pay dividends in the long run since police officers, like the rest of us, are frequently overworked and under-resourced.

Frequently *you* will locate your youngster before the authorities do. However, you may expect a return call from your local police station, to check the veracity of your information and, frequently, a house call the following day. The officer(s) will want to see the child and may use this opportunity to give them some good advice about the dangers of running away, causing *distress* to your family and creating more work for an over-stretched police force. Sometimes this can be an effective deterrent.

A child who is accommodated with a foster family or in a children's home is protected under the Children Act from many of the restrictions you might wish, as her adoptive parents, to see imposed for her own safety. This could include physically restraining a teenager who wishes to go out late at night, even if it is clear that she is going to put herself, or others, at risk by doing so. **Whilst you must be certain never to abuse your power, you are in a better position, as parents rather than 'carers', to give your youngster the safe *boundaries* she needs, and for longer.**

Of course a fifteen-year-old can be six foot four and weigh twenty stone, but if you are successful in establishing who holds healthy control in your home, you will have a great *psychological* advantage. **Some parents have found that the determination to keep their youngster safe has empowered them to hold quite large adolescents through their resistance, into a quieter time when reasonable thought becomes a real possibility.** It is an act of faith and of love. If you would like to know more about this option, please get in touch with Adoption UK for more information and to speak with experienced 'holders'. **This is something you should not contemplate without sound preparation and on-going support.**

Running Away

Since running away can begin as a reflex response to threat, encouraging your child to take up running for fun can be a very effective therapeutic strategy. Very young children actually cannot run away from the dangers in their families. 'Body workers' and psychotherapists are finding that this can lead to persisting physical problems, alongside the emotional ones, which can be freed up by running through choice. Even running on the spot can 'free your child up' and help her lose her muscle tensions.

Talk to your youngster about this, so that she can begin to make sense of her life. Running free can also become part of her arsenal for coping with stress, allowing her to move from high emotional *arousal* into relative calm (see illustration on page 34). Try it yourself!

As with 'staying out', your messages of caring concern can become *distorted* in your youngster's mind (see Speaking the Same Language, pages 38–42). **Expressions of anxieties for her safety are easily misinterpreted as indications that you don't trust her to take care of herself** and hence that, as she is deemed irresponsible, she may as well *be* irresponsible!

Although you may know from experience that the young person often acts without thinking, gravitates towards danger and tends to get carried away, bear in mind that the other side of that is that **this kid is a survivor** (see 157). Moreover, you are trying to work towards helping her grasp the concepts of cause and effect, of consequences and of personal responsibility. **If you do the worrying for her, she does not have to work out these things for herself** (see also point 4.4, Units of Concern, on page 66).

There CAN be room for drawing attention to the dangers a young person may meet, if you take a more indirect approach, keeping the conversation short, snappy and preferably humorous. You could draw an analogy with the way you sometimes worry about your partner's driving. You trust his/her driving but you may need reassurance that the car has been carefully serviced and that regular checks are done on tyres, oil, brakes and so on. Your main concern is probably that other drivers on the road may be unpredictable or dangerous and that, however careful one is, accidents do still happen.

In discussing some of the potential risks of being on the streets, you might emphasise the external issues beyond both your control, rather than focusing on the youngster's shortcomings (however wild he can be at times). Having drawn attention to specific areas of concern, such as street violence or under-age drinking, you can then offer to point him in 'the right direction' for more information or advice, as and when he chooses, implying that you believe he is capable of sorting things out himself.

You cannot say a lot more, without running the risk of *triggering* arguments and denials, or setting off a defiant 'I'll do it anyway, just to show her' reaction – but you can 'keep the doors open' and go on finding ways of making yourself feel O.K., despite the inevitable, and frequently justifiable, worries.

If you are around when a young person is preparing to run, and he seems un-stoppable, try giving him a genuine good luck message – he may well need it. Remind him that you love him, that he knows how to find you, and that you hope you'll see him again soon. If you have a chance, slip the same sort of message into his coat pocket or bag; add some chocolate hearts or teddies to make your point even more tangible.

You may like to offer to make your young person some sandwiches, to find some buns or biscuits, or some fruit and a drink or two. Perhaps a few (large) cans of baked beans wouldn't go amiss, since he can't be sure where the next meal is coming from! Keep a supply of 'iron rations', black bags and cardboard boxes handy – you never know when they might come in useful. With tongue *very* much in cheek and a *real* sense of the absurd, you may well be able to defuse the whole situation – and at least he will know that you care!

There are times when you MUST report runaways to the authorities. Exactly when this is necessary is a matter for your judgement but the younger the child, the more common the pattern, and the longer the absence, the more concerned you are likely to be. However, the boundaries between staying out late and running away can often be blurred – as what began as an evening out turns into an overnight stop, or even extends to several days. This may mean that you begin by adopting a 'wait and see' attitude.

In other circumstances you may wish to spend some time looking for the youngster yourself, before you alert the police. Sometimes the whole episode may seem very amusing, if not a little pathetic, in retrospect, but at the time you will be very **distressed**. **Take a little time to breathe before you do anything,** then check out what has gone missing. **This may give you an opportunity to think** and provide a better idea of how serious the runaway attempt may be.

Where threats, and melodramatic acting out, of running away are becoming regular you cannot afford to ignore them – even if you know your child well enough to guess that she's probably only gone down the road to the park. You may be able to work out what the real problem is and begin to talk to her about it – at a quieter 'thinking' time (see point 3.5 on page 63).

Sometimes the most effective way to stop a youngster 'doing a runner' is to help him to pack! You will be the best judge of when this could be appropriate and you will need to make sure you appear calm, respectful and loving at this time. You could say something like: 'I don't want you to be cold, or wet or hungry (or whatever) whilst you are out, so let me help you do your packing.' Have a sense of humour, drag it out, lay it on with a trowel. The child may well change his mind whilst you are 'helping' – either because he's lost interest, because he's amused or intrigued by your response, or because he doesn't intend to do anything you want him to. So if you want him to go (which you don't *really*), then he'll stay (which you do want).

Conversely, putting locks on outside doors and windows to prevent your child getting out may do the trick for some children. For others, however, this is like giving an open invitation to defy you and leave! If this is the case, then there is little point in going to all the trouble and expense of fitting locks – and then being faced with an additional repair bill! This is *your* youngster and *you* are best placed to know what is *really* going on. Then it's all about 'choosing your battles', so that you *all* win (see pages 67–68).

There are times when *holding* your child, firmly but gently, until she is calmer and more reasonable, can be a good choice. It may take considerable effort but it can make a difference at so many levels that it can be well worth it (see above).

Often you will have a good idea of where your runaway has gone. If she has contact with her birth family, or has been showing a pronounced interest in their whereabouts or welfare, that could be her first stop. **Youngsters often have quite *unrealistic* expectations about 'rescuing' birth family members, or 'being rescued', especially by their birth mother.** Sadly, some birth parents may be stuck with similar rescue fantasies – they can then feed each other. Make sure that you get some help on this one, since anything you do or say could be interpreted as 'being jealous', hostile or over-possessive.

It will all hopefully work out, once the *realities* of a reunion begin to sink in. Your youngster may need to do this 'piece' of her jigsaw: finding out for herself where she came from and who her birth mother is. **Almost all adoptees who do so, do come back home,** sooner or later. Meantime, you may be able to work on building a working relationship with the birth family yourself. **No-one benefits from a 'tug of love'.**

Even if you child has been *accommodated*, you should still be notified if your youngster runs away. Legally it seems that you are responsible for any damage your young person may incur whilst on the run. Be prepared for a night visit from the police and probably a follow-up visit the next morning. It is hoped that the foster parents, or the social or residential workers, will keep you well informed of developments. If your child is in the habit of running away, you may begin to feel like old friends!

Don't feel that you have to accept responsibility for picking up and returning your youngster to his foster home or residential home/school, especially if he is a 'regular runner' and tends to go a long way. **After all, if he is old enough and clever enough to get there, he is old enough and clever enough to get back again.** You also have responsibilities towards your other family members and to yourself.

At critical points such as this, you need to be even more than usually careful to look after yourself and your partner and family. It is so easy to expend all your energies on worrying about one youngster and to forget you have lives of your own. **Where there** are other adopted or foster children in the family, their insecurities can also be *aroused* by a sibling's absence from home, yet they may feel unable to worry you further, when you are obviously 'stressed out' already.

By finding time to relax and even having some fun yourself, you are showing your other children good ways of managing difficult times, looking after your own well-being and making yourself more ready and willing to listen to their worries too.

I suspect that it is only the most desperate of youngsters who truly feel that they have nowhere to turn, who do not come back home once the *realities* of living rough begin to bite. **Most of our children know somewhere deep down that there IS a home and family ready and waiting for them and do return, sooner rather than later.** You don't have to do the 'prodigal son' bit, as long as you have plenty of water ready for a hot bath and something filling and comforting to eat – once he's clean!

Perhaps the single most essential thing you might like to have ready for a returnee is a great big hug! Yes, you may have to take a deep breath first (to hide the tell-tale cigarette smoke if nothing else) but I believe you can't beat one of the oldest, tried and tested ways of showing you are pleased to see someone after a time apart.

Facing a returnee who is recalcitrant, defiant or ready for another argument can be particularly problematic. You will probably still be feeling *hurt* or angry and may be tempted to say something about your 'house rules', which is likely to set off another row or walkout. Both of you may get caught in a game of 'not losing face' which can easily spark yet more disagreements.

Instead you could try throwing your arms around the errant youngster exclaiming 'I'm so glad to see you!' Sometimes the more over the top you can be with this the better you can both handle it. This is genuinely part of how you feel anyway, and it can often defuse an otherwise tense situation. It may also be so far from the hassle your youngster expected that you catch him unawares and may allow you to slip through his defences and touch a more vulnerable part – especially if he has had a tough time or is tired from lack of sleep. This can even be effective in front of his mates: they may think you are a mad mother but they will also see that you are not the harridan you have been painted!

It is essential that you keep on reminding yourself that you are not to blame for whatever has caused your child to run – even if he tries to make out that it is. Be ready to listen, to be genuinely sympathetic about his trials and tribulations of being away from home, and to hope out loud that he can find other ways of working things out for the better next time.

Addictive Behaviours and Self-Harm

Almost all parents dread the possibility of their children getting caught up in activities which are self-destructive and hope it will never happen to them. In most cases it doesn't. For children who *hurt* the likelihood is unfortunately greater but, thankfully, problems are neither inevitable nor insurmountable.

Some youngsters do not feel comfortable with their lives. They perceive the world as threatening and their own behaviours tend to reinforce this **distorted**, but understandable, viewpoint. Their bodies, too, seem to be working against them – they often seem unable to relax and let things happen. They have never learned techniques for effective **self-soothing**: even as young children they may have been 'rockers' or 'headbangers' or 'twirlers' or 'pickers'. (See *First Steps*, pages 57.) Often they remain impulsive, highly reactive, constantly on the go, always looking for the 'next thing' in the hope that *that* will make them feel good. Conversely they may appear depressed, or 'spaced out' in a fantasy world which can feel more comfortable than **reality**.

Most of these disturbing behaviours are more readily associated with adolescence and young adulthood but they can occur in a much younger child. Whenever they occur they should *never* be dismissed as 'just a phase kids go through' or as 'she's young, she'll grow out of it'. On the contrary, the likelihood is that a youngster will grow into, and get stuck in, *more* self-destructive or self-defeating behaviours – unless you all find the help you need.

Although the behaviours themselves may appear to have a manipulative quality, we must remember that the youngster has a SERIOUS UNDERLYING PROBLEM and that their acting out is a way of communicating their pain to us. It is unlikely, when asked, if the young person will have any *real* idea of what this is – although she may well blame us. It is also unlikely that she will be able to let go of self-defeating behaviours without first gaining some understanding of their roots.

The range of behaviours which come into the categories of addiction or self-harm is almost endless: even something which seems healthy, like eating plenty of greens, can become dangerous if we overdo(se) it! I shall confine myself here looking *very briefly* at some of the most prevalent addictive and self-harming behaviours, including:

> **drugs and alcohol; eating disorders; suicidality; cutting, burning and hurting the body; sexual acting out and promiscuity; difficulties with money, including compulsive spending and gambling; engaging in other dangerous, thrill-seeking activities – such as taking and driving away or deliberately picking fights.**

Many of these issues deserve much more attention than is possible within this volume and will hopefully be the subject of separate 'occasional papers' in due course.

What You May See (The 'Presenting Problem')

A young person who persistently puts himself at risk, despite being aware of the potential dangers. He seems actively to be drawn towards such activities and even to revel in the thrill of challenging death. There is often a 'just watch me' quality to the behaviours, as if we, the parents, are being invited to participate as voyeurs, as helpless and powerless 'lookers-on' in a bizarre tragicomedy. This emphasises the power, albeit destructive, which the youngster seeks and which can give him a sense of 'being someone', in a world where once he was treated as if he didn't exist or didn't matter.

Conversely some activities are more likely to be concealed – especially if the youngster is more overtly bound in *shame* than into control battles with parents. Anorexia, bulimia and compulsive eating tend predominantly to be highly secretive activities, although parents are likely to become aware of the situation eventually. Then control can become a major issue. Similarly with drug and alcohol abuse and gambling. Some kids who cut will also go to great lengths to hide their behaviour. In these cases, the youngster's 'relief' or 'satisfaction' may come from the process itself, rather than from the effect it has on you.

As the 'responsible adult' you are likely to blame yourself for your youngster's behaviours, or to try to be protective and 'take control' at all costs. Confrontations typically escalate and the young person then openly blames you for her difficulties, or accuses you of being an 'interfering old battle-axe'. **She cannot afford to 'let you in' to her life and you feel you can't afford to stay out of it.** You reach stalemate, or the young person escalates the behaviour to show you she doesn't care, or that she is the one who runs her life. Sadly, life seems to be running away with, or from, her. Occasionally the pain becomes too great and she breaks down, perhaps even allowing you to try to comfort her, or to help her out of her current difficult situation. Then she's off and doing it again and you're left, at best, feeling knocked sideways, at worst, feeling used and abused.

Beyond the Looking Glass (or What May Lie Beneath)

- To most young people death is still a life-time away: they are young, death belongs to the elderly. It is hard for any youngster to be *realistic* on this one.

- The tendency to *self-harm* or to self-medicate is a predictable, although not inevitable, outcome for a child who has been seriously *hurt* in the past. The brain and body have already accommodated to a stressful early environment and they continue to function as if those stresses still exist.

- A child who was neglected or ignored for long periods will not have developed a normal perception of, or expectation about, relationships. Such a youngster has not had the opportunity to associate bodily discomforts, such as hunger, with the appropriate relief: food. She may ignore hungry feelings completely, or not know when to stop eating, or interpret feeling hungry as something else (such as fear), or she may eat whenever she feels *anything*.

- The neglected or emotionally abused child has also had to learn to rely on herself and not to expect comfort from other people. Hence she drastically limits the subsequent opportunities for learning about **self-soothing** activities and continues to use the strategies she learned as an infant and which brought her some measure of relief (see above).

- Physical abuse leads a youngster to expect pain and to **associate** pain with love. If he feels unloved he is likely to look for pain; the **endorphins**, naturally occuring morphine-like neuro-chemicals, which are released then make him feel good – just like getting an external 'fix' of heroin would. This can be the beginnings of a truly addictive behaviour.

- A child who has been sexually abused has also experienced pain and powerlessness, although excitement and **shame** may have been very powerful companion feelings. Young people often turn to sex as a way of gaining a sense of control over other people. However, in their attempts at exploitation, they inevitably exploit themselves too.

- As with other **self-harming** behaviours, subsequent feelings of **shame** can be overwhelming. The youngster is therefore likely to try to **dissociate** herself from such feelings. However, as they build up again, which inevitably they will, she may repeat the cycle of sexual self-exploitation in a continuing attempt to escape from the unbearable emotion.

- Engaging in frenetic or promiscuous sexual activity can become a habitual way of handling **distress**, including feelings of anger, loneliness and depression, as well as **shame**. Some youngsters learn that the thrill of the encounter is followed by a tremendous release, as **arousal** is raised and then dramatically lowered. They may have no other effective means of producing this powerful effect. This has both **psychological** and **physiological** rewards in the short term and can therefore become highly addictive in the longer term.

- Children who have survived repeated abuse are constantly on the alert for further **hurts**. Anticipating further (and seemingly inevitable) abusive situations can be so intensely **distressing** that a youngster may deliberately provoke further abuse 'to get it over with'.

- All children who have been **hurt** and **shamed** may hurt themselves because they believe they deserve to be punished. The **distorted** thinking which enabled them to survive in early childhood stays with them and can continue to cause them **real** pain.

- Much addictive and *self-harming* behaviour has a **dissociative** element. Whilst the moment lasts, pain can be inflicted without actually feeling it, danger can be faced without experiencing the fear, money can be gambled, stolen or spent without guilt or thought of the consequences.

- Sometimes the child has a punitive side, **modelled** on a previous **primary caregiver**, which will often try to punish the **part** of her which feels vulnerable and frightened, in the distorted belief that by doing so she is strengthening her defences – and that this is the only way to survive.

- Children and young people who have not developed a good awareness of their bodies may actually feel that their bodies are in some way separate and to blame for all the pain and *shame* they feel. *Hurting* the body, or not taking good care of it, may be the understandable result of this lack of connection between mind and body.

- There can be a cleansing element in some children's self-wounding. Drawing blood may be like bloodletting – allowing out the 'toxic' element which the youngster believes lies within. For others, making oneself bleed is life-confirming, proof that the body is not just an empty shell, that the life force still flows. Self-induced vomiting or purging may be used to similar effect.

- The *hurt* and helpless child often builds a counter-image of himself as all powerful. (See Superkid, Scared kid, pages 46–50.) He may swing from feeling useless and all bad to feeling that nothing can *hurt* him (which was exactly why this *part* of him came into being). For such a youngster, the normal rules do not apply; the belief that 'it will never happen to me', or 'I'm tough, I can handle anything', can lead him into all sorts of unseen dangers.

- Some children feel 'dead' most of the time, since their bodies and minds have been raised on very high (or extremely low) levels of *arousal*. Their nervous systems may actually need more stimulation than individuals with normal levels of *arousal*, so they engage in scary and exciting activities to 'up the ante' and to start feeling 'alive'.

- Other youngsters find peace and quiet very threatening, because it gives them time to think and to feel. This can be a totally overwhelming experience and a child may try anything to escape from it. These kids are constantly on the go: they seem unable to rest – and the truth is they are not 'programmed' for rest; they just don't know how.

- Some youngsters make the 'wrong' choices in the heat of the moment because they don't 'do' thinking very well. Their early experiences mean that they have not made the 'right' inner connections and are weak on cause and effect thinking. They may feel the world is one big lottery and that they stand as much (or more) chance of winning as anybody.

- These are the youngsters who will, say, be offered a drug and not refuse – despite your attempts at getting the health messages across. They are in double jeopardy, because once they find that the tobacco, or the dope, or the vodka, actually makes them feel better, fills a piece of their body chemistry which is missing, they are unlikely to find it easy to stop.

- Some kids get their 'buzz' not only from their own fear and excitement but also vicariously, from *distressing* others. If they can see that we, as their parents, can be upset or can be dragged into control battles, they will endeavour to make this happen – even if it means they are putting themselves at risk in the process. The more concern you show, the more they feel they have 'won', the less they actually feel cared for, and the less they seem to care about themselves (or anyone else).

- Any or all of these behaviours may be set off by feelings of *abandonment* and rejection. The youngster may get into a doubly vicious cycle: his anti-social behaviours bring out negative responses from others, which in turn trigger overwhelming feelings of *abandonment* – which in themselves are likely to drive a young person into further self-destructive activities, including promiscuous and dangerous sexual relationships.

- The *dissociative* element in a youngster's behaviour may be powerfully reinforced by the approach of adolescence – a time when a young person is working to separate (dis-associate) to some degree from family and when he may only wish to associate with his peer group. Social pressures to conform with the 'in crowd' can combine with hormonal changes to such an extent that the 'nice side' of your child, becomes totally submerged by the more anti-social aspects of his behaviour.

First Choices

If things have got this far, many of the 'first choices' have already been taken from your youngster and from you. Clearly you will have tried to give your child a stable, loving home and to show her that she can make choices about her life. You will also have tried to set a good example, to encourage your child to take care of herself and to educate her about the potential dangers in the world. Sadly, the earlier lessons she learned of pain and *shame* may still have a greater hold over her life.

You may well feel that you cannot deal with the issues around addiction and SELF-HARM on your own, that your young person needs effective therapeutic help to make sense of her past and to come to terms with the present. You, too, are probably needing to talk about your feelings and to find some effective support. This is easier said than done. Child and adolescent mental health services are under-resourced and overworked. Often 'brief family therapy' interventions are the only ones available. These tend to focus very firmly on the present and only offer a limited number of sessions. Whilst for some families this can be all that is needed, for children who **hurt**, who have a very **real**, long and painful history, it may simply alleviate some of the symptom behaviours, rather than deal with the underlying causes.

However, in some cases, behaviours in a younger child may point the way to possible later difficulties – stealing of food, refusal to take part in family meal times or behaving unacceptably at the table need to be dealt with early on, if they are not to contribute to later problem-eating behaviour. (See also section on Eating Difficulties in *First Steps*, pages 75–77.) In a similar way, children who begin to engage in **hyperactive**, impulsive or dangerous activities will be more easy to help at a young age than older adolescents who have had more time to become hooked on risk taking.

Early Eating Problems

Family meal times are, obviously, about more than just eating – they are part of an essential socialisation process. Try to establish a good pattern of shared meal times as soon as you can. It is vital that you keep meals low-key, comfortable and fairly short but at the same time expect every member of the family to join in. Begin by setting a good example yourself, of sitting down to a relaxed meal at least once a day, rather than grabbing a quick snack on the run.

Often a youngster will carry on playing when you call her to come to the table. Then you may simply offer her 'two choices': to join you right away, or to wait until the next meal time for something to eat. Complaints of hunger pangs in between can be listened to sympathetically, with a gentle comment that you hope she'll bear that in mind next time you call her. Do make sure there are plenty of drinks available in the meantime.

Some children regularly stay in their rooms and are unwilling to join you for a meal. If you feel this is a deliberate ploy, either to avoid being with you, or to avoid eating, it may be helpful to 'take the table to Mohammed'. Have ready a good supply of picnic equipment and join your child in his room now and again. Make it as much fun as you can for everyone – and don't forget to thank your 'host' for his kind hospitality when you leave. The most usual way that guests do this is by giving the host a hug or a kiss on the cheek – try it!

Remember that *real* picnics, in the open air, can also make communal eating more pleasurable. The food you provide at such times can be more 'fun size' and will probably be more acceptable in any case out of doors. Messy eaters will be in their element!

If quantity of food is a problem for your child, try using smaller plates. For poor or 'picky' eaters this can be encouraging – especially if they can always see something they particularly like laid out – and over-eaters might just be tricked into thinking they have 'lots and lots'. Providing a selection of food, on a 'help yourself' basis, can also be helpful in allowing a youngster to choose how much she eats, whilst still implying that you do expect her to eat something with you.

Always keep a plentiful supply of healthy foods, such as fruit and bread, available as fillers. Unless you are specifically working on achieving participation at meal times, making some 'good' snacks readily accessible gives your child your blessing to 'fill herself up' with your food, without having to 'take' it.

Children who make rude comments about your food, cannot sit still long enough to eat, or behave badly at the table are not just 'trying to get at you', although that may be part of the *looking glass* picture. **Set your own house rules for meal times, as you would for anything else, and be ready to keep to them.** Remind your youngster that if someone acted like that in a restaurant, they would be politely asked to leave. They certainly wouldn't be given something else to eat because they were still hungry!

Faddy eaters may benefit from being more actively involved in selecting menus and food preparation. There's nothing like feeling that you've made something to encourage you to appreciate it! Even if it is simply chopping up some carrots, or opening the tin of beans, it can look and taste so much better.

Some children appear to be deliberately messy eaters. Food throwers and droppers can be encouraged to clear up any mess after the meal and might do well to be confined to the kitchen area, where there are no expensive carpets to ruin. You could give recalcitrant 'pigs at the trough' the choice of eating in another room until they improve. Perhaps they could eat their meal whilst you do the washing up, preferably close to you but out of direct vision! That way you can still talk and spend time together, without the potential for being offensive.

Sometimes a child's messy eating may be related to trying to master feelings which belong to a much earlier time. If this seems to be the problem, you could consider providing some *real* opportunities for regression – preferably when you are on your own with your youngster. At other times they will be expected to 'act their age' at the meal table.

Often children can gain great comfort from being allowed to bottle-feed, or to eat baby foods (with their fingers or being spoon-fed by you) – if it is with your support and approval. A child's difficulties frequently arise because he just did not get the emotional (or even the physical) satisfaction which goes with these life-giving activities. By allowing him to try this now, you are offering your youngster a second chance to get what he has missed first time round. Ample opportunities for 'getting dirty' may also be helpful. (For further discussion on regression and messy play, please see *First Steps*, pages 77–78 and 51–52 respectively.)

Early Impulsivity and Risk Taking

Children who always seem to be dashing out into the middle of the road, doing handstands on their bikes or falling headlong into deep rivers may lack an appropriate awareness of danger. They may genuinely not recognise dangerous situations or they may be so used to 'living on the edge' that they keep on putting themselves at risk. Some may also have some difficulties with co-ordination or with *associating* what they do directly with what happens to them.

Where this is the case, please re-read the relevant sections in *First Steps*, as many of the suggestions may still be suitable, with minor changes to make them more age-appropriate. It may then be possible to lower a child's threshold of excitement and improve their *regulation of arousal* and physical *self-awareness*, so that their difficulties are considerably reduced.

In addition you may wish to look for safer, or more socially acceptable, activities which still supply a large degree of excitement. Obviously such things as Disney World spring to mind – but these are highly expensive and not likely to be readily available. Similarly bungy jumping, abseiling, wind-surfing, skiing, snorkelling, parascending and pot-holing may be out of your youngster's reach much of the time, as yet.

Instead, how about encouraging your youngster to mountain bike or sail with a club, or to join the basketball, cross-country running, or line-dancing team? There are often committed adult leaders who are only too willing to be encouraging and can also set some safe limits for your youngster (which he may be less likely to kick against!).

Make it clear to your youngster that you wish him to take as much care of himself as possible – and provide all the safety helmets, goggles, knee and elbow pads, wet suits, buoyancy aids and padded gloves that you can get hold of. **If you start as you mean to go on, by insisting on basic precautions, in the same way that the 'professionals' do, you are doing your best to minimise dangerous outcomes.** Then your child can be free to be fast and furious (and there is a *real* exhilaration in feeling the air rushing past as you slide, cycle or sail along) without *you* going quite so grey!

If Things Still Don't Change …

If your youngster is putting himself seriously at risk in any way, you are still likely to blame yourself and will try to work out what *you* did wrong that has made him act this way. Society in general, along with many child care practitioners, may reinforce this viewpoint, to the detriment of your whole family. **You are not to blame for your youngster's *distress* any more than he is. Blame, guilt** and *shame* **keep us trapped and prevent us moving on** – when what we need, more than anything, is to find new ways of looking at things and new ways of handling what we see.

Your child does *not* need to see you acting self-destructively, wearing yourself into the ground worrying, even though his behaviours may give you good cause. **He needs to see confident, self-assured adults who can take control of their own lives, who can find new ways of coping, and who can look after themselves, even when they are under great stress.**

This is the point at which you may need reminding that your first responsibility is to take care of yourself. You will need to be feeling good about yourself if you are to change the old messages in your child's thoughts, which are so destructive. **Your good example may not appear to be having any obvious effect yet – but later you may be surprised at just how much of it your young person has been absorbing.** Moreover, it takes an enormous amount of emotional energy to live with, and through, the pain of someone close – so you will need to build up and maintain your personal reserves.

Give yourself repeated reminders that trying to protect a young adult from the consequences of his own actions is in fact enabling him to maintain his habit. Your love has to go beyond 'search and rescue', has to have very firm *boundaries* and has to encourage the youngster to acknowledge and take responsibility for his life. This is an essential principle, irrespective of the particular problems your teenager may show. *Yes* he had a lot of *hurts* in the past and he is in no way responsible for those and *no* that is no excuse to go on allowing himself to be *hurt* or to blame everybody else.

You may need to take on board an additional set of principles in parenting *young adults* with addictive and *self-harming* behaviours, which I have called DOUBLY ASSERTIVE.

DOUBLY ASSERTIVE PRINCIPLES FOR MANAGING SELF-HARMING BEHAVIOURS IN YOUNG ADULTS

Keep these DOUBLY ASSERTIVE principles at the front of your mind constantly, as you remind yourself that your own role in changing your young person's *addictive* and *self-harming* behaviours is limited – but it is also vital.

- ACKNOWLEDGE the problem and ACCEPT the young person's version as her *reality* for the moment.

Whatever your youngster's problem, do not be dismissive or blaming when she does let you in on the problem. Acknowledge the situation for what it is and be sympathetic about how bad it must feel. That helps the youngster feel validated and can help her to move on to dealing with her difficulties.

Although you may see a very different version of *reality* from your young adult, *part* of her at least believes the story she tells you, that she is a helpless victim, or that it was all someone else's fault. You can accept that for the moment, whilst not losing touch with the subtitles!

- Be SUPPORTIVE but stand your ground. Stay calm, stay sane and STAY OUT.

Be clear on what support you are willing to provide *if asked* and what you can offer in practice. Always bear in mind that this is not your problem and you are not responsible for solving it. Recognise your limits; do not become over-involved.

Your young person needs to hear that you believe he is capable of sorting things out himself but it may *not* be helpful to offer much advice, unless you are asked for it – and unless you are also prepared to see him do something completely different! You can, however, be a powerful source of information, or a guide to other advice resources. Try saying 'some young people have tried so and so when they are in this kind of situation' and leave him to think about it.

- EMPATHISE with the young person's situation and ENCOURAGE them to work it out for themselves.

Even the gravest situations can seem more manageable if you believe someone else can see and recognise the problem. By empathising, you are letting the young person know you see and care about what happens to them – then they can stop shouting about it and get on with *doing* something about it!

A good way to approach a problem is to say: 'Yes, I can see that is going to be difficult but I am sure you can work it out. Do you have any ideas of how you are going to handle it?' Hopefully the answer will be a (qualified) 'yes'. If not, you can suggest they take their time to think and that you'll be around when they have some suggestions they'd like to share with you. Either way, wish the young person good luck – and mean it!

- REASSURE the young adult of your belief in them and then RETURN THE RESPONSIBILITY for the problem to them.

Although it is very tempting to scratch your head and say 'Well, Stanley, this is another fine mess you've got (yourself) into!', it isn't likely to help. When in distress a young person needs the reassurance we can give them that things *can* be sorted out and the confidence to believe they can do it themselves.

Although handing back the responsibility for a crisis to one's child is never easy, it will get harder, for both of you, the longer you leave it. Remind yourself that your child is also a young adult, with all the rights and responsibilities that confers.

- TAKE YOUR TIME and TAKE GOOD CARE of yourself.

Do not feel that you have to respond immediately to a cry for help. Be ready to use your judgement and to allow time to work on your side. Some youngsters seem to go from crisis to crisis as a way of life and come to rely on other people to pick up their emotional mess. You could offer to talk to the young person 'tomorrow' in the hope that by 'tomorrow' something will have intervened – it very often does! This can help *you* avoid becoming **distressed** over something, only to find that the youngster no longer considers it a problem.

Never forget to look after the most important person in your life – you! If you don't, no-one else is likely to. Being vulnerable and needy is part of being human – embrace your humanity and get a hug from someone else as soon as you can!

Let us now see how being DOUBLY ASSERTIVE can work out in practice.

Money Issues

Take money issues, for example. Many of our young people have great difficulties managing their money, due to weak cause and effect thinking, and the enormous emphasis they place on the material things in life, as if to compensate for their emotional (and physical) emptiness. This is a heady combination and one which can lead them into problems with mounting debts – and eventually with the law.

Typically the youngster tries to take advantage of all the credit which is available to today's teenagers and spends 'as if there were no tomorrow' – which, in their *distorted* way of thinking, is actually the case. For a while everything goes well, they derive pleasure from their spending power and some, though usually short-lived, from their acquisitions. Then the bills start coming in, piling up until they can no longer be ignored.

This may be the point at which the youngster lets us in. He needs a loan and who better to ask than his parents. He argues that they have plenty of money (probably not the case!) and will want to help him, if they love him (almost certainly true!). The parents are concerned that their son should not be chased by irate bankers, or 'blacklisted' for future credit – although they may not yet realise that their own credit rating could also be affected. Their dilemma is that they know that if they do not lend the money, their son will get into further difficulties and that if they do they are unlikely to see any of it back. They may well decide to 'help him out just this once, he has enough problems already'.

Unfortunately it is rarely 'just this once'. More typically the young person takes greater and greater financial risks, believing that his parents will go on 'bailing him out'. If they become reluctant he turns nasty, accusing them of not caring about him, threatening to steal the money if they don't help, or terrifying them with tales of unsatisfied money lenders. However, this doesn't usually stop him running up more debts. On the other hand, if they keep on paying, he just keeps on spending, confirmed in his *distorted* belief that they 'owe him'. Feelings can run higher and higher, yet the spending pattern does not change.

The only way to escape this cycle is out! The young person certainly needs to know that you love him and he needs the benefit of your understanding, support and (some) advice. He also *wants*, but does not *need* your money! The sooner the youngster faces up to the effects of his actions, the sooner he is likely to recognise these as the **real** cause of his problems, instead of being angry with you, or anyone else. **Your child needs your sympathy, not your pity. He needs to face** *reality*, **not to have someone buy into his fantasy.** He does not want, or need, long lectures on the puritan ethic – so why not save yourself the *distress*, the time and the trouble!

Next time you are asked for money try saying: 'I'd love to help you out but I know how difficult you will find it to pay me back. I don't want to make that a problem for you, or between us.' Debts can keep you as 'the bad guy' and leave you both with a grudge – he because he wants to be spending his money, not giving it to you; you because you hate having to keep on asking for it. This can mean that your youngster starts trying to keep out of your way, to avoid being reminded of what he owes you, and you lose what little contact there still exists between you.

You could, in lieu of handouts or loans, negotiate jobs to be done *before* handing over money as wages. If your youngster is unwilling to collaborate with you on this one, he is depriving himself of the money and has only himself to blame. Alternatively you could suggest that you might act as a 'banker', holding a certain amount of cash for your youngster, against the next time he is in desperate need. Sadly, since most teens don't have a penny, this is unlikely to happen – but again it does show you are willing to be supportive!

You may be prepared to go with your young person to visit their bank manager, or whoever, to discuss their debts. Get your child to make the arrangements if you possibly can and let him know you expect him to do most of the talking. **You are there as an objective adviser:** not to apologise or make good the debt but to empower the youngster to work things out. **You all need to be clear on this before you go into the meeting.**

Be ready to allow the consequences of the young person's actions do the talking. You can listen and reflect what you see is happening. If you know he is also an ace at wangling money out of other people, you can be sure he can work his way out of this one too.

Drug and Alcohol Use

Providing money for a drug user can be even more problematic. Parents may recognise that their youngster has a chemical addiction, which she will try to feed at all costs and they know the risks involved in continuing drug use. She has probably stolen from them already on numerous occasions and they fear she is also committing petty crimes, or prostituting herself, to support her habit. She may have run up debts with dealers and be in physical danger if she does not pay up.

In the *distorted* thinking of the child who *hurts*, your willingness to try to protect her from the dangerous world in which she has placed herself may be seen as weakness or stupidity, or as 'her right' as your child. Trying to talk her out of her addictive behaviour, by pointing out the dangers, is also unlikely to be effective, since you will be taking all the 'units of concern' (page 66) and allowing her addictive side free rein. For the regular drug (or alcohol) abuser, her thinking will inevitably be further impaired by the chemical toxins in her brain. There is little value in lengthy arguing at this point. **She may have set all reason aside right now, she does not need you to do the same.**

Experience has shown, over many years, that **the only way that an individual who has an addiction is likely to stop is if she recognises for herself the suffering she is causing TO HERSELF.** You can be there, you can go on loving but you cannot make her change until she hits 'rock-bottom' – and she will not reach that low point quickly if you enable her to keep up her habit. **You cannot take her pain away by 'rescuing' her – you will only *hurt* both of you more.** When you feel the pain of her *hurts*, look after yourself first and foremost, and remind yourself that she has already proved she is a survivor. Then, as and when she is ready to face up to the *realities* of her life, you will be in the best position to support her and encourage her efforts.

There is a wealth of material which has been written about addictions and co-dependency – the part people who care can unintentionally play in perpetuating addictive behaviours. Some of it is good, some of it can make you feel even more *hurt* and guilty than you do already. Whilst it is important to draw attention to the dangers inherent in becoming over-involved in another person's problem, I believe this approach is unfair and unproductive; it feels like 'blaming the victim' and blame, to repeat, is very destructive.

If you know where your youngster is obtaining his drugs, or that he is buying under-age tobacco or alcohol at certain shops or pubs, don't keep it to yourself. It is not just your youngster who is at risk from these unscrupulous vendors. The police also need to have this information, if they are to do their job well.

Consider taking a recent photograph of your adolescent and showing it to officers at the local police station, so that they can recognise him on the streets or in the clubs. It can also be helpful to visit such places yourself, with photographs, and let the proprietors know if your child is under age. If they continue to give him admission or to supply alcohol, for example, tell them that you will have no compunction about informing the police. Licences can be put at risk!

If you know someone who has been through this and come out the other side, talk to them. Other parents can be very supportive and can suggest topical tips for survival. Young adults who have 'been there and done that' are often willing to talk to another young person and are ideally placed, as poacher-turned-gamekeeper, to get across the dangers *realistically*. They are also more likely to be listened to than 'old wrinklies' like yourself.

You are entitled to a drug and alcohol-free zone where youngsters are concerned – your own home. If you do find traces of illegal drugs, be prepared to inform the police, since permitting your home to be used for such activities is an offence in itself. Let the adolescent know this in advance, so that they are making an informed choice. It could just be that a caution from the police will deter further infractions. If not, continue to be persistent in maintaining your own boundaries.

One of the worst side-effects of teenage drinking, beyond the damage the kid is doing to himself, is the mess she may cause. Vomiting all over the living room carpet is definitely 'in your face' but angry lectures will go unheard. Although she may be in no fit state to do anything about it right away, allow her some time to sleep it off and then matter-of-factly provide bucket, cloth, disinfectant and so on, and leave her to clean up.

Young people often argue that you drink, so why can't they? You could quietly inform the young person of the difference in your ages and remind him that you only spend your *own* money on drink. Unless you are in the habit of 'getting legless' yourself, you can also point out that you act reasonably and responsibly after a few drinks. Suggest that once he reaches eighteen *and* is able to do the same you will rethink your position.

Young people approaching adulthood may be coming to a point where they may do better living on their own, or with friends. Although you may have major concerns, you can take the view that this will give you back your peaceful home and allow you to establish a different, less strained, relationship with your youngster. **Often the challenges of managing their own lives and their money can be a very useful learning experience for acting-out youngsters.**

Sexual Acting-Out

Clearly there are no easy answers to *any* complex questions, and dealing with a youngster who is sexually acting out is no exception. **Not only is this a deeply personal issue for all of us, it may well go deep into the roots of a child's early history of *hurts*.** Again, all caution may go out of the window as powerful, unrecognised forces overtake a youngster's reason, and action becomes ***dissociated*** from thinking.

Young female adoptees often become sexually active very early. Sometimes this seems to be a re-enactment of their birth mother's history, at an unconscious level; sometimes the youngster desperately wants to conceive a baby, someone to whom she can feel connected. Often the teenager will shun all your well-intentioned advice about not rushing into relationships and engage in a whirlwind of short-lived sexual encounters. A new generation is often the direct result.

Being a grandparent before your time can be very challenging, especially as you watch a young person, who is not yet mature or responsible, trying to take responsibility for a tiny baby. It can bring up many issues for you, not least because you may fear that the cycle of maltreatment may be repeated. There is insufficient space here to deal with this issue in the depth which it deserves. I hope that it will be covered more fully as one of the set of 'occasional papers' to be published by Adoption UK beginning in 2000. (See page 12.)

Where the adolescent has previously been a victim of childhood sexual abuse, the whole idea of sexuality may be extremely difficult for her. It may be that she becomes very inhibited about sex and goes to great lengths to avoid sexual encounters. She may, on the other hand, throw herself into meaningless relationships to overcome her own sense of *shame* and embarrassment, or to silence the criticisms of her more mature peers. She may also believe that her body is worthless, or feel she has no *real* choices in this area.

Her confusion will escalate and her self-esteem will fall further as she repeatedly meets *abandonment*, *hurt* and further *shame*. Either way, she needs your encouragement and support to handle these challenges and come through. In particular she needs to know how you feel on these issues and guidance on how other young people may deal with them, since her own view is so confused.

Perhaps more commonly, an adolescent survivor of sexual abuse will feel that her (or his) body has no value or that sex is the only way to get close and feel loved, so she will repeatedly seek out sexual relationships and will repeatedly be *hurt*. She may get hooked on the 'thrill of the chase', only to discard a lover as worthless once 'caught' or because, conversely, she feels he is getting too close. She may use sex as a way of managing her distress and become *physiologically* addicted to the act itself. It may be far harder to live with and support your youngster in such circumstances, **but however uncomfortable you may feel with her activities try to hang on to a positive memory or image of her which can carry you through.**

Like any other behaviours in young people's lives you cannot always prevent them from getting *hurt*. You can try to provide them with the knowledge, guidance and support to face the world, show them by example the courage it takes to look after yourself and give powerful messages that you believe everyone is capable of finding the good within themselves, if only they are prepared to look. **Never mind what the neighbours, or the church, or your relatives may be thinking, you should not be judged by what your children do, any more than you would wish to judge your children solely on their current mistakes.**

Talking over your child's own history can be particularly relevant here: often youngsters are very aware of the suffering of the unwanted child they once were and may be able to act more responsibly by looking at their own behaviours in this light. Being clear on how much you are personally prepared to take care of a tiny baby can help you to be *realistic* and can help a teenager to see what pregnancy may actually entail, beyond the fantasy.

Be prepared to set and maintain house rules with which you feel comfortable. 'No sex in my house' may be enforceable up to a point. However, if you do find evidence of sexual activity, the best thing you can do may be to ask the young person to clean up after herself and to take responsibility for washing bed-linen and so on. This can give you some feeling of control, letting your teen know that you know, without an angry confrontation. If the behaviour seems deliberately to escalate, this might be the time to start thinking about helping a young person find their own accommodation, where at least you don't have her behaviours thrown in your face. (See Part 7: Staying a Family and Being Apart.)

You may feel that 'the evidence' – used condoms or wrappers, discarded underwear and so on – has been deliberately 'planted'. This is quite possibly so. A young person may be asking for your help in dealing with her own ambivalence (even asking that you say 'no' for her!). Conversely, a child who **hurts** may be saying 'Look what I've been doing and there's nothing you can do about it!', or trying to hook you into becoming upset and angry. **You are the best judge of which of these is relevant to your family and only you can know what is the most appropriate choice of response (or lack of it).**

Providing information about sexual relationships and encouraging the appropriate use of condoms and other contraceptives such as the pill is of course essential, yet fraught with potential problems. You know your youngster best and should be best placed to decide where, when and how you approach this sensitive issue. Some good advice is readily available from doctors' surgeries and family planning clinics. Read it together and talk it through if you can – choose a quiet time when feelings are not running high and you are both able to think reasonably.

For boys, the *realities* of the Child Support Agency should also be discussed. Few adolescents would willingly confer part of their income on someone else for the best part of their lives. This might *just* have a sobering effect on current sexual activities!

Continuing Impulsivity and Addictive Risk Taking

Often, children who are impulsive and take risks become more reckless with age. They may graduate from legitimate to highly illegitimate thrill-seeking, as their body chemistry becomes increasingly habituated to high levels of excitement and danger. This form of addictive risk-taking behaviour can become very difficult to manage because it also involves the very *real* risk (and perverse excitement) of being apprehended by the police.

Youngsters who take and drive away cars, for example, appear to derive a major part of their 'fun' from the thrill of the chase – being pursued over long distances by a number of police vehicles. They put themselves, their pursuers and innocent bystanders at risk of injury or death. In such circumstances you will undoubtedly wish to give all the help and information you can to the police, even if it means 'grassing' on your 'joy-riding' teenager, to avoid unnecessary tragedy.

Make sure that you set a good example by never driving your car when you have had a drink or two and that you are scrupulous about speed limits (at least when your youngster is a passenger). The more unambiguous you can be on these sorts of issues, the more likely they are to have *some* impact on your wayward adolescent – even if there is no evidence of this yet!

There is a good deal to be said for 'looking after your own' here – your own car keys, your own vehicle and your own peace of mind. If your youngster is under seventeen years old, you cannot condone her using your car, even to 'practise' around the local car park. You will also need to make it clear that you will not sanction any 'borrowing' – keeping your 'I' statements brief and neutral (see also point 23 on page 61).

It would probably be a very good idea to check out your personal accident insurance cover. You need to be sure that your own cars are fully covered for 'accidental' damage and that your youngster is insured for causing injury both to himself and other road users and for damage to other vehicles and property. You may not be able to prevent misdemeanours on the road but at least you can minimise the damage to your pocket.

Youngsters who get into fights are certainly over-impulsive. They are readily provoked into anger and do the ***adrenalin***-charged 'fight' part of ***fight and flight*** as an habitual response. They may also provoke fights because they have not acquired adequate social skills, or because they get a 'buzz' out of it: it makes them feel big. (Remember that in the ***distortions*** of the ***looking glass***, they feel small and powerless, somewhere deep down, so *acting* big and powerful can be just that, 'a front'.)

In addition, a minority of young people may derive some inverted pleasure from getting ***hurt***. Not only are they replaying their childhood victim role, they may also be ***triggering*** off the release of those addictive ***endorphins*** (see also page 168). This may be the best way they know of dealing with stress and making themselves feel better. In this case it may be more useful to look at alternative ways of helping your child get his needs met (see for example, page 173).

Whatever your adolescent's 'risk of choice', try to avoid the common pitfalls, including showing too much ***distress*** about his behaviour, however justified your feelings are. In all likelihood he is also getting a 'buzz' from winding you up and from deliberately going against your stated wishes. When you are battling against risk taking, you are also battling against established ***neuro-biological pathways***.

Sometimes the best you can hope for is that your youngster receives his 'come-uppance', in this case a bruising he will never forget, sooner rather than later. It is a very hard lesson for him to have to learn, and for you to watch. Hang tough and hang in there. **The more that natural, external consequences can do the teaching, and the more you can be the empathic observer, the quicker the lesson is likely to be learned.**

Once you have made your position plain, steer clear of giving long lectures, time and time again. Either the young person heard you the first time, but has no intention of taking any notice, or he effectively ***switches off*** from any perceived nagging from 'the olds'. You also run the risks of pushing him further into acting out – 'just to show you' – and of taking on ALL the worry and responsibility for your youngster's anti-social behaviour – leaving him with none.

Self-Injury

Drawing too much attention to your youngster's cuts or burns on her body is unlikely to be helpful. If she wishes to be secretive about her behaviours, this can drive her further underground and may exacerbate her self-injury. If she is getting gratification from your reactions, your teenager is also more likely to keep it up. It is important, however, that you let your adolescent know, quietly, that you can see what she is doing. Try to get her to talk about her feelings and to look at safer or more comfortable ways of expressing her *hurts*.

Encourage your youngster to treat her body more kindly – perhaps by allowing you to massage her with relaxing essential oils. Serious nail biters might be helped by the challenge of a brilliant nail varnish (where to paint it?) and skin pickers by healing creams, such as Nelson's Calendula Cream (made from, and smelling deliciously of, marigolds).

More serious injuries may need medical treatment; they certainly warrant therapeutic intervention from a practitioner experienced in working with children who *self-harm* **and their families.** Effective support will empower you to help your child and look beyond the 'presenting problem' to the real issues underneath.

Try to find ways of giving your youngster the message that you love him and want to take care of him – other than tending to his wounds. It may be that he has learned that he can only be touched or fussed over legitimately if he is sick or injured. Providing lots of opportunities for closeness and genuine concern, unrelated to incidents of *self-harm*, may help him to manage the behaviour better.

For some young people the big pay-off is not so much the direct *distress* they cause, more the power they experience in having numerous adults running round in circles after them. Sadly, they may learn to play one off against another, to elicit sympathy from one by claiming the other does not care. **You may have to walk a very fine line between showing that you care enough to want her to stop** *hurting* **herself and** *realistically* **giving her some sense of control over her own body – but not yours.**

A few youngsters may go as far as making unfounded allegations of physical, sexual or emotional abuse against you, pointing to their injuries as evidence of their pain. Hospital staff, teachers and social workers are rightly on the alert for any indications of child abuse and may be highly-sympathetic to such claims, perhaps setting child protection procedures in motion without fully understanding the situation. This helps no-one. It makes the child a victim of his own *distorted* thinking and allows him to victimise the very people who are doing their best to help him – *you*. **Please do not try to handle this alone – get in touch with Adoption UK for further information and advice as soon as possible, before things escalate.** Most youngsters, however, do not go on to injure themselves seriously. The temporary relief they get from their own actions can help them keep their current distress at manageable levels. If they can begin to make sense of their *hurt* lives they can begin to find more healthy ways of reacting over time – as long as you are there for them.

Suicide and Suicidality

A small but significant minority of children and young people *do* make attempts on their own lives. **Suicide is always a serious issue, whether or not the attempt itself seems serious.** Treating a suicide attempt as 'just attention-seeking' is very unhelpful, even when there are clear indications that the youngster had little intention of killing herself.

Often the individual is trying to escape unbearable pain – to that extent she wants 'to end it all' NOW – and can think of no other way of making that happen. It is a sad contradiction that the only strategy she can find to try to survive is to put her life on the line. This actually makes most sense if we think about *dissociation* and how different *parts* of an individual appear to want or feel very different things (just as a youngster can apparently love you and hate you simultaneously).

In more extreme cases of *dissociation*, one part of the person may actually believe that she can kill another *part* (through fatally harming the body) whilst remaining alive herself. Although this may sound fantastic, **it has been this ability to 'be fantastic' which has allowed the *dissociative* survivor to keep the unbearable truth of her life even from herself** – at least for manageable periods of time.

Such a destructive part of the *self* can feel omnipotent and indestructible, able to inflict pain and suffering on others, including other *parts* of the *self*, in order to keep herself safe. **It is unhelpful to criticise this *part* or fail to give it credence – since that side of the young person's character will probably feel forced to try even harder to be 'protective', in a *distorted* show of strength.** However, it may be possible to encourage this part to find less harmful ways of being protective (see Part 4: Through the Looking Glass), especially if you can acknowledge the very *real* role that *part* has played in the young person's survival to date.

There may be a *part* of your youngster which believes, in its depressed state, that there is no hope; which experiences the world as just too dark and painful. It can be very distressing and scary to allow this *part* to 'tell it like it is', at this moment, to this particular *part* – and very tempting to try to move the young person to a more comfortable place. However, sometimes giving your child safe time with you, to feel the *really* bad, terrifying *parts* can empower her to face her 'darkest demons'. Being able to say 'it was that bad *and* I can survive' can begin to break down the barriers between the powerful but contradictory feelings which are currently tearing your youngster apart.

Clearly if you believe your youngster has difficulties to this degree you will wish to obtain effective outside help. You may find that the International Society for the Study of Dissociation (ISSD-UK), telephone number 01244 390121, can advise you on locally available support for your child and your family. It may also be helpful to get in touch with other families on the Network who are experiencing similar difficulties, through telephoning Adoption UK at Lower Boddington.

Never try to take over and be that *part* of your young person which wants to live. One way of understanding this is in terms of 'units of concern' (see Part 4.4 on page 66). If *you* do all the worrying about trying to stop a youngster from **hurting** herself irrevocably, *she* doesn't have to. Instead, she can expend all her emotional energy on wanting to die – knowing that she can leave the responsibility for keeping herself safe to you. In addition, if she has a tendency to be **oppositional**, she may push herself into 'having a go' to maintain an illusion of having some control, where otherwise she feels she has none.

Once again, however, you will need to strike a *balance* between allowing your youngster to feel some measure of control and still showing that you care about the pain in her life. Some individuals respond well to being told, 'I know you feel terrible and you want to stop the pain. There are **parts** of you which you do wish were dead. What about the **parts** who want to live?' After all, if your young person did not have some will to live she would have died long ago! In this way you are both acknowledging the depths of suffering your young person may feel *and* guiding her towards her own internal resources for survival and healing.

In the final instance, personal safety is down to one person – the young adult. **Again, you can make your home as safe as you can for a young person, but you cannot prevent a determined suicide.** You are, however, in the best position to work out whether hiding all the knives, razor blades and prescription drugs in the house will help. Some depressed youngsters may benefit from having such temptations removed – especially if they can also be very impulsive.

On the other hand, a youngster could interpret your legitimate concerns as indicative of how dangerous you perceive him to be. He *may* rise to the challenge and take responsibility for himself, or *conversely* he may try to live up to your perceived 'expectations', with potentially disastrous results. **Given that you can't predict every eventuality or stand guard over your youngster twenty-four hours a day, seven days a week, you would do better to encourage protection and self-care from the inside, not impose it from the outside.**

It may be unclear from moment to moment where your child is 'coming from' and you may sometimes get it wrong: your youngster may feel so confused that it isn't possible, at that moment, to 'read' his motives clearly. **Please do not allow yourself to accept the blame or the pain of even the saddest outcome. Perhaps your youngster will now find the peace he has not found in life.**

Voluntary organisations such as Childline, Samaritans, Young Minds, SANE and MIND offer telephone counselling for young people who feel depressed or suicidal. Some also offer group or individual support for children and for other family members, as well as publishing some useful material. Often their approach may seem more appropriate, as well as more immediate, than that of the statutory sector, with its long waiting lists and drug orientation.

It is essential that you find support for yourselves and for your child, with which you feel comfortable. You do not want to feel excluded from therapy or undermined within your family; your youngster does not need inexperienced workers or superficial work. Do not allow yourselves to be pushed into something of which you are uncertain: take time to look, listen, explore and think – even in a crisis!

You may wish to consider the use of medication, such as antidepressants, for your youngster. There are many new drugs coming on the market, making even greater claims about treating depressive behaviours than Prozac. Overworked clinicians are often only too keen to write a prescription, particularly when faced with threats of *self-harm*. **Such drugs can be very useful in the short term, if prescribed with care and with a clear recognition of the possible side-effects.**

However, one of the greatest dangers lies in allowing a young person to come to rely on medication to 'get him through the day', instead of giving him coping and problem-solving strategies so that he can master his life. You may be able to obtain up-to-the-minute information on new drugs coming onto the market through organisations like MIND. They may also be able to suggest viable alternatives, including group and individual counselling sessions.

Complementary medicines such as homoeopathic remedies also have a good deal to offer – and can help stressed-out parents too! Try speaking to other adopters on the Network and see what they have tried and with what success. St John's Wort is currently receiving a good deal of favourable publicity just now, both in the treatment of depression and 'agitated depression' – which looks and feels like just the opposite, on the outside! It is hoped that a 'occasional paper' on the subject of depression will be published in due course.

There are some children and young people who use the threat of suicide to feel more powerful in a world in which they feel powerless. This can make it difficult for parents to hold on to the deep vulnerability of such a child, in the face of what feels like gross emotional manipulation. Reminding yourself that feeding your youngster's obsessive compulsion for control is as unhealthy as handing over money to feed his drugs habit can help sustain you through difficult times and help you see the *real* issues beyond the *looking glass*.

Most children know their rights these days. A few also soon learn that if they shout 'suicide' everybody jumps! **You know your youngster only too well and are best placed to recognise when a threat is a *distorted* manipulation rather than genuine.** *Yes*, the child is feeling pretty bad at present, but *no*, he is not *really* going to leap out of the bedroom window from which he is hanging.

In such circumstances, **a low-key approach may be most effective, as long as you also seek out the right sort of in-depth help for a youngster whose perception of her world is so painfully** *distorted.* Perhaps saying something along the lines of 'I'm just going to put dinner on the table. I hope you don't miss it' might be effective – as long as you are genuinely caring and can avoid sounding sarcastic or dismissive. **Once the immediate situation is over, and passions are not so high, you may be able to get in touch with what is** *really* **distressing your child.**

Alternatively, go for the funny side! If you can raise a laugh you will raise everyone's sense of well-being and lower the potential for damage, *in the short term.* I like the image of Rabbit hanging his washing on the 'South End of Pooh', when the bear became caught in Rabbit's doorway. I also like the idea of Christopher Robin reading 'sustaining stories at the North End of Pooh', although it might not be everybody's cup of tea! You know your youngster's sense of the absurd better than anyone, so trust your intuition here.

Whilst behaviours which are openly attention-seeking or centre on control need to be discouraged, it is important never to lose sight of the intensely vulnerable *parts* **which they have been developed to protect. Then you will need to find healthier, more acceptable, ways of giving your youngster the attention they deserve and the personal empowerment they seek – so that they can feel more at ease with the world.** (Look out for the proposed 'occasional paper' on suicide and suicidality from Adoption UK. More details will be made available in due course through the Journal *Adoption Today*.)

Compulsive Eating Disorders

Anorexia nervosa and bulimia are at the more extreme end of the continuum of compulsive eating disorders and can in themselves become life-threatening. The severity of anorexia is often misrepresented, as in the term 'the slimming disease'. Whilst over-concern for individual appearance *is* one manifestation of the 'presenting problem', it is *not* the fundamental issue; nor is it accurate to see this as a 'disease', nor as a disorder which affects only girls and women. A sizeable

minority of individuals with eating disorders are male. **The unhappiness which a youngster displays about her outward appearance, or self-image, can be understood as a metaphor for the unhappiness she feels on the inside:** for the deep lack of self-worth derived from her very earliest life experiences.

Many problems around eating itself can be traced right back to infancy: patterns learned at the mother's breast (or powdered substitute formula in many cases) can become deeply ingrained, since they are so fundamentally *associated* with parental care and love (or the lack thereof). For these very reasons such patterns can take a great deal of time and effort to change.

There is an important issue of control which can underlie eating disorders – to the youngster it may seem that controlling what goes in or comes out of her body is the only thing which does lie within her control. This is particularly true of children who have been abused or maltreated in the past – when abusive adults have appeared to take control of every aspect of the child's life. Understanding this makes it easier to see why it is 'a matter of life and death' to a youngster that she *feels* she is in control – and that **you should not take what little power she has retained from her, by force-feeding or over-vigilance of her consumption and elimination.**

It is also clear that, like most other *self-harming* behaviours, eating disorders frequently have a *dissociative* component. Often the apparent normality of a young person's life hides the *looking glass reality* of her inner thoughts and suffering. Getting in touch with the *inner child* parts of your youngster, which feel *abandoned*, alone, terrified, unloved and unloveable, can help you all to begin to make sense of this seemingly 'crazy' behaviour and to find more healthy ways of her getting what she *really* needs.

Many of us can identify with the need to eat sweet, carbohydrate-loaded foods when we feel stressed out or tired, or even very excited. We are often trying to 'fill ourselves up' with something – and it is no coincidence that the foods of choice are usually sugar-based (and fat-loaded). Over and above the powerful *associations* between sweetness and love, evident in so many of our terms of endearment, sugary foods reach *parts* others do not – in the short term! And of course chocolate has very similar properties to some natural, mood-elevating chemicals in our bodies, such as *serotonin*.

I cannot hope to do justice to the complexities of eating disorders in this brief space. However, I hope that the issue will be addressed in one of a series of proposed 'occasional papers' to be published by Adoption UK beginning in 2000. Please contact Lower Boddington for further information or watch out for further information in *Adoption Today*.

Staying a Family and Being Apart

The *reality* for some adoptive families, especially as their youngsters approach adolescence, is that they cannot carry on living the way they are. The family of a child who *hurts* can all too easily become the ever-present battleground for past childhood suffering. Try as parents may, they may not be able to heal the child's wounds, or alter his *internal working models* of family life well enough to allow him to feel comfortable, safe or at home within his adoptive family.

Sometimes these unhealthy patterns of relating have become so ingrained that parents feel they are being sucked into their child's *looking glass reality* faster than they can draw their child into their own, more 'normal' way of being. The well-being of every family member can feel seriously threatened by such challenges, yet requests for help from **distressed** parents, at this stage, can easily be misinterpreted. You *feel* crazy, you *sound* crazy, you even begin to *look* crazy – so is it any wonder that outsiders think you *must* be crazy? Then it is not a far cry from being seen as 'crazy-making' rather than the 'crazy made' – and child care practitioners are understandably hypervigilant for evidence of crazy-making behaviours in adults, not children!

Clearly, you are not going to be at your best to convince people otherwise at this point. That is one of the reasons why it is essential to take such good care of yourselves right from the start and why it is equally important to 'know your limits'. **Asking for support sooner rather than later can be a sign of strength, not of weakness.** A request for respite, for example, should *always* be recognised as a serious 'cry for help' and any support should actively empower parents to continue to do the job they elected to do – to be *good enough* parents for their children who *hurt*.

Even when your adopted child is living away from your family, whether she spends short periods of time in respite care, has been accommodated, placed in a residential school or therapeutic community, is in a mental health facility or prison, or has just moved herself out of your home, **she is still your child – and always will be.** The expectation of still belonging is important to us all but is *vital* to a youngster who has already experienced painful separations and losses. Remember that it is not so much the continuing to live together which links family members, it is more a *feeling* of being connected, of sharing something unique in life, which is on-going – as if we each carry a *part* of that other person within us. When these connections are strong enough they can withstand the longest distances and the lengthiest separations.

Belonging is often a very difficult issue for children who *hurt*, who experienced their first families as rejecting or *abandoning*, and who may still feel they do not belong anywhere. It can also be a tough one for adoptive parents, who may be willing to go to almost any lengths to protect their youngster from further rejections. It is very easy to feel that you are letting your child down if she is being looked after elsewhere, even if it is only for a few hours each week, with a family down the road. This sense of not being ***good enough*** parents may be made worse by the reactions of wider family and friends, who have not experienced your problems first hand, and by child care practitioners, who understandably wish to protect a child from what they see as further painful rejections.

However, trying to carry on in an intolerable situation can make us less able to be the loving, accepting, enabling parents our children need us to be and may make it increasingly likely that a painful break will come eventually – and in the least well-managed way. Feelings may have risen so high on either side, too many ***hurtful*** words may have been spoken or too much emotional damage done, for parents or youngsters ***realistically*** to go on feeling committed to each other. **Necessary breaks,** whether they be short or extended, **must be well planned, so that essential family links,** however tenuous they may feel, **are kept intact and can be built on for the future.**

The dynamics in the family of a child who ***hurts*** are very powerful but they are *not* one-way. It may *feel* as if your youngster does everything he can to keep you at bay – and you can understand this in terms of his ***distorted*** expectations of being ***hurt***, in particular by close family members. Remember that 'for every action there is an equal and opposite reaction' (Newton's third law of motion); that is, you are tied into a powerful pull–push situation. (See also page 33.) **The closer you seem to be getting, the more threatening you can seem to the child and the more he will find ways of pushing you away** – whether it is by biting, kicking, not washing, refusing to eat your food or follow your rules, hurling abuse at you, or running away – whilst all the time what he ***really*** needs is to feel safe enough to let you into his life of isolation.

Whilst you are living together it is very likely that the urge to push you away will feel stronger than the urge to get close. Keep reminding yourselves that this strategy kept your child alive in the past – and he believes it is still the only way to live. **Amazing as it may seem, the innate drive for closeness is still there too, although it may not be activated until you are apart.** Then additional major obstacles for getting in touch can be anger, pride, a continuing sense of rejection, poor communications and firmly closed doors. This is why it is absolutely essential that, however bad it feels, you need to try to part on good terms, to keep in touch and to leave your family doors open and welcoming (within reason, see below). Moreover, substitute carers, residential workers, social workers and therapists *must* play their part in encouraging the young person to maintain links with your family and to give the message that she is still your child – both legally and socio-emotionally.

What You May See (The 'Presenting Problem')

A child who *hurts* may *hurt* everybody, including themselves, to try to avoid getting *hurt*! A younger child may steadfastly refuse to let you into her life and seem to prefer anyone else's company to yours. She may reject your food, destroy your precious possessions, ***hurt*** your other children and try to destroy all semblance of family life. Yet despite her apparent indifference to, or abhorrence of, you she cannot let you go – try arranging a visit from friends, or an evening out, and you will face an escalation of 'bad' behaviour, in an attempt to sabotage your plans. Baby-sitters need to be 'industrial strength', to cope with the tantrums and mayhem thrown at them and you may soon run out of suitable, co-optable adults! It then becomes very tempting to give up on having a social life altogether. Your youngster may also refuse to go to friends' houses to stay, even for a few hours, or to take part in the sort of trips or organised holidays which most children love.

Adolescents may begin to use their greater physical weight to intimidate you, and use their growing freedoms to distance themselves from you in a growing variety of ways – through both their actions and their words. Then, just occasionally, you may see a glimmer of ***real*** childlike neediness, which can be enough to keep you struggling to reach your youngster – until the next time! This takes its toll. You may begin to dread getting up in the mornings: your home and your life no longer seem your own. Your health is beginning to suffer. You feel like a human punchbag – emotionally and physically – and you are rapidly losing what remains of your ***self-esteem***. You may find yourself wondering why you adopted in the first place – whether your child would have done better in another family, or even whether there is any way out of this intolerable situation. **It seems that your youngster cannot live with you but you are painfully aware of how ill-equipped they are to live without you.**

Beyond the Looking Glass (or What May Lie Beneath)

- Children without a ***secure base*** may appear less needy, more independent, more precocious and more mature than their peers but, as you know, appearances can be very deceptive. To survive successfully in an unsafe world your child had to convince herself that she did not need anyone except herself. She has seen and felt the dangers of trying to get close to people and is determined that she will never expose herself to those dangers again.

- Sadly, as you know, this view of the world does not change when a child is placed in a safe family – in fact this can seem even *more* dangerous, because it doesn't feel like 'home'; that is, what she is used to. The child does everything she can to make the outside world fit her inner world, to ***distort*** the new ***reality*** to fit the old ***looking glass distortions***. You need to be able to recognise these ***distortions*** if you are to make enough sense of the child's world to bring her fully into yours – and all the time those two opposing forces are fighting within her for supremacy.

- Nature gave your child the drive to search for intimacy; nurture has bequeathed her a legacy of striving to remain apart. This can lead to quite mercurial changes in your youngster's behaviour – from toddler to teenager, from helplessness to control, from love to hate and back again in seconds! *I Hate You, Don't Leave Me*, the title of a popular paperback on adult borderline disorders (see the Reading List), may accurately sum up your youngster's conflicting and confusing feelings.

- In many children, however, resisting closeness *appears* to outweigh the need for intimacy. Almost all of a youngster's behaviours can appear to be based on anger and hate; it can be hard to believe that your child needs anything from you, that you have ever been, or will ever succeed in being, *part* of his life. **Remember that if YOU are feeling confused or scared or overwhelmed by living alongside such feelings, how much more confusing, scary and overwhelmed must your child be feeling, deep down inside?**

- A child who feels unloved and rejected re-creates a world empty of love and filled with rejection. **It is often not until he has left your family that he can begin to recognise what he had, and what he has now lost.** This can also provide you with new opportunities to relate to your youngster in healthier, more comfortable ways.

- A child who has experienced the total vulnerability of loss, neglect or abuse may create for himself an alternative image of himself as indestructible and capable of anything (see Superkid/Scared kid on pages 46–50). **He has to believe that he can take care of himself better than anyone else.** Even though you may see an immature, irresponsible and easily led youngster, he may well perceive himself as *perfectly* competent – and may not be able to be *realistic* about the dangers in which he places himself.

- Since an adoptee's life has been predicated on change, the youngster may feel that to move on again is just another step in her life – and she may be dazzled by the mirage of greener grass elsewhere. She may even return herself into 'care' in a misguided attempt to find the missing pieces in her life, or to gain illusory freedoms.

- Some adopted children cling to the fantasy of being reunited with members of their birth family – if only this could happen they believe they will 'all live happily ever after'. This can *really* get in the way of the child allowing themselves to become part of their adoptive family and making good connections with you.

- Even where this does not seem to be the case, the adoptee may feel innately different from her adoptive family and wish to separate herself physically from it as soon as possible, to try to locate her '*real*' place in the world. Again, it may take a period of painful separation before she realises that you are the closest thing she has to a *real* family and that she belongs with you.

First Choices

A number of strategies for getting close to young children are discussed in *First Steps*. Many of these are amenable to adaptation, to make them more appropriate for growing youngsters and young adults. **The basic glue** *of attachment* **is an essential component of healthy relationships** and initially demands that you be there *consistently* for your child – until he 'gets the hang' of the fact that you will always be there, as *part* of himself, even when you are separated. (If you are having your own difficulties 'getting your head round' the idea of each having several *'parts'*, this is a great place to start – think how things your mother said or did when you were small can still pop into your mind and affect the way you behave even now!)

However, being there consistently for a child does not mean having to be there constantly. In many animal species, parents have to forage for food over extended periods, leaving their offspring alone or with 'relatives'. It is also a common sight to see very young animals *following* their mothers around for safety, rather than the mothers following their young ones: this is *adaptive* behaviour. Although comparison with other species can only go so far, it can help us to identify a pattern of increasing self-reliance over time and to see that **closeness in relationships has to flow both ways** – a dance of *attunement* and *attachment*.

How much time you and your child spend together or apart depends on many factors. It often involves you walking a delicate line between giving your youngster opportunities to try out new things, whilst simultaneously continuing to consolidate her weak sense of belonging. **Bowlby's two elements of** *attachment*, **the creation of a** *secure* **base and the encouragement of exploration, are frequently less clear-cut for children who** *hurt*, **so that expectations based on 'normal' chronology may be of little help to you.**

You may need to rely increasingly upon your gut-feeling about what your child needs – and what YOU may need to retain your sanity! If you feel the need for a short break, don't discount the idea – just look at ways of easing the separation and bear in mind that if your child *does* become upset when he is away from you, he will be pleased to see you when you do meet up again! **For some children this could be the first time they have shown any commitment to the relationship and it can be a unique opportunity for getting closer.**

There is some evidence for a *psycho-biological* basis to *reunion*. According to Allan Schore (see the Reading List) **a baby reunited with her mother after a temporary separation re-experiences the 'joy state' of** *attachment*, **through the release of** *endorphins*. This can be *triggered* by the approach of the mother's smiling face. The heightened discomfort of separation may have to be experienced in order for this experience of elation to occur – for both mother and child.

Certainly, from what we know of the addictive properties of these morphine-related compounds, the desire to repeat such an experience is likely to increase. This would in itself be *adaptive*, since it ensures that mother and youngster actively seek each other out, after being apart. **Hence reunion after these brief separations appears to enhance the *attachment* process;** in fact, some experience of separation may be an essential part of a healthy *psycho-social developmental* process.

Another way of looking at separation is to understand that only by *not* being with the ***primary caregiver*** all the time can the infant explore her own uniqueness and find out where you end and she begins. This is an essential developmental step towards greater ***self-awareness*** and eventual independence. For an older child who *hurts*, you might better reframe separations as fresh opportunities to find out where you both begin!

With a child who is genuinely anxious about separations, you can find all sorts of little ways of keeping in touch whilst you are apart. This could be the natural place for *transitional objects* – those teddies, blankies, plastic dinosaurs or whatever, which small children clutch to their chests when going to bed, or staying with granny for tea. An older child may not have an identifiable *transitional object* – but this could be a creative opportunity for both of you! Something personal of yours (though don't risk anything valuable) could be just the thing – and may prevent your child from having to 'borrow' something without asking.

Begin by making sure that your youngster understands where he is going, with whom and for how long. Try marking the hours or days on a calendar and let him keep them for reference. Even some older children may not yet have grasped the concept of time and may need additional, concrete help to make sense of 'a weekend', for example.

Your child may want to know exactly where you will be for every minute of the time apart – don't worry if you can't be that definitive, just let him know you'll be thinking of him and will be there when he needs to come home. Remember that once he is away, and 'gets carried away' by the novelty and fun of being away, he is less likely to be worried. A reassuring telephone call in the evening, when a child's anxieties may rise again, could be extremely useful here.

Try writing little messages to your child and popping them in all sorts of strange places for him to find during the time he is away. 'I love you' or 'I'm thinking of you' can reach even the 'toughest' heart – especially if the child has actually begun to miss you! Adding a chocolate heart or two can help too!

Consider buying your youngster a 'phone home' card and encouraging him to use it. Have a word with relatives, or the staff or leaders who will be caring for your youngster, and make sure they understand that it is important for your child to call you – even if it is usually discouraged, in the latter case, for most children. Parents *really* do know best on this one.

Some parents have even been known to include photographs of themselves in the packing – just to remind their child who they are and what they look like! **If they haven't got a good picture of you inside their heads, at least they can have one on the outside.** Remember that if you can see the warm and funny side of this, the likelihood is that your child will too.

Drop a postcard or note into the letter box the minute your youngster leaves the house – so that she receives it the following morning. All you need to say is: 'Hi! Thinking of you, see you on … Love …' **It is not what you say, it's the fact that you've reached out and said it that counts.**

Once you've paved the way with short periods apart, probably with friends or relatives locally, you can begin to take advantage of any 'natural' breaks which school trips, Cub camps, play schemes, PGL-type holidays and the like, can offer. Yes, you may feel concerned about your youngster's behaviour but don't let that put you off giving it a try. Unless your child actively refuses to go, or the organisation is unhappy about taking him, don't feel that 'it isn't fair to send him'. As Sheila Fearnley, director of Keys Attachment Centre, has reminded us, **the 'coming back' – both the message and in practice – is VITAL to your becoming, and remaining, a family.**

If Things Still Don't Change …

I am sure that you would not willingly put yourself in the position of having to decide that you and your child cannot go on being together on a permanent basis. It is likely that you have tried and tried to make changes within your family which would allow you to go on parenting your youngster 'in the usual way'. Only when you feel that all other options have been exhausted can you begin to acknowledge that you may have little choice left but to begin to live apart – at least for brief periods, or in the shorter term. You may then feel you must say something to your child along the lines of: 'I will always love you but there may be times when I cannot live with you.'

In an ideal world you and your child will have had the opportunity to practise separations in managed ways and to grow comfortable with the idea of being apart, yet staying together. In an ideal world you will also have had the opportunity to explore your choices for therapy and support for children who have continued to struggle with these issues. (Practical support could well include the use of short-break respite facilities on either an informal or a formal basis (see below).) **However, the *reality* is that most of us don't live in an ideal world** and that you may have had to struggle in isolation for much too long.

INFORMAL ARRANGEMENTS

Ironically, the informal breaks with relatives or friends which most families use are much less feasible, if not impracticable, with children who *hurt*. You know from experience that they are more than likely to end in tears – usually yours and not the child's! You would also like to stay on good terms with your family and friends, so it is tempting to stop asking for their help – which leaves you with even less time for yourself at the very time when you need it most!

It is sometimes possible to link up with other adoptive parents informally and to provide each other with support – who better to look after your stroppy teenager than a parent who knows what it is all about and sees things the way you see them? This could take the form of an exchange deal – 'You have mine this weekend and I'll have yours next' – or it could be something that an adoptive parent whose young adults have left home is able to offer, because she has more time and because she remembers how desperate she once was.

Don't spend too much time worrying about what your child is up to during the breaks you are able to arrange. Remember that most of the time, especially with people she does not know well, your youngster's behaviour will be much better. Moreover, with informed supporters you won't be greeted with comments like 'she was no trouble for me', which can make you feel so demoralised. Instead, you can allow yourself to relax, relieved that you have had some time to find out that you are quite a nice person, whilst your teen has also had some time finding out that she can be quite nice too, sometimes. It's all good practice!

Difficulties around living together, under the same roof, frequently escalate as a youngster moves through adolescence and, of course, once she turns sixteen the legal position can differ markedly. It may become even less possible to access residential or respite arrangements and yet your young adult may be pushing very hard for a 'final separation'. Sometimes it is still possible to find creative alternatives to the formal provision of accommodation, once your adolescent has turned sixteen.

Some parents have used an old caravan in the back garden to provide a separate space for their young adult. With access to water and electricity he can live a semi-independent existence and **yet still feel part of the family.** You can *choose* to set a 'reasonable' rent for the pitch (to give practice in managing money in the *real* world) and make up your own mind about how much access to the house and its facilities you will encourage. That way your young person can feel freer to 'do his own thing' in terms of cleanliness, night hours and so on and you can feel freed from some of the more 'in your face' behaviours you have had to put up with.

Almost all young people leave home eventually. Often this is linked to going to college or university, getting a job or setting up house with a partner and eventually starting a family. (An occasional paper on issues relating to teenage pregnancy and adoptive grandparenthood is planned to follow in 2000. Please contact Adoption UK for more details.) **However, the more socially acceptable moves towards independence often do not come easily (or only too easily but in the 'wrong' way, see below) to young adults who** *hurt.* Sometimes it *is* possible to find meaningful alternatives, such as Community Service Volunteers, where accommodation, personal support and some income are provided, even for young people with few qualifications and fewer positive experiences.

Where this, or other opportunities, are not feasible you may need to take the initiative in encouraging your youngster to take that vital developmental step into the wider world beyond your family. The message you need to be giving here is one of helping him to make a positive move forward, not of pushing him out or rejecting him (even if you have had more than enough of his anti-social behaviour already). Once the initial step towards independent living has been made, with your support and encouragement, you can then hand over much of the responsibility to the independent liver!

You might consider helping your young person find accommodation for himself and even contributing directly to the first month's rent, as long as you are clear as to the limit of your financial commitment. **Being prepared to subsidise a young adult, in the longer term, may undermine his ability to manage his own finances and discourage him from taking appropriate responsibility.** In the meantime, you can provide as many hot meals, food parcels, hot baths and laundry facilities as you wish, for as long as *you* wish. The rest is up to him!

If his subsequent non-payment of rent means that the young person loses his accommodation, you can be truly sympathetic. Give him the message that you know he can, and that you expect him to, work out how to handle it himself. (See pages on being DOUBLY ASSERTIVE on pages 174–177.) Sleeping on other people's floors, squatting (or even sleeping rough) are not usually life-threatening conditions. On the contrary they can provide excellent lessons in coping with *real* life, especially for youngsters who tend to spend most of their lives in a fantasy world.

FORMAL ARRANGEMENTS

Sadly for most of us formal respite facilities are not readily available and may only be accessible if you can demonstrate that things are *really* desperate – by which time you may be even more over-stretched and exhausted, and less able to find the *resilience* you need to carry on. It is tempting to feel you should be doing this difficult job of parenting better, and doing it alone – especially if you receive criticism or rebuffs from child care agencies, who are often seriously under-resourced and may have other service priorities. **However, you do deserve a break, so please do not give up.** Bear in mind that if you don't go on asking for help with respite, agencies may *never* realise that there *is* a demand for such facilities or begin to adjust their budgets accordingly.

If you do strike it lucky and receive an offer of respite, do not be deterred by the formality of the official process. Agencies are now using Looked After Children (LAC) forms, which can seem quite inappropriate for respite situations; fill in only what you feel comfortable with! **It is also important that you aren't so overcome with gratitude that you take anything that is offered – even if it doesn't 'feel right'.** Your child will not benefit from being looked after by inexperienced respite carers who allow themselves to be manipulated or who unwittingly undermine your position as parents. Perhaps your local authority would like to set up a training programme for carers using material from Adoption UK's 'It's a Piece of Cake?' – which would benefit all user families and not just yours.

Sometimes your home situation can become so unbearable that you ask for your child to be looked after, or **accommodated**, under the Children Act of 1989. These terms have superseded the use of in care – which was frequently a **real** misnomer, as recent court cases have shown. In other cases, particularly with older children, the request may come from the youngster herself, through her actions or her words. Either way you will have to face the formal bureaucracy of the social services (or social work) department and will be requested to support your child financially after an assessment by the department.

Some parents have argued that if they had been given all the relevant information about their child at placement, or had received the help their family needed sooner, they would not be in such an intolerable position now. They have been successful in resisting pressure to make such payments, which can often feel like penalising parents for their original, altruistic motives in taking on a child who **hurts**.

Reactions from social work staff and substitute carers (in the main, foster parents) can also be difficult to handle. These can be judgemental and over-simplistic and can seriously undermine your continuing position as a parent. Sometimes it seems that this is especially the case where the child is adopted. Whatever the circumstances, **it is important not to over-react when you are feeling at your most vulnerable, since you may then come across as volatile or vindictive,** which will certainly be counter-productive!

From experience, some parents have worked out that they can handle meetings with social workers more easily on neutral ground, or in the agency offices. At home they feel bound by convention to be polite and to act reasonably; elsewhere they can speak more freely and end the interview as and when they choose.

It is often difficult to speak openly about your child who **hurts**, when they are present at meetings with agency workers or substitute carers. Often you do not want to say negative things about the youngster in her hearing. You may also wish to discuss strategies for working collaboratively with other professionals, to prevent her playing you off against each other. In such circumstances, **consider requesting further meetings where you have more time to speak openly without your youngster being present.** For further information, contact Adoption UK, or try networking amongst the parents on the After Adoption Network. Local After Adoption co-ordinators are listed at the back of the Adoption UK journal *Adoption Today* and will be glad to talk to you, or put you in touch with someone who has been in a similar situation.

Some adoptive parents have found that boarding school facilities can provide a buffer between themselves and their difficult youngsters, whilst keeping family connections intact. It may be possible to obtain a statement of Special Educational Needs for your child, which specifies that her needs should be met through residential provision, although current budget restrictions and weak inter-agency collaboration are making this option less viable.

You may find that you have to argue a very strong case to convince the powers that be on this one – and do your own homework on which residential schools and communities, in and out of county, can best meet your youngster's emotional and educational needs. **Some establishments are better at including parents in decision making and maintaining school–home, child–family links than others. Check out, too, the staff's approach to discipline: that they can provide safe, enforceable boundaries, as well as creating a nurturing environment.** It could also be that a residential placement 'out in the wilds' would help a wayward teenager stay safe, where an urban establishment would not.

There are a very limited number of places in secure accommodation throughout the UK, for young people who have committed serious crimes, or who are deemed outwith parental control (Scotland), or in need of care and control. These are very costly units to run and local authorities may be more reluctant still to fund such a placement, even if it seems the most appropriate, than to pay for other residential accommodation. **Some young offenders may end up on remand or in prisons, where they are at far greater risk, simply because of an agency's financial constraints.**

It can feel, by this stage, that you have very little say in where your youngster lives and you may be feeling that you have let him down badly. **Please keep in mind that you have probably spent years trying to keep him on the right track and, if he has strayed off course, it is not for want of effort on your part.** Sadly, he may need the appalling experience of being detained 'at Her Majesty's Pleasure' to face up to his own actions. You don't have to condone what he has done, accept the blame for it or to go on protecting him from the hard lessons of life: *as long as you remain there for him*, he has the choice to 'come home' again.

Visiting a child who is living away from home, in local authority accommodation, in a residential community or school, in a mental health unit or in a young offenders' institution, can be very painful for many parents. You may feel that enormous walls have been erected between you and your, once small, child – often the child feels she has to erect them to save herself from further *hurt* too.

Foster parents, residential and clinical staff may reinforce these barriers unnecessarily – through misguided efforts to 'protect the child' or because of their understandably stereotypical perceptions of parents as abusive or rejecting. It becomes so hard to remain loving and to maintain your self-esteem when all around you there are messages that you have 'failed' or that you are no longer needed, no longer a valid part of your youngster's life. **Remind yourself, when it comes to the crunch and the system begins to fail her, that you are the only one who will still be there. That makes you essential and indispensable, on your own terms, not only in the future but now.**

Your responsibilities and rights relating to your youngster also change with age. These are particularly important to get to grips with in the case of medical or clinical treatment for a young person where the doctor may take the view that a child or young person is sufficiently mature to give an informed consent in their own right. Whilst as a parent you will inevitably be concerned for your child's well-being and will wish to be involved in her treatment plan, remember that once she is eighteen years of age, she is legally an adult and entitled to treatment confidentiality. Ultimately it will always be her choice which treatment she accepts or rejects. It is always advisable to seek legal advice on rights and responsibilities in relation to parents and young people. Family Rights Group and the Children's Legal Centre are good sources of accurate advice. Contact Adoption UK on 01327 260295.

However, like every other 'next of kin', you are part of the young person's life and should be provided with adequate information and be included in decision-making processes, IF YOU SO WISH. (The recent Inquiry chaired by William Armstrong specifically highlighted the need for the involvement of relatives and carers in mental health decision making.) Since care in the community is likely to be perceived as you, your partnership at all stages of any treatment programme would seem to be indispensable – although it is also vital that your personal boundaries are accepted and respected.

You may feel that expecting a young adult to return home to you at this time is unlikely to work well. It is far easier to remain on good 'speaking' terms with some space between you, when your *expectations* of each other can move on from those of 'needy child' and 'responsible (or punitive) adult', which may haunt your mutual past.

Remind yourself that a crisis, according to Chinese characters, **represents both danger and opportunity.** This critical time in the young person's life may require you all to take more risks and chances – especially if the young person is to take increasing responsibility for herself. **Becoming responsible is, literally, becoming more able to respond,** both in facing up to one's feelings and learning to get one's needs met appropriately. Therefore it is essential that you allow your young adult the time and space to develop these skills for herself.

Visiting a child (even a young adult one) in prison can be particularly hard, not least because of the body searches, the locked doors, the institutionalised atmosphere and the degradation which is integral to such places. **You may decide that you 'don't do prisons', or any other type of secure establishment for that matter, and that's fine – as long as you can find other ways of *really* keeping in touch.**

Think of it like this: if your young adult elected to take a trip round the world, you wouldn't beat yourself up if you couldn't fly out and visit him – although you would avidly await postcards, reverse charge calls or poste restante addresses. So why should you feel duty-bound to visit a young person in less salubrious surroundings, just because he has chosen to do something less socially acceptable and is experiencing the consequences? In both cases you may only be able to hope that he will come home (in the broadest sense) one day – **meanwhile you can get on with your life and know that you'll be ready and waiting for the prodigal's return.**

Wherever your young person is living, try to keep the connections going. Even if he has told you he never wishes to see you again and is three hundred miles away, you can still send 'thinking of you' cards (see above), or small parcels of inexpensive goodies, which might reach his heart through his mouth!

Picture postcards of places you both know well, with just a few poignant words of reminder about the better times, can also be very touching. **If you go over the top on how much you are missing him, your young person is likely to be turned off.** He may not be into long letters any more than he was into long lectures about behaviour at home – so spare yourself the pain and the effort.

Of course, your young person may well not appear to acknowledge your existence, let alone your notes. However, that does *not* mean that you are wasting your time, although it can make it much harder to keep up the very one-sided contact. Providing writing paper, envelopes and stamps (in kind rather than in cash, which is so easily used for more 'essential' requirements) may help your young person stay in touch.

Some parents have been known to go further and send their youngsters stamped self-addressed cards with pre-prepared replies, such as: 'I am/am not having a good time (please delete as appropriate).' Light-hearted humour often reaches *parts* that more intense approaches cannot (in our child and in ourselves). This way you can get across your message that you would like a reply, are interested in your child, know that he finds letter writing a bore and that you are *not* going to fall apart if you get nothing back.

And finally, remember that almost all our children do eventually come home. It may be after years, they may have gone through many extremely distressing experiences, but at some point they realise where they belong and join us once more. **Be there – but don't hold your breath, or put your life 'on hold' in the meantime. What you do beyond that is up to you!**

And Finally – Letting Go ...

Many adoptive parents go through times of believing their child might have been better off being placed with someone else, or left with their birth family. However, the *reality* is that they are with you – and you are now their family for life! **It is not only essential that you are allowed to 'claim' your child as your own, so that she can feel close and that she truly belongs, it is**

**equally vital that you are allowed to begin to let go, at times which are appropriate to
you.**

Sometimes the physical and emotional distance between parent and child can become too intense
for comfort, either through a youngster's over-dependence, his rejecting behaviour or his repeated
challenges to your self-esteem. Clearly this is not a healthy situation for either of you. Even the
utter dependency of infancy forms part of a *changing*, developmental process; **getting stuck is not
getting on. Hence, letting go can also be part of a developmental process, for all of you.**

Once a young person approaches adulthood and prepares to separate her life from yours, in so
many ways, parents can become freer to be themselves again. Try to use this freedom well – and
not get tied up in continuing to fight unwinnable battles. For example, if your young person is
accommodated and is repeatedly absconding, or has been excluded from school, is it still *your*
problem? Is there anything that you can **realistically** do to change the current situation, or are you
more likely to get hooked back into the old, uncomfortable ways of relating?

If you expend all your available energy on trying to change something you cannot **really**
change, you may have little energy left for yourself, or for trying to rebuild your relationship with
your youngster in newer, more positive ways. Sometimes you can only truly see a problem if you
stand back from it. Similarly, it may only be from standing back from a problematic relationship
that you stand a chance of doing something about it.

This might mean, that for a period of time, you set some limits on your contact with each other.
It might be that you don't see each other face to face at all but communicate by letter or by talking
on the telephone. This not only keeps you from being 'in each other's faces', it may allow you to
get closer in different ways. Often you can say things more easily on paper. You may also find that a
youngster's defences are down and that they are more relaxed when they use the telephone.

The idea of putting some distance between you can also work well if you begin to think of your
son or daughter along the lines of a slightly more distant relative. You wouldn't usually give a long
lost cousin weekly handouts if they were abusive, spend your life worrying about what they were
doing, or repeatedly bailing them out of trouble. Remind yourself that **freeing yourself from the
constrictions of an uncomfortable relationship is also freeing for your child.**

Again, once a young person has moved away from home, you all have the opportunity to do
things differently – and I guess if you had both been 'getting it right' more often than not, then
you wouldn't be in this position now. Although the family home will always be your child's home,
it may not always be the place where she lives. So too, **though there will always be a place for
her in your heart, you may wish to set some limits on when she comes back, how often
and on what terms.**

If the parent–child relationship has been a tricky one, then you can choose, actively, to set your
relationship on an alternative footing. You would expect a guest in your home to behave quite
differently from a permanent resident – and, technically, this is the young adult's position now. You
could point this out to her and talk about some of the advantages and the differences.

These could include expecting a guest to knock before they come into your house, to ask before they help themselves to food from the kitchen and to offer some help with the washing up. You in turn would expect to treat a guest with a greater degree of deference, to make time to talk to them and, perhaps, to cook a special meal.

You may, rightly, be anxious about recurrent angry and violent scenes, or of your possessions going missing, or being damaged. In such circumstances you need to take care of yourself first. Protecting yourself may mean that you change all the locks on the house, so that a young person comes in only at your invitation. You might also consider having a friend there with you, to help you reach some measure of agreement on important issues. You are both likely to feel more relaxed, and the young person to behave more reasonably, in the presence of someone else.

Alternatively, you might choose to meet the young adult on neutral ground. A cup of coffee or lunch at your local restaurant can be pleasant, as you are both more likely to observe the rules of etiquette in public. Neither of you need to feel threatened by the intensity or intimacy associated with home and you are able to leave more easily, should the going get tough.

If you receive a frantic call from your young person, asking for help with a problem and insisting they need to see you immediately, consider suggesting that you meet later, rather than right away. This can give her time to work out the difficulty for herself and can save you being 'dumped on' yet again. **That way, you help her to feel better about herself and preserve what remains of your rather sticky relationship.**

The secret is to be able to live separate lives, yet to remain connected. Since your eventual aim is always to establish a healthier relationship with your son or daughter, finding better ways of getting along has a major part to play. It can only work against both of you, in the long run, if you allow your youngster to continue to treat you disrespectfully, under the misconception that setting these sorts of limits is unfair, or you let yourself feel used, and then start to react out of frustration. In particular, the young person needs more practice in accepting reasonable limits and in taking responsibility for himself – which doing it 'the old way' may not have provided. **Letting go, and changing the way you get on, can let you all get on with your lives.**

However much you are able to let go, 'losing a child' can be an intensely painful experience. In the past, Adoption UK has run 'healing weekends' for adopters whose children have left home under difficult circumstances. Parents who have attended have gained a good deal from sharing their *hurts* with others and from having access to skilled facilitators and counsellors. For more information about forthcoming 'healing' workshops, contact Adoption UK on 01327 260295.

I wish you well on your continuing journey with your child.

Caroline Archer, January 1999

Glossary

A

abandoned

Children who are 'given up' for adoption may experience this as being abandoned. Similarly, extended or repeated periods of being left in infancy are perceived as abandonment. This comes to form part of the child's internal working model.

accommodated

'Looked after', 'taken into care'.

AD – Attachment Disorder

Both ICD 10 and DSM IV carry descriptions of Reactive Attachment Disorders, with onset before five years of age due to gross maltreatment. Many children who have been fostered or adopted have developed distressed or distorted patterns of attachment, as a result of their early traumatic experiences, which continue to influence their current social and emotional relationships.

ADD/ADHD – Attention Deficit Disorder/Attention Deficit Hyperactivity Disorder

These are common medical terms for a cluster of symptoms/behaviours including impulsivity, poor attention, and usually hyperactivity. Emphasis in diagnosis is given to pervasive symptoms (of at least six months' duration). ADD/ADHD diagnoses are required to exclude both disorders due to developmental delay and disorders of traumatic aetiology (e.g. dissociative disorders).

adaptive

Facilitating survival, on an evolutionary or personal level.

adrenalin

A neurotransmitter. Its release is associated with the response to perceived threat. It raises respiration, heart rate, and reduces digestive processes. Primes for action.

arousal

The body and mind's responses to everything which goes on inside and out. Vital within normal 'comfort' limits. Unhelpful when there is too little or too much.

associated

Connected, integrated on many levels.

associations

The establishment of connections between senses, behaviours, feelings, awareness, memory processes and areas of the brain and nervous systems.

attachment

A persisting relationship between two individuals. For a child the attachment relationship initially involves complete dependency and facilitates survival at the biological level.

autonomic nervous system

The part of the nervous system responsible for involuntary responses. Made up of the sympathetic system, responding to stress and preparing the body for action, and the parasympathetic system, involved with rest, relaxation and stimulating digestion. Includes a network of glands and hormones mediating experience and behaviour.

avoiding/ant

Tending to evade close contact, relationships. Stems from early, hurtful experiences which generate model of intimacy as dangerous.

B

bio-chemistry

Functions and interactions of the chemistry of the body.

body rhythm

Your natural body patterns, including diurnal (waking/sleeping).

body-work therapist/body-worker

Some therapists work on the body and its sensations to get in touch with, and release, feelings and 'body memories' which may be causing physical distress.

boundaries

Personal limits by which an individual can define herself, experience herself as separate from others and having personal agency.

brain stem

Developmentally the 'oldest' part of the brain, which regulates our breathing and heart rates (and basically defines whether we are alive or not).

C

CD – Conduct Disorder

This (descriptive) diagnosis is frequently given to children and adolescents who demonstrate serious aggressive, violent, criminal or destructive behaviours (often alongside ADD). It does not refer to aetiology of the individual's difficulties but current literature tends to make significant links with experiences of dysfunctional parenting.

child, inner

Psychological representation of the persisting inner feeling states which can influence current beliefs, thinking and behaviours (Parks, P).

child, inside

See above. Often used in the field of dissociative disorders, e.g. by Colin Ross. May appear subjectively to an individual as being a totally separate self. Behaviour may reflect this 'as if' quality.

cognitive

Conscious thinking processes, correlated with (cerebral) cortical functions of brain.

compliant

Tending to please others. Can be problematic to excess, since it involves placing others before oneself.

containment

The provision of security, either emotional or physical, usually by an attachment figure.

core self

The innermost essence of self which remains untainted and undamaged by even the worst abuses, although it may remain silent and hidden.

critical periods

These are periods of maximum growth and development, when the greatest interruption to development may occur from minimal adversity.

D

dance of anger

The tendency for one partner to respond with anger to anger from the other partner.

DD – Dissociative Disorders

Dissociated sensations, feelings, thoughts and behaviours in childhood are included in diagnoses such as PTSD, Dissociative Identity Disorder (DID, formerly Multiple Personality Disorder) and Dissociative Disorder Not Otherwise Specified (DDNOS). Dissociative processes may also occur in other disorders e.g. CD, ODD, anxiety and eating disorders (and as part of personality disorders in adulthood).

development

The process of moving from the total dependence of a new-born towards the (relative) independence of adulthood. It implies growth and change at physical, emotional, psychological, intellectual and spiritual levels.

developmental

The on-going maturational process through which every child moves, albeit at a unique pace and in her own way. 'Normal' developmental progress implies functioning abilities matching chronological abilities.

developmental delay

Any slowing down or interference with normal developmental processes.

dissociate

To fail to connect (to associate), or to disconnect from, one's thoughts, feelings, actions, memories or part of one's self (usually temporary).

dissociated

Lacking or losing connection or meaning. Out of touch with some element of normal awareness.

dissociation

Loss of connections between senses, feelings, knowledge, behaviours, memories or neurological processes, leading to a weakened ability to make sense of self or others or to learn from new experience.

dissociative response

An adaptive, protective response to being overwhelmed by number, or content of, incoming stimuli. Becomes maladaptive if used excessively or when environment alters for the better.

distorted

Skewed, 'out of true', e.g. as in 'distorted perceptions'.

distortions

Alterations from the norm or reality due to early traumatic experience.

distress

Literally dis-stress, unhealthy or uncomfortable levels of stress.

diurnal rhythm

Rhythm of day and night/wakefulness and rest.

dysfunctional

Poorly functioning, unhealthy.

dyspraxia

Often described as 'clumsiness', it is a difficulty of co-ordination, involving the planning, and carrying out, of movement tasks, both small and large.

dysregulation

Lack of, or weak, regulation of basic body processes, e.g. respiration, body temperature, heart rate.

E

EBD – Emotional and Behavioural Difficulties

Tends to be a 'catch-all' term used mainly in an educational context to describe children whose social and emotional behaviour is 'challenging' in the school setting.

empathy

Sharing/getting in tune with another's feelings, thoughts, needs.

endorphins

These are morphine-like substances occurring naturally within the body, for relief of pain or distress.

explicit (memory)

Verbal or narrative memory processes, which are usually able to be recounted. Mainly a function of the left side of the brain.

expressive therapy

As opposed to psychoanalytical or 'talk' therapies, these therapies encourage expression in many dimensions such as art, music and drama. They may therefore access thoughts, feelings and memories not readily available to the child.

F

feeling states

These are compartmentalised ways of feeling which are embedded in an individual's experience.

fight, flight or freeze

Primitive survival mechanism in event of perceived threat – either to stand ground and defend, run away or become immobilised.

flashbacks

These are intense, anxiety-producing images from the past which intrude without warning into present awareness. Can be visual, auditory, olfactory or body-based.

functional

Offering some kind of advantage to survival.

G

good enough

A parent does not have to (cannot) be perfect. As long as we 'get it right' enough, the child will thrive.

gratification

The experience of pleasure, relief, satisfaction, comfort.

H

hold/ing

Containing, providing security and comfort for a baby or small child – can be physical or emotional.

holding for nurture

Elective holding time to provide safe containment and enhanced opportunities for closeness and communication.

holding therapy

An expressive therapy which employs physical holding by a trained psychotherapist to facilitate effective healing.

holding time

First used by Martha Welch, to describe time deliberately and regularly set aside, for the child with the parent. It involves physically holding the child in close, face to face, and allowing free expression of feelings in order to enhance closeness in the relationship.

homoeostasis/static

The maintenance of 'normal' balance or function in our body processes.

hurt

Greg Keck and Regina Kupecky used the term 'hurt' in the title of their book *Adopting the Hurt Child*. It implies the 'wounding' and pain which traumatised children still carry with them from their earliest times. It also, in the context of this book, implies their potential to hurt others as a result of their inner pain.

hurting/ful

See above.

hyperactive

Extremely 'busy', overactive, 'on the go' non-stop.

hyperkinesis

Another word for hyperactivity, especially physical activity.

hypersensitive

Greater sensitivity and responses to experience than 'normally' expected. Often sensitised due to earlier trauma, including in the womb and at birth.

hypervigilant

Intensely watchful, unable to relax vigilance for fear-producing events/stimuli, due to persisting internal arousal.

hyposensitive

Less than 'normally expected' responsivity.

I

implicit (memory)
> Non-verbal or pre-verbal or 'automatic' procedural memory patterns and processes (utilising predominantly the right brain).

impulsivity
> The tendency to react without thinking of the consequences.

inner child
> The concept of the childlike part of self within.

integrated
> Brought into the system and being part of a coherent whole.

internal working model
> The internal 'map' which an individual builds up about the world and about herself from her experiences (Bowlby). Once established it tends to be fairly resistant to alteration, since perceptions are 'selected' to fit what is expected.

K

kindle/ing
> Over-arousal effects of even minor, or positive, experiences (such as having a good time) leading to exaggerated (fear) responses.

L

left brain
> In most people this hemisphere of the brain controls the right side of the body. It is thought to be predominantly logical and language orientated.

limbic system
> An important part of the mid brain (or animal brain) which controls, amongst other things, emotion and motivation.

looking glass
> In context: implies the persisting distortions of reality due to poor early mirroring (see below).

M

mid brain
> Younger than the brain stem in evolutionary terms and responsible for functions such as diurnal and circadian rhythms, emotion, motivation, sexuality and fight, flight and freeze.

mirror/ing
> Responding and reflecting back to the child aspects of her expressions, movements, feelings, thoughts – leading to greater self-awareness.

model
> To demonstrate through example. An infant learns initially through observing and responding to parental modelling and mirroring.

modulation of arousal
> The ability to moderate reactivity to internal and external stimuli within comfortable limits.

mothering figure

This is the single most important person in a very young child's life. In our society it is still usually the mother. Whatever their gender, this is the person who provides the mothering which is essential to an infant's survival and well-being.

N

neural network

The complex linkages, or connections, between cells in the brain and nervous system (neurons), which become established and organised around individual experience.

neural pathway

Neural networks which become selectively reinforced through repeated use. An adaptive process.

neuro-biology

The study of the biological structure and function of the brain and nervous systems.

neuro-hormones

Internal bio-chemical secretions, including neurotransmitters such as adrenalin and serotonin, which enable transmission of information along neural pathways.

neurological connections

These are the links between individual nerve cells and specific areas of the brain and nervous system which need to be laid down and reinforced through repeated use.

neurological organisation

The developmental organising of connections within the nervous systems.

neurological system

This is made up of central nervous system and autonomic nervous system and includes the structures of the brain.

neuro-physiological

Relating to the biology of the brain and nervous systems.

neuro-physiology

The study of the functioning of the brain and nervous systems.

night terrors

Flashback-like intrusions within sleep, producing intense fear even though the individual is not fully awake.

normal

A relative term, which implies a shared, or 'collective', reality.

O

object constancy

The establishment of an internal way of thinking which allows an individual to know something exists when it is not actually visible, tangible, audible etc.

ODD – Oppositional Defiant Disorder

Used predominantly to describe youngsters whose behaviour is 'difficult' and confrontational but which does not reach the anti-social levels of CD. Often diagnosed in conjunction with the ADDs, it makes no reference to aetiology, although received wisdom 'blames the parents'.

oppositional

Used to describe a child who tends to resist conforming to adult wishes and appears to be deliberately disobedient.

oral sensitivity
A specific sensitivity within the mouth or around the lip area.

over-compliance
An exaggerated willingness to please, at the expense of personal needs, the self. Often derives from inner feelings of self-worthlessness or badness.

P

paediatrician
A medical consultant who specialises in the health of children.

part
In the text, used to describe different 'sides' of the self – such as the angry part, sad part, thinking part, little child part. In healthy individuals these are well integrated and balanced. In a child who hurts they may be quite extreme and disconnected. Note that in all cases, the individual is always greater than the sum of these parts.

passive-aggressive
Tendency to act in ways which provoke anger in others whilst appearing impassive oneself.

passive resistant
Behaviour which is not openly defiant but which is, in effect, obstinate or disobedient.

perceptions
The reception and organisation of incoming sensory information.

physical prompts
The reminders given to a child through touch/movement.

physiological
Relating to the biology of the body – how it keeps us alive and responds internally to what is going on around us.

post-traumatic stress reaction
A complex pattern of physiological and psychological/emotional responses to overwhelming or chronic stress.

predisposition
A tendency to particular characteristics or traits, can be carried in the genes.

pre-frontal cortex
Part of the 'higher' (uniquely human) brain associated with, for example, abstract thought.

primal wound
Term introduced by Nancy Verrier to denote the intense, original pain of early separation from the birth mother.

primary caregiver
The child's main source of physical and emotional security, the main attachment figure (mother figure).

proprioception
The awareness of one's physical body, its sensations and movement capabilities.

psychological containment
Winnicott proposed that in order for a young child to develop a sense of security, she needs to experience being emotionally held by the parenting figure. In that way she also learns to manage her own feelings and emotions.

psychological representation

A structure or framework to 'map' internal patterns of belief, thought, behaviour: an internal working model.

psychological trauma

The (long-term) effects on behaviour, feeling and thinking of overwhelming experiences.

psychotherapist

There are many different styles of therapy aimed at getting in touch with our thoughts and feelings. Some (like psychoanalysis) focus predominantly on words. It is now being recognised that non-verbal expressive psychotherapy (and body-work) can play a major role in increasing the well-being and self-knowledge of survivors of trauma (where 'wordless terror' is a common experience).

PTSD – Post-Traumatic Stress Disorder

Once used predominantly for adults with distressing symptoms following a single-incident trauma, this has now been developed to include repeated (chronic) traumatic experiences and to include children and young people. It includes three categories of disturbance: a) intrusive – repetitive thoughts and play, dissociative flashbacks, nightmares, somatic symptoms; b) constriction or numbing – avoidance of painful reminders or thoughts and numbing of feeling; c) persistently raised levels of arousal (and hypersensitivity to minor triggers).

R

RAD

See Attachment Disorder.

real

The term used (in context) to imply differences in perception due to distortions in perception.

realisation

Recognition of what is real.

realistic

Used in the text to highlight differences of perception between different individuals (as below).

reality

Used in the text to denote possible divergence of expectations, perceptions, understanding of the world due to patterning of early experience.

really

Used in the text to emphasise the subjective nature of perceptions.

referent looking

Infants derive a sense of security and a sense of themselves as individuals by regularly 'checking back' at the mother's facial and body expressions. Toddlers also look back at a familiar figure to gain the reassurance and confidence needed to move away and explore the unfamiliar.

reflecting back

Acting as a mirror to another's actions/feelings.

reflections

Feedback from another (initially the mother) which can profoundly influence self-perception.

reframing

Using an alternative way of looking at something, e.g. 'my glass is half-full' is a positive reframing of 'my glass is half-empty'.

regress/ion

Going back to 'earlier' developmental patterns of behaviour.

regulation

The ability to monitor and maintain within comfortable limits, feelings and emotions, and body functions and responses.

reinforce

To make more likely to happen again, accentuate.

resilience

The inner durability and flexibility which allows an individual to adapt and survive.

resilient

Having functional adaptability.

right brain

In most people this hemisphere of the brain controls the left side of the body. It is thought to be predominantly emotion-based, intuitive, and responsive to perceived patterns.

S

safe holding

Elective holding to provide additional nurturing, security, comfort and opportunities for closeness and communication.

SD – Sensory Defensiveness (Sensory integration difficulties)

A diagnosis used mainly by occupational therapists and clinical neuro-psychologists to indicate over- or under-sensitivity to one or more of the five senses. Onset may be traumatic – e.g. due to overwhelming exposure to sensory input in an immature individual.

secure base

Physical and psychological 'place of safety' (see Bowlby).

selective attention

The ability to pick out important, striking or frightening aspects of the surroundings and focus on them to the exclusion of less important stimuli (highly adaptive).

self

who we are, our awareness of self, is derived from the experiences we have. Hence our sense of self may be fluid and responsive to present as well as past happenings. However, early experience seems to carry the most weight and profoundly to influence future perceptions and interpretations.

Some aspects of self definition are listed below. They all contribute to our knowledge of, and acceptance of who we are and how we react, in response to our self (self-reference, our sense of self) and to others:

> self-aware/ness
> self-care
> self-competence
> self-confidence
> self-consciousness
> self-constancy
> self-control
> self-destructive
> self-esteem
> self-expression

self-harm/ing
self-identity
self-possessed
self-regulatory/ion
self-respect
self-soothing
self-stimulation

sense of self

see above; derived in major part from reciprocal and mirroring experiences within the attachment relationship

sensori-affective

The tendency for all early perceptions through every the sense to become linked (in implicit or procedural memory processes) to particular feeling states – whether positive or negative (see state dependent below).

sensori-motor

Perceptions and responses of the senses and/or of movement.

sensory soothing

Calming activities which relax any or all of the senses.

serotonin

This is one of a group of important neurotransmitters. Serotonin tends to 'put a brake on' impulsive behaviour and confer a sense of well-being.

shame

Feeling bad about who we are – as opposed to guilt, feeling bad about what we have done. In small doses it can bring about healthy change, in excess it becomes toxic, affecting our sense of self-respect, self-worth, self-esteem.

shame reaction

The overwhelming physical state which accompanies above. May include flushing, trembling and looking down (gaze avert).

slow-motion response

By moving your body *very* slowly through an action (such as punching an imaginary brick wall) and making the appropriate sounds (under your breath) you can 'burn off' aggressive feelings safely – leaving you calm and de-stressed.

soothing

Calming and comforting from inside or from outside.

state dependent

Denotes learning or recall which is only accessible whilst the body is in a specific state of arousal, or is exposed to certain external stimuli, e.g. smells, sounds.

stimulation

The raising of levels of arousal.

stimuli

The incoming information of every sort which can influence perception and responses on an internal or external level.

switched

This is used to denote a swift change of physical or emotional state.

switched off

> The shutting down of feelings, responses and interactions in an attempt to avoid further fear or pain. A dissociative technique often used by avoidant children.

switching off

> A child who feels threatened or afraid or ashamed may respond by distancing herself psychologically from her surroundings, temporarily, through dissociating. This can become habitual and prevents the child learning about the comfort and security of closeness.

switching out

> See above. Tendency to move awareness away from the current environment, often going 'inside', into another part of self, as a protective response to perceived fear-provoking stimuli.

synchronic attunement

> The harmonising effect seen between parent and infant, which has been shown to enable an infant to alter her body rhythms and internal responses to match the parent's and hence to learn to regulate her own. Hence to 'get in sync with'.

T

time in

> These are brief periods spent together during which quiet reflective communications are encouraged.

time out

> These are short periods of time spent quietly (and usually alone) – they allow time to think/calm down.

transitional object

> This usually takes the form of a concrete representation of the security and comfort of the mothering figure, which is available to the infant at times of brief separation.

trauma

> Literally, a wound. Normally taken to mean an overwhelming experience, which does not allow the individual to return to a 'normal', comfortable state of being. There are demonstrable biological and bio-chemical changes associated with feelings of powerlessness, lack of control, panic or numbing.

traumatic

> This adjective is used to describe experiences and responses to trauma.

trigger

> According to trauma theory, once a pattern of behaviour has come into being, a much smaller stimulus of a similar type may produce the same level of response, over and over again.

U

unreal, unrealistic

> Contextual use: implies distorted 'out of true' perceptions, expectations or responses.

W

withdrawal

> Going into oneself, disconnecting from people/surroundings. Originally protective, can ultimately interfere with ability to relate.

Reading List

Ayres, Jean A. (1994) *Sensory Integration and the Child*. WPS.

Black, Dora; Newman, Martin; Harris-Hendriks, Jean and Mezey, Gillian (1997) *Psychological Trauma*. London: Gaskell.

Bowlby, John (1988) *A Secure Base*. London: Routledge.

Brady, Maureen (1991) *Daybreak*. USA: Hazelden.

Brière, John (1992) *Child Abuse Trauma*. London: Sage London.

Chennells, Prue and Morrison, Marjorie (1995) *Talking about Adoption*. London: British Agencies for Adoption and Fostering.

Delaney, Richard (1991) *Fostering Changes*. Fort Collins: WJC.

Delaney, Richard and Kunstal, Frank (1993) *Troubled Transplants*. Maine: University of Southern Maine.

Fahlberg, Vera (1994) *A Child's Journey though Placement*. London: British Agencies for Adoption and Fostering.

Field, Tiffany and Reite, Martin (1985) *The Psychobiology of Attachment and Separation*. New York: New York Academic Press.

Goleman, Daniel (1996) *Emotional Intelligence*. London: Bloomsbury.

Goulding, Regina and Schwartz, Richard (1995) *The Mosaic Mind*. New York: Norton.

Green, Christopher (1995) *Understanding Attention Deficit Disorder*. London: Vermilion.

van Gulden, Holly and Bartels-Rabb, Lisa (1993) *Real Parents, Real Children*. New York: Crossroad.

Howe, David (1996a) *Adopters on Adoption*. London: British Agencies for Adoption and Fostering.

Howe, David (1996b) *Attachment Theory for Social Work Practice*. London: British Agencies for Adoption and Fostering.

Howe, David (1997) *Patterns of Adoption*. Oxford: Blackwell Science.

James, Beverly (1989) *Treating Traumatized Children*. Lexington, MA: Lexington Books.

James, Beverly (1995) *Handbook for the Treatment of Attachment Trauma Problems in Children*. Lexington, MA: Lexington Books.

Keck, Gregory and Kupecky, Regina (1995) *Adopting the Hurt Child*. Colorado: Pinon Press.

Klein, Josephine (1995) *Our Need for Others*. London: Routledge.

van der Kolk, Bessel; McFarlane, A and Weisaeth, L. (1996) *Traumatic Stress*. New York: Guilford.

Kotulak, Robert (1996) *Inside the Brain*. USA: Andrews McMeel Publishing.

Kreisman, J. and Straus, Hal (1993) *I Hate You – Don't Leave Me: Understanding Borderline Personality.* Somerset: Avon Books.

Krieger, Dolores (1993) *Therapeutic Touch.* Santa Fé, New Mexico: Bear and Co.

Lewis Herman, Judith (1992) *Trauma and Recovery.* London: Pandora.

McIntee, Jeanie (1992) *Trauma: The Psychological Process.* Chester: DTP.

Montagu, Ashley (1986) *Touching – The Human Significance of Skin.* New York: Perennial.

Munroe, Catherine (1993) *The Child Within.* London: Children's Society.

Perry, Bruce (1993) 'Trauma' I and II 'The Advisor', *American Professional Society on the Abuse of Children 6,* 1 and 2, 14–18.

Peterson, Janelle (1994) *The Invisible Road.* (US) DTP.

Pithers, Gray, Cunningham and Lane (1993) *From Trauma to Understanding.* Brandon, VT: Safer Society Press.

Putnam, Frank W. (1997) *Dissociation in Children and Adolescents.* New York: Guilford Press.

Randolph, Elizabeth (1994) *Children Who Shock and Surprise.* Evergreen, Colorado: RFR.

Ross, Colin A. (1997) *Dissociative Identity Disorder.* Chichester: Wiley.

Sach, Penelope (1996) *Take Care of Yourself.* London: Penguin Books.

Santoro, Joseph (1997) *The Angry Heart, Overcoming Borderline and Addictive Disorders.* Oakland, CA: New Harbinger Publications.

Schore, Allan (1994) *Affect Regulation and the Origin of Self.* Hillsdale, NJ: Lawrence Erlbaum.

Sykes, Lenni (1995) *The Natural Hedgehog.* London: Gaia Books Ltd.

Umansky, W. and Steinberg-Smalley, B. (1993) *ADD – Helping Your Child Untie the Knot of Attention Deficit Disorders.* London: Warner Books.

Verny, Tom (1982) *The Secret Life of the Unborn Child.* London: Sphere.

Verrier, Nancy (1994) *The Primal Wound.* Baltimore, MD: Gateway.

Waites, Elizabeth, A. (1993) *Trauma and Survival.* New York: Norton.

Waites, Elizabeth, A. (1997) *Memory Quest.* New York: Norton.

Welch, Martha (1988) *Holding Time.* Hemel Hemstead: Simon and Schuster.

de Zulueta, Felicity (1993) *From Pain to Violence.* London: Whurr.

Hope against Hope

You offered me new hope
Wrapped up in cotton wool,
Tenderly, gently,
As if you really cared;
I threw your loving gift back,
Like sprats into the sea.

You whispered words of hope,
Yet I saw only fear;
Reached out your touching fingers:
I slammed them in the door,
Afraid that opening up one crack
Would break my world apart.

I led you a merry dance;
Goose-stepping to your two-step
Stepping out of line,
Deliberately stepping on your toes:
So uncertain of the real step,
So afraid of losing hope.

Yet you stayed out on the floor;
Feet firmly on the ground,
Keeping your rhythm and your balance
Long after the music stopped;
Hoping that I would still hear it
And join you in your time.

And so our dance goes on;
On times, in tune and time,
I am able to take your hand;
On times, so off the wall,
So lost in past echoes,
That we seem to lose our touch.

Yet slowly I dare to breathe,
Loosening the distortions of doubt,
The harsh frost-bites of fear,
Holding on to the present,
In touch with more of my past:
Your hope becoming my reality.

Caro Archer 1998

Index

abandoned 205
abandonment 123, 140, 170, 188
abuse
  allegations of 139, 151, 183
  lying and stealing 143
  see also emotional abuse; physical abuse; sexual abuse
accommodated 205
acknowledgement
  of feelings 79, 128–9
  self-harming behaviours 174
actions
  accepting responsibility for 33, 65, 146
  focusing on 70–4
active listening 134, 156
activities
  modulation of arousal 82–3
  offering excitement 173
  working through anger 129
adaptive 206
ADD/ADHD *see* attention deficit disorders
addictive behaviours 165–88
adolescence
  challenging issues 22–3
  intimidation by 191
  running away 154
  separation at 153
  sleep problems 122
  stealing 141
adoption 15–23
Adoption UK 7, 16–17
adoptive parents, links with other 196
adrenalin 40, 129, 132, 206
adulthood 202
After Adoption Network 16
aggressive behaviour 92–110, 127–40
alcohol use 144, 161, 177–9
all or nothing thinking 64
allegations, of abuse 139, 151, 183

allowances, sleep problems 127
anger 83, 127–40
anxiety, expressions of 162
arousal 206
  patterns of 34
  sleep problems 123, 124
  thrill seeking 168
  see also modulation of arousal
associated 206
associations
  anger 131, 134–5
  bedwetting 116
  defined 206
  eating disorders 187–8
  impulsivity and risk taking 173
  sleep problems 123, 124
atmosphere, sleep problems 125
attachment
  defined 206
  push-pull experience 33
  and separation 193–4
attachment disorder 205
attention deficit disorders 27–8, 205
autonomic nervous system 132, 206
avoiding/ant 206

baby foods 172
baby-sitters 191
balance, finding right
  introducing change 22
  personal expectations 19
  suicidality 185
balance of power, perception of self 50
battles 67–8, 158
bedtime, distinguished from sleeptime 124
bedwetting 114–22
behaviour swings 80
behavioural patterns 139
behaviours *see* problem behaviours
belonging, sense of 189–90
benign autocracy 58
bio-chemistry 206
biorhythms, inverted daily 155
birth families
  fantasies about 192
  rescue expectations 164

blame 141, 165, 167, 173
boarding school facilities 198–9
body awareness, problem behaviour 116, 169
body language 71, 135
body rhythm 206
body-work therapists 129
boundaries 206
  addictive behaviours 174
  containing anger 133
  search for secure 21
brain
  organisation of 44
  resilience of 26
  see also left brain; mid brain; right brain
brain stem 43, 206
breaks 59, 188–201
  see also separation
breathing, practising 134
bullying 138

challenges, to authority 67–8
change
  adolescent reactions to 192
  introducing 22
  in strategy 88
charge, taking 58
chauffeur, offering services as 159
child development 25–30
Children Act (1989) 161, 198
children who wait 17
choices
  addictive behaviours 169
  in anger 128
  eating problems 171
  offering limited 73
cleansing, self-wounding 169
closeness
  innate drive for 190
  in relationships 193
  resistance to 192
cognition 38
cognitive 207
communication
  being heard 70
  dealing with anger 136
  maintaining 190
  pre-verbal 82
  respect and humanity in 71